Large Gardens and Parks

Large Gardens and Parks
Maintenance, Management and Design

T. W. J. Wright,
B.Sc. (Hort.) London, A.L.I. (Management)

GRANADA
London Toronto Sydney New York

Granada Publishing Limited - Technical Books Division
Frogmore, St Albans, Herts AL2 2NF
and
36 Golden Square, London W1R 4AH
866 United Nations Plaza, New York, NY 10017, USA
117 York Street, Sydney, NSW 2000, Australia
100 Skyway Avenue, Rexdale, Ontario, Canada M9W 3A6
61 Beach Road, Auckland, New Zealand

British Library Cataloguing in Publication Data

Wright, Tom
    Large gardens and parks: maintenance, management
    and design.
    1. Gardens   2. Parks
    I. Title
    711'.3   SB453

    ISBN 0-246-11402-9

First published in Great Britain 1982 by Granada Publishing Ltd,
Technical Books Division

Typeset by V & M Graphics Ltd, Aylesbury, Bucks
Printed in Great Britain by Mackay of Chatham, Kent, Great Britain.

Granada ®
Granada Publishing ®

Contents

To Shirley, Geraldine and Jane for their help, encouragement and forebearance.

Acknowledgements

I would like to thank the following for their invaluable help and assistance:

Bridget Cue for her patience and hard work in typing the manuscript; Shirley and Geraldine Wright for proof reading the drafts; David Butler, R.I.B.A., M.Sc. (London) for the figures and line drawings; and the owners and head gardeners for their generous help and advice, especially with the case studies.

I would also like to acknowledge with thanks the following for permission to reproduce photographs, tables and extracts:

The Metropolitan Museum of Art, New York (plate 1.1); the University of Reading, Institute of Agricultural History and Museum of English Rural Life (plates 1.2, 1.3, 1.4); G. S. Thomas (plates 3.4, 3.5, 3.6, 3.7, 3.8, 3.9); Cambridge University Collection: copyright reserved (plate 8.7); Royal Horticultural Society (table 2.2 and extract p. 53); William Heinemann Ltd (table 2.7); W. W. Johnson & Son Ltd (table 3.8); Scotland's Garden Scheme (table 7.2); Dame Sylvia Crowe (extract p. 25); Blackwell Scientific Publications Ltd (extracts pp. 49, 54); John Murray Publishers (extract p. 121); Royal Society of Arts (extract p. 127 from a paper on 'The preservation of historic gardens' and extract p. 135 from a paper on 'Creative conservation' (both papers from *Journal of the Royal Society of Arts*, **CXXVIII**, No. 5285); Save Britain's Heritage (extract p. 136); and H.M. Treasury (extracts pp. 147, 149).

Foreword

by Lawrence Banks

Hon. Treasurer, Royal Horticultural Society (since 1981)

Chairman National Council for the Conservation of Plants and Gardens (from its formation in 1979)

Ex Chairman Historic Houses Association Gardens Committee (from formation 1976 to 1981)

Vice Chairman: International Dendrology Society

Owner of Hergest Croft Gardens in Herefordshire, 'one of the world's finest collections of tree and shrubs' (Hugh Johnson, *The Garden*, 1980)

I welcome this important and practical contribution to the preservation of Britain's gardens. Anyone who is involved in the management of a large garden or park is only too well aware of the serious problems of maintaining it to a satisfactory standard. Labour costs inexorably increase, always it seems, at a faster rate than the income available to meet them. The problem is not confined to the private owner but affects equally the National Trust, local authorities and other institutions who are responsible for gardens.

Tom Wright is well qualified to write on this topic since he has run the Landscape Management course at Wye College since September 1978. He has shown a particular interest in Britain's unique heritage of gardens. He has organised two seminars on the management of larger gardens and parks which brought together owners and gardeners to explore how to preserve gardens in an era when staffs have had to be reduced to a minimum. Those who attended know how valuable these meetings were and I am delighted that this book makes Tom Wright's work available to a wider audience.

The book offers no instant solutions to the intractable problems, but its thorough research and sound guidance should be invaluable to all concerned in the management of gardens, whether owners, administrators or head gardeners. It does not confine itself to technical horticultural aspects alone but covers such areas as management and cost control. I am delighted to see a section on taxation and grants, subjects on which many owners are ignorant and seek advice and information. The analysis combines well with the case studies to give a clear understanding of the wide range of considerations which must be taken into account in running an important garden.

Tom Wright's work will be, I am sure, an essential reference book for all involved in this field.

Preface

Throughout Western Europe, large gardens and parks are becoming increasingly expensive and physically more difficult to maintain. Costs continue to rise and manpower whether skilled or semi-skilled is now the most expensive single item of most garden budgets. There is also a shortage of skilled, trained gardeners so necessary for proper garden upkeep, and although their place to a certain extent is being taken by a plentiful range of machinery, equipment and chemical aids, selecting the most suitable and cost-effective machinery and the safest and most efficient chemicals to use, are important and often difficult decisions. Garden owners, garden managers and amenity horticulturalists with similar responsibilities, must be able to make these decisions and many others, including the preparation of management and maintenance schedules, and the planning of effective planting schemes, as well as dealing with public visiting and perhaps income-raising ventures also.

This book is about many of these things, and is as far as I am aware the first text-book or handbook on the theme of the maintenance, management and design of large gardens and amenity areas.

No handbook or text-book on this subject can attempt to draw up rigid blueprints or rules to follow since one of the great rewards of gardening is to evolve one's own methods to suit a particular site, situation or personal taste. There are underlying principles to all maintenance operations, and these are explained in the early chapters following a short historical introduction which recognises the long-established traditions and skills of British gardeners.

Since garden visiting has become a major leisure activity for so many people, including overseas tourists who flock to see English gardens, I hope this book will also have an educational value in revealing more about the business of running large gardens, and the work of those often unseen and usually all too few staff, whose duties appear to be always 'behind the hedge' or in the 'potting shed'. So many of the otherwise attractive and informative guide books to historic houses and gardens provide very scanty information on these aspects. A closer look behind the scenes in gardens of different periods and style can be found in Chapter 8. In September 1981 a unique conference was held at Wye College for the owners and the head gardeners of large gardens on the theme of garden management. A large attendance of dedicated owners and senior staff was an indication of the demand for information and guidance in the face of increasing difficulties. I was very impressed with the enthusiasm and the determination to keep going among so many who came. Maintenance and management are now critical considerations for all those who own or work in gardens and parks.

I hope this book will provide some of the answers and I also hope that it will encourage students and others to take up a career in the fascinating business of amenity horticulture.

1

Introduction

An ironic and disturbing situation has been developing in the realm of ornamental parks and gardens ever since the end of the Second World War and going back still further to the reverberations of the 1914-18 war. This situation concerns the upkeep and the well-being of many fine gardens and estates in Britain and the important buildings usually associated with them. The irony lies in the fact that whereas, on the one hand, garden visiting and gardening itself have never been more popular than at the present time, with millions of visitors and participants taking part; on the other hand, it is only too evident that the actual manpower and resources available for the essential maintenance of so many of these large gardens and stately homes has been dwindling dramatically, to the point where many of these places face extinction altogether and some indeed have already disappeared.

A combination of factors is responsible; e.g. death duties, taxation and the changing ambitions of land-owning families have eroded away the wealth and the family continuity, while urban development and industrial expansion have swallowed up others or altered them beyond recognition. Wages and running costs, after a steady rise over the last twenty years, have risen more steeply in the last five years, and at the same time the supply of skilled gardeners has fallen. There are many young horticulturists leaving colleges and training establishments but they tend to be more attracted by jobs in the production industry or in research. For the owners or agents responsible for large gardens and parks there is the prospect of having to manage with dramatically fewer people than in the past resulting in a growing dependence on labour-saving machinery and equipment and the many modern technical aids now available. Owners themselves are willingly becoming far more closely involved with the selection and purchase of these aids and the day-to-day running of their gardens, and there are many instances where they are managing their gardens single handed. Management and organisation have become disciplines in their own right; to be studied carefully.

Another serious maintenance problem is that of the constructed element of formal gardens. The steady, but insidious decay and erosion of the brickwork and stonework, such as steps, balustrades, walls, fountain basins and statues, often centuries old and frequently lacking the continuous care of masons and craftsmen to keep them in good order, presents a formidable problem. Air pollution and vandalism also aggravate this damage and decay. Again new techniques are available to deal with stonework, but costs are inevitably high and in some gardens there is a formidable backlog needing attention. Visits to the great Renaissance gardens of Italy and France reveal only too obviously the enormous task now facing those involved with such restoration work.

If the buildings and stonework are ageing and decaying, one must remember also that the planted elements of the great gardens, the trees, hedges and shrubs, are not immortal and eventually need renewing. This can be a major undertaking when, for instance, an historic avenue of trees has to be felled and replaced. The current epidemics of Dutch elm disease and beech bark disease are also adding to the formidable task ahead of renewing some twenty-five million parkland and amenity trees in the next decades in England and Wales alone.

However, excellent restoration work of historic parks and gardens is taking place in Britain with several notable examples by the National Trust; those at Erddig, and Claremont are outstanding achievements. In Chapters 5 and 6 the restoration and maintenance of gardens is examined in more detail. The situation regarding gardening staff is certainly now more encouraging. In the National Trust, for instance, there is a career structure emerging, and a team of very capable and dedicated gardeners and maintenance staff is being built up. Remedies and answers to the upkeep problems are also being eagerly sought by many owners. An enterprising range of income-raising ventures is in operation today exploiting the character and the attractions of the house, park or garden. There is also the possibility of tax relief concession, grants and loans. These economic aspects are summarised in Chapter 7. One must not forget, however, that success in terms of large numbers of visitors can also bring problems of wear and tear, some of which are considered in later chapters. There is also the important fact that gardens themselves are constantly changing in character and condition and always have done, as societies evolved and the fortunes of the landowning and garden-owning families fluctuated, so this was reflected in the growth or decline of their seats or dwellings and the estates and gardens with them.

Until the second half of this century there was a steady appearance of new and substantial private houses with designed gardens to match. For example, impressive great houses of the high Victorian era and the more traditional large country houses of Lutyens and Blomfield, all with fine gardens, which are considered very important today. In Britain we are now contributing very few contemporary fine houses and gardens, and one has to look to the United States for the most inspired contributions.

Historical aspects of maintaining gardens

Roman
The gardens of Rome were famous for their size and richness. Pliny the Younger wrote in detail about his garden in the first century A.D. One feature he describes:

'is a sort of terrace, embellished with various figures and bounded with a box hedge, from which you descend by an easy slope, adorned with the representations of divers animals in box ... into a lawn overspread with the soft Acanthus ... and a plantation of shrubs, prevented by the shears from shooting up too high ... On the outside of the wall was a meadow, that owns as many beauties to nature as all I have described within does to art.'

This account well illustrates the practice of clipping and shaping evergreens, especially box (*Buxus sempervirens*), in many Graeco-Roman gardens. A gardener skilled in this art was known as the *Toparius*. The practice of topiary is still a feature in many gardens and parks today. Pliny's description of his lawn and meadow also shows that grass mowing was another feature and his appreciation of the natural beauties of his meadow is reflected in current trends in garden design which advocate *meadow gardening* (see Chapter 4).

Monastic horticulture and gardening became important aspects of the many religious foundations that evolved in Western Europe in the ninth and tenth centuries A.D., with the creation of highly functional and productive gardens to provide the necessities of the community life. Fish and duck ponds, poultry yards, orchards, vineyards and kitchen and physic gardens were common to many establishments. Manual labour was obligatory as were many horticultural skills including those of grafting and training fruit trees, the cultivation of herbs and the distillation and production of herbal extracts and high quality wines.

Medieval

Pleasure gardens and the gardeners who made them really began to emerge in the thirteenth century. At that time, and for the next four centuries continental influences tended to dominate the design, styles and the maintenance crafts of gardens in England, craftsmen and gardeners being brought over to England to help build and maintain the houses and the gardens (plate 1.1).

In the larger towns all classes of people began to have gardens and by the end of the thirteenth century many were well stocked with fruit such as peaches, apples, plums, quinces, strawberries and gooseberries.

*Marhus, Aprilis, Maius, funt tempora ueris · * **VER** *Pueritiæ compar* · *Vere Venus gaudet florentibus aurea fertis ·*

Plate 1.1 Spring by Pieter Brueghel, the Elder. Engraved 1570. The details of the formal intricate beds, the cultivation in progress and tools used are worthy of note in this very labour-intensive scene (The Metropolitan Museum of Art, The Harris Brisbane Dick Fund, 1926. All rights reserved. The Metropolitan Museum of Art)

Tudor

The first detailed references to gardeners can be found in the records of the great Tudor establishment of Hampton Court built originally by Cardinal Wolsey in 1514 and dramatically enlarged and redesigned by Henry VIII. 'The garden to be weeded and watered by women at two pence a day' is an entry in the Royal accounts in Henry VIII's time. There is also reference to a payment to:

'Harry Corantt of Kyngston ... for carving thirty eight *Kyngs* and *Queenys Beestes* at twenty six shillings the piece and for the supply of many plants ... 600 *cherry trees* at 6d, 200 *roses* at 4d ... and a border of *rosemary* 3 years old to set about the mount.'

Andrew Borde wrote in 1540 his *Boke for to Lerne a man to be wyse in Bylding of his House* in which he includes some very practical advice on siting and layout of the gardens. The garden and orchard for instance, were always to be located as near as possible to the house, and to be considered as an integral part of the same premises. Features of these gardens involving much maintenance are also referred to, such as mazes, knots, arbours, topiary, hedges, trained fruit trees, as well as the arts and crafts of cultivating new arrivals of colourful flowers.

Elizabethan

Promenading was a popular activity in this period and generally wide gravel walks were considered more important and more suitable than grass, surely due to the climate and the wear factors.

Gervaise Markham, who produced several entertaining and original books on garden layout from personal experience, in the early seventeenth century recommended for walking, paths of 6 ft width, sanded over coarse gravel or rubble. Fine yellow gravel mixed with pebbles and coal dust was recommended, the latter to discourage weeds. These sanded or gravel paths would be raked daily or at regular intervals.

The continental influences on English gardens and horticulture received a fresh impetus in the mid-sixteenth century with the arrival of Flemish, Walloon and French refugees during the Hugenot persecutions in Holland and Flanders. These included skilled and very knowledgeable gardeners and growers as well as craftsmen and weavers and they settled predominantly in East Anglia and south-east England. The gardeners would have been trained in the styles of the period creating and maintaining knot gardens, and topiary, as well as having a wide and detailed knowledge of plant cultivation. They may have influenced William Harrison (1534-93), Dean of Windsor, remarking on 'how wonderfully is the beauty of our gardens increased not only with flowers but various and costly workmanship'. (He defines gardens incidentally as '*all spade-dug grounds*'.)

Seventeenth century

In the late seventeenth century the famous Royal gardener, John Tradescant the Elder was involved with the development of the gardens at Hatfield House, Hertfordshire. He was head gardener here under Robert Cecil, Earl of Salisbury (1550-1612). Hydraulic engineers were introduced from France and Holland to create highly elaborate fountains and water features under the direction of the famous garden architect De Caus. Tradescant was responsible for importing large numbes of exotic plants especially from France. Thirty thousand vines were presented by the wife of a French Minister for the Hatfield vineyard, and French gardeners were employed by John Tradescant.

French and Italian renaissance gardens established in the seventeenth century and reaching heights of magnificence and splendour in France under the great 'Sun'

King Louis XIV, strengthened the already marked influence of continental gardens in England. It was after the restoration of Charles II in 1680 that gardening in the *Grand manner* became a widespread fashion. Some features of these gardens were, however, in vogue during the Commonwealth period (1649-60), and one is indebted to Sir Thomas Hanmer for his detailed writings on gardens and gardening in his *Garden Book*, completed in 1659 but not in fact published until 1937. Even at this time Hanmer comments that the cosiness of the earlier gardens is being replaced by spaciousness. More elaborate and exposed knots were the forerunners of the *parterres* (of French gardens) and another feature was the alleys between the parterres surfaced with coloured gravels, sands and dusts. Labyrinths formed of hedges 5-6 ft high were also a feature of large gardens with long tree-lined walks or allées. The trees would have been 'pleached' as is still practised today. A particularly interesting reference by Hanmer is to the 'winter house' or 'winter room', called by the French *La Serre*, which was to become the orangery and the forerunner of the glasshouse.

For a reference to the tools of the trade used at this time we are indebted to John Rea, 'Gentleman' of Worcestershire, for listing and describing in detail garden tools in his work *Flora, Ceres and Pomona*, written in 1665. Here is his list: A screen (or sieve), a fine wire riddle, two spades, a bigger and a lesser; shovels, hoes of several sizes, a pruning hook, grafting knives, a saw, chisel, mallet, a small penknife for 'inoculating and layering gilliflowers', a line and rule, trowels of several sizes, two iron rakes, several baskets of twigs and besoms to sweep the garden.

Gardeners of the larger establishments were by this time important and respected experts in their own right and such great men as the Tradescants, Royal gardeners to Charles I and Charles II and the Mollets (Charles II) are household names in the annals of British gardening. One must also note one John Field, head gardener to Woburn Abbey about 1663. He had a sound reputation and like other fellow head gardeners he was allowed to engage in business on his own account. He was one of the original partners in the firm that eventually became the famous London and Wise team in London.

The economics of running royal gardens and the wages paid to gardeners in the late seventeenth century can be discovered in the accounts for the Royal gardens at the time of William and Mary in 1699 and the accession of Queen Anne. The total costs of running the gardens at Hampton Court, Kensington, St James and Windsor were about £5000 per annum, of which nearly half went on Hampton Court. The maintenance of Hampton Court at this time was divided between three superintendents each paid £20 per annum. The labour force consisted of nine men paid at £14 per annum, ten at £9 and ten at £7.10s. per annum. This totals twenty-nine men. There were also twenty-seven men each paid at £15 per annum plus ten casual men whose daily rate was from 2s. to 1s. and 6d. So we already have three superintendents and sixty-six men and to those we have to add the weeder women paid at 8d. a day (remember 150 years earlier they only got 2d.) and a mole catcher at £16 per annum. So there must have been a total gardening staff of over seventy people. It is interesting to calculate that even in 1696, labour costs amounted to about 75 % of the total expenditure, with materials like fuel, and dung only amounting to about 8 %. These figures are remarkably similar to those for running a large garden or park today (see Chapter 7).

It is sometimes suggested that it was the high costs of running formal gardens like Hampton Court, that helped to bring about the revolution of taste and styles of garden design in the eighteenth century when so many great formal gardens were swept away to be replaced by the extensive English landscape style with its incidental low maintenance requirements.

Scarcely any vegetation seems to have escaped the tonsuring effects of the shears and clippers at this time. In June 1712 Joseph Addison was prompted to write 'British gardeners ... instead of humouring nature love to deviate from it as much as possible. We see the marks of scissors on every plant and bush.'

Eighteenth century landscape gardens

The great change of taste was also strongly influenced by the literary men of the period like Pope and Addison and the coffee house and Burlington House intellectuals. An admiration of nature and the simple unadorned beauty of landscape became the great mission, with a consequent strong reaction against the extremes of symmetry and formalism of the French designs. The quest for more restrained, quiet and less eccentric pleasure gardens must have become a widespread movement and Hadfield observes that the excesses of professional gardeners laid themselves open to ridicule by the more literary minded and the ambitions of prevailing taste.

In the ensuing half century or more a great revolution gradually transformed many of the larger English parks and gardens into the designed pictorial scenes of a pastoral landscape. Of course, there was not a total transformation, and some of the larger and many of the smaller gardens where in any case the landscape style was really inapplicable, continued in the more traditional styles, with the skills of horticulture still flourishing in the kitchen gardens and orchards.

There is no doubt, however, that from the maintenance point of view landscape parks in the new style, such as were laid out at places like Blenheim, Stowe, Petworth and Castle Howard, once the construction work and planting had been completed, would have involved fewer staff than those employed in the old style. The most concentrated work would have been in the kitchen gardens and limited flower gardens near the house, while much of the parks would be grazed by cattle or deer, with the ha-ha or sunken fence to prevent such animals reaching the house.

Foresters would have dealt with the trees and woodlands, and masons the stonework and buildings. The new version of designed English countryside as implemented by the two great landscape gardeners of the eighteenth century Lancelot 'Capability' Brown and Humphry Repton became known on the Continent as 'Le Paysage humanise' and its impact was sufficiently strong to see examples of this style being created in many Royal and prestigious establishments in France, Holland, Germany and Italy. Among the aristocracy and 'anyone who was anybody' 'Le Jardin Anglais' became the 'thing to have' and examples can still be seen today throughout Europe.

Late eighteenth century

New plants arrived in increasing numbers into the country from the mid-eighteenth century onwards and their arrival presented botanists and gardeners alike with the challenge of growing them successfully.

The nineteenth century

During the next century we move into the great Victorian era of gardening with all manner of new and traditional styles being adopted, but in general a return to the more formal French and Italian style design made colourful with the new exotic bedding plants and a great range of new hardy plants arriving in large numbers in this country in this period. This movement began towards the end of the eighteenth century when that great successor to Capability Brown, Humphry Repton, acknowledged that Brown, despite all his great concepts and fine landscapes, did leave the house exposed on a low grassy platform without immediate shelter or pleasure from flowers.

With the wealth accruing from entrepreneur industrialists and landowners in the industrial revolution, so many new 'seats' and gardens were coming into being that

Plate 1.2 William Cobbett would probably have approved of the apparent order and industry of this early nineteenth century gardener at work in a walled garden

William Cobbett felt compelled to write his book *The English Gardener* which was published in 1829. This was a very useful and practical book, with an obvious preference for the utilitarian rather than the pleasure gardens. He was a great expert on the kitchen garden in all its emerging magnificence and had some very sensible comments on the relationship between the size of the vegetable garden and its production. He also gives fascinating and very detailed instructions for the laying out of kitchen gardens including the planting of the box edging also with thrift, strawberry, daisy and grass, the design and siting of tool sheds, glasshouses and frames, and the detailed making of hotbeds. There is also a great deal on the cultivation of specific crops including fruit trees. Plate 1.2 shows a gardener of the early nineteenth century among his tools and plants.

Victorian gardeners

The education of gardeners was also anticipated by the rapidly enlarging Royal Horticultural Society. Founded in 1805, a decision was made in 1838 to admit no young men into the Society's experimental gardens (one and a half acres was first acquired in 1818 at Kensington with a move to a twenty-two acre site at Chiswick in 1822), as *journeymen*, who had not had some school education. It also decided to recommend no one from their gardens for situations as head gardeners who had not been regularly examined in scientific knowledge and had not received a certificate stating his degree of proficiency.

Nurseries and botanic gardens developed in the nineteenth century and the demand for hardy garden plants increased dramatically in the second half of the century as more gardens came into being.

Plate 1.3 Alexander Shanks grand advertisement of his various new horse, pony-drawn and hand-propelled mowing machines on the lawns of Balmoral. Queen Victoria was one of his first customers. This picture probably dates from the 1860s

The mechanical arts and aids to gardening also made quite an impact during this century, the greatest probably being the introduction of Mr Budding's 'machine for cropping or shearing the vegetable surface of lawns, grass or plots, etc.', in other words, a lawn mower. This was in the year 1832 and its design bore quite a remarkable resemblance to modern machines. Before its introduction, all grass was mown with scythes or grass hook or hand shears. In 1860 Green's of Leeds introduced a mower which mowed, rolled and collected the clippings (plate 1.3).

Made with Long Wooden Handles for Clipping Box Border.

Plate 1.4 One of the many gadgets invented for elegant gentlemen to 'manicure' their elaborate gardens in the late-Victorian era

Lawn mowers were not the only mechanical aids to meet the demand by the gardeners of the Victorian era. By the end of the century a vast range of gardening tools and sundries flooded the shops and stores (plate 1.4). The advent of the internal combustion engine and electric power also had tremendous effects enabling very high standards of garden maintenance to be achieved with a gradual decrease in the numbers of gardeners employed.

The period 1870-1920 spans the high Victorian and the Edwardian eras when styles of architecture and garden design became incredibly mixed and confused. There was a strong revival of gothic and formal renaissance styles on the one side led by the architects Charles Barry, George Devey and Reginald Blomfield with gardens in a pompous French and Italian manner, while ranged against them were the 'natural' school of gardeners led by William Robinson, Gertrude Jekyll and Reginald Farrer who advocated the more natural woodland, wild and cottage garden styles.

In the post-war era 1920-1939, successful blends of the architectural, the natural, and the 'cosiness' of the Elizabethan garden were evolved in such gardens as those at Hidcote Manor, Gloucestershire, Sissinghurst Castle, Kent and Great Dixter, Sussex. This was still the era of cheap and plentiful labour and generally very high incomes 'above stairs', but low wages for gardeners, estates staff and domestic households. Gardeners may have basked in the reflected glory of this period, but there was no time to sit about and certainly little time and money for leisure activities. A ten hour day was not uncommon and a sixty hour week with frequent weekend duties was the general rule.

The Second World War (1939-45) had a profound and irreversible impact on the lifestyles of garden owners and gardens. On the large estates most of the able-bodied staff were drafted into the armed forces, leaving the maintenance to a handful of individuals. For example at Petworth Park in Sussex, only three or four gardeners were left from an original staff of nearly thirty. Elsewhere, parklands and pleasure grounds were turned over to vegetable and farm crop production.

After the war, there was no real return to the hierarchy and manning levels of the vintage gardening years. Lack of skilled, dedicated staff and rising costs of upkeep enforced smaller numbers of gardeners without a general return to the high standards of maintenance and production of the pre-war days.

2

The Principles and Practices of Contemporary Garden Management

Introduction

In order to restore, conserve and maintain ageing houses, buildings and gardens and the ever-changing elements of vegetation that usually comprise the gardens, and to do this with fewer and fewer staff, the role of management and of machinery and equipment becomes a key factor. Another important point, of course, is the size and character of the garden. Owners and occupiers of the many millions of smaller gardens that are the norm today (probably averaging 400–800 m² (approx. 500–1000 sq yd) usually take a great pride in keeping up high maintenance standards. They are usually able to do this because of the limited size of the garden and the tasks involved, their leisure time available, and because the actual gardening activity offers a relaxing occupation in itself. For many, then, gardening is a pleasure, and a challenge, but because the garden is reasonably small maintenance can be kept within bounds. Where a garden begins to become less of a pleasure, and more of a worry, is when its sheer size and maintenance requirements begin to exceed the normal man hours available to keep it going in the way the owner would like. There are more and more instances, of gardens of, for example, 0.2–0.4 ha (½–1 acre) or even larger which have been well maintained (and perhaps even started) by the owners with or without the help of a full- or part-time gardener. As the owners grow older or develop an infirmity they are naturally able to do less in the garden. The garden then indeed can become a burden and a great worry and I think this is one reason why all too often such gardens are abandoned or sold off for development.

The principles of garden maintenance and management

There are two definitions that will be useful to bear in mind throughout most of this book:

(a) *Maintenance* – the routine, day-to-day or week-by-week operations involved in the upkeep of gardens, such as grass mowing and weeding, or the clipping and pruning of hedges and shrubs.
(b) *Management* which is more concerned with the longer-term planning and policies and the organisation of staff and equipment to achieve efficient maintenance. Long-term decisions about vegetation management will also be a factor.

Principles as primary sources and fundamental truths

Years of trial and error in the first place established set courses of action which were then followed as a regular code of practice. Generations of gardeners followed these practices and made new ones or modified old ones. They seldom wrote them down, but passed them on by verbal instruction, and practical demonstration. Gardeners and owners of gardens of today, however, especially those coming new or untrained into the business, are usually without one of these skilled old timers to turn to, or work beside, and so do need to consult some sort of reference source for these guidelines for the maintenance and management of gardens. Despite the very diverse nature of gardens and gardeners, the underlying principles that follow should provide the guides to action that are described in later chapters. Let us look first of all at the fundamental laws and truths underlying gardening.

The plant environment

The influence of weather and climate

If we accept the fact that a garden for many people is primarily concerned with growing a wide variety of plants whether for pleasure, utility or profit, then a highly critical factor will be the kind of plant environment that exists or that can be created or encouraged in any particular site or situation. The plant environment consists of a complex of physical and chemical factors all of which influence the way in which plants establish and grow.

In an excellent Masters Memorial lecture given to the Royal Horticultural Society in October 1967 Professor Hudson distinguishes between *weather* as the current meteorological conditions at any particular place including short term fluctuations, and *climate* as the longer term average weather conditions.

In terms of garden and plant growth therefore the climate will determine which plants are worth trying to grow depending on their hardiness or resistance to winter frosts and exceptional weather conditions, and the probability of them growing well in most years. The weather will largely determine how well the plants will do in any particular season. The hardiness factor will also determine the longevity of borderline plants and special cultural and management conditions needed to grow them successfully in the first place and the remedial measures to apply if damaged after a severe winter.

As 90% of the British population live in towns, and suburbs, we are in danger of losing contact and first hand acquaintance with the full realities and effects of climate and weather. Generations of farmers and gardeners in the past built up a keen awareness and sensitive appreciation of weather, and, in their own localities they developed shrewd powers of observation and forecasting which enabled certain courses of action to be taken as precautions, perhaps against frosts or storms or for harvesting of crops.

However, there are some quite distinctive and almost dramatic variations in the British climate depending on the particular region in which one lives, and it is now necessary to look rather more closely at these variations and the causes of them.

Latitude and temperature

Temperature is the major limiting factor on growing ornamental plants in the British Isles, assuming that they also have enough water. Temperature is closely related to latitude, and as we shall see later, to altitude. Generally speaking the range of plants that one can grow outdoors with reasonable safety decreases as one travels from south to north and to a lesser extent from west to east. Thus if one moves from a garden in Sussex or South Devon for example, to one in Lincolnshire or Northumberland (unless the microclimate is exceptionally favourable), one would expect to have much more difficulty in growing and overwintering half-hardy exotic evergreen shrubs such as ceanothus (California) or cistus (Mediterranean) and hebe (New Zealand). The altitude factor may also be very important in either accentuating the extremes of temperature, or modifying them. Temperature will also have a marked effect on the growing season of actual number of days in the year when plants are making growth. These are defined as growing days by the Ministry of Agriculture, i.e. those days in the year when the mean air temperature does not fall below 6.1°C (43°F). This means that there is quite a difference in the number of growing days between one part of the United Kingdom and the next. This is well illustrated in table 2.1. From this table one can see that the south-west peninsula of Britain has nearly one hundred more growing days a year than Northumberland, an advantage for growing ornamental plants but a different matter if one has much grass mowing to do!

Altitude
Some very dramatic variations in localised climate can be caused by marked changes in altitude. Since, for every 300 m (1000 ft) rise in height above sea level, there is a decrease in mean air temperature of 1.7°C (3°F) this means in effect that hilly areas even in the south and south west will have a cooler climate than the valleys nearby and often a windier and more robust climate too. If one lives in a sheltered valley (allowing for frost pockets) one may enjoy nearly two weeks more growing days throughout the year than in gardens only a mile or so away 150 m (500 ft) up in the hills. Table 2.1 also shows this effect of altitude on temperature. Altitude effects are very common in the British Isles affecting not only temperature, but wind speed, cloudiness, rainfall and winter snow-fall. All these in turn affect gardens and rates of growth and may call for planting for shelter and enclosure and special attention to windbreaks and hedges as well as siting of garden features.

Wind and exposure
It is a well-known fact that Britain is a windy island and that there are very few days in the year when there is little or no wind. The strongest winds are usually on the sea coast or in the hills and mountains and there are also regional and local variations which in terms of plant growth, can be categorised by the following two examples:

East Kent, East Anglia, north-east England. Residents, especially farmers and gardeners have been suspecting what meteorologists are also finding out, that there has been a tendency over the last fifteen years or so for a decline in the traditional prevailing mild south-west and westerly winds and an increase in the frequency of the colder, north, north-east or easterly winds, especially in March or April. Such winds can often be very strong, persistent and desiccating, and in winter, bitterly cold, associated with Scandinavian anticyclonic high pressure systems, or low pressure systems over France. Their effect, especially in the early spring is a retarding, and desiccating one and where temperatures are below freezing such 'black frost' winds can cause devastation to susceptible evergreens, far more serious than the low temperatures of still night radiation frosts. Shelter and windbreaks are essential to moderate the effects of these winds (see table 2.1).

South and south-west England, west Wales, south-west Scotland and Ireland. Protected from the cold air blasts from the north and east, and benefiting from the warming effects of the north Atlantic drift, these regions generally have favourable climates for plant growth, despite the frequency of sudden gales from the south-

Table 2.1: Regional variations in the plant environment in England and Wales. (Adapted from *Technical Bulletin*, No. 35, *The Agricultural Climate of England and Wales*, M.A.F.F. 1976 averages 1941-70.)

Region	Latitude	Average height above sea level	No. and period of growing days	Last frost (mean)	Average daily sunshine hours	Monthly average rainfall
Durham Northumberland Cumbria	55.6°N	67 m (220 ft)	237 April 4th - November 27th	Late May	3.75	54.2 mm (2.1 in)
N. Pennines Upland zones	54.4°N	315 m (1033 ft)	189 April 25th - October 31st	Late May	3.25	89 mm (3.5 in)
Merseyside Cheshire Wirral	53.6°N	28 m (92 ft)	258 March 23rd - December 6th	Late April	4.1	69.75 mm (2.75 in)
Lincolnshire Wolds	53.2°N	42 m (138 ft)	248 March 27th - November 30th	Early May	4.0	54.2 mm (2.1 in)
N. Midlands	52.0°N	83 m (273 ft)	251 March 23rd - November 29th	Late April	3.9	55 mm (2.2 in)
Norfolk	52.6°N	33 m (108 ft)	248 March 26th - November 29th	Late April	4.2	52 mm (2.0 in)

Region	Latitude	Altitude	Days and period	Season	Value	Rainfall
Severn Valley S.W. Midlands	51.6°N	91 m (300 ft)	263 March 19th - December 7th	Late April	4.0	64.6 mm (2.6 in)
Surrey E. Berkshire	51.0°N	107 m (351 ft)	258 March 22nd - December 5th	Late April	4.3	64.6 mm (2.6 in)
S.E. England	51.2°N	58 m (190 ft)	266 March 18th - December 11th	Late April	4.3	48.1 mm (1.9 in)
South coast	50.8°N	64 m (210 ft)	268 March 19th - December 12th	Late April	4.5	52.5 mm (2.1 in)
S.W. England Devon, Cornwall	50.2°N	83 m (272 ft)	322 February 20th - January 8th	Early April	4.6	87.25 mm (3.4 in)

west. Such gales are usually mild and accompanied by cloud and rain so that given adequate shelter from physical damage such as salt spray near the sea coasts a wide range of interesting plants and especially evergreens and conifers, can be grown. Some of the finest gardens and plant collections in the British Isles can be found in these areas. The effect of wind on gardens is more likely to be a problem with seaside and coastal gardens where so many people tend to live, and planting for shelter is absolutely essential. Without this, soft plants can get battered and even killed by intensive salt-laden gales, and maintenance work becomes uncomfortable and tiresome. Living hedges and screens take longer to establish under these tough conditions and are better planted in the lee of a constructed windbreak like a wooden fence, or even a post and wire fence with netting mesh to reduce the force of the winds.

Microclimate
Table 2.1 shows the broad variations in climate and weather in England and Wales, the figures representing a mean of those from 1941 to 1970.

Further modifications and ameliorating effects of these regional climates can be brought about by exploiting or developing microclimate or small-scale climates in gardens and parks in order to create more favourable habitats for people and plants.

Figure 2.1 shows a bird's-eye view of a house and garden where a fascinating range of microclimates and plant habitats has been created. The use of walls, hedges and changes of level have all been fully exploited.

At the same time it is important to understand that all species of plants introduced into cultivation in this country and usually the cultivars and hybrids derived from them, have evolved over very long time periods in their countries of origin, and have certain ecological preferences or habitats. These habitats are determined by such factors as microclimate, altitude, soils and location, with examples ranging from the cool leafy temperate woodlands of Japan or North America, to hot, dry stony slopes of the Mediterranean or West California. Temperature and sunshine are often the most critical factors in these microclimates and in cultivating and maintaining the fantastic range of introduced plants in our gardens it is very helpful, and indeed often essential, to try and match the original microclimate and habitat preferences as closely as possible.

Garden walls, or the walls of houses and outbuildings are very effective features on which to exploit these microclimates and table 2.2 shows the relationship between walls and their microclimates and the possibilities of plant selection. This, is, of course, a generalised table but I hope it does show the potential for a large range of ornamental and also fruiting plants associated with the different aspects.

The city microclimate
It is now widely recognised that cities tend to be warmer than the surrounding countryside and there are other distinct differences, some of which have already been mentioned, such as wind turbulence. The city itself is the cause of these differences. Its compact mass of buildings, hard surfaces of roads and pavements presents a very different landscape to that of the original countryside, and the activities of its inhabitants also generate a considerable amount of heat.

In terms of plant environments and garden maintenance the temperature effect is the most important. Research carried out in the U.S.A., in Germany and in London all show that cities have higher average temperatures in winter and summer than

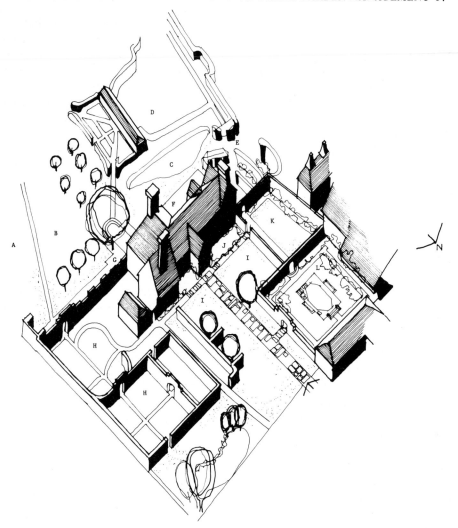

Fig. 2.1 The microclimates and plant habitats of a garden in southern England

A   Some exposure to prevailing south-west winds. Open site full sun. Rather windy. Gentle slope to south

B   Part shade of apple trees. House protects from north winds

C   Damp, sheltered habitat

D   Open lawn. Good protection from planted shelter belt on west/north-west side

E   Enclosed intimate areas. Sculptured hedges

F   Very warm terrace area. Dry, full sun. Half-hardy plants here

G   Warm, fairly protected border, except for south and south-west gales. Important background hedge on north and north-east side

H   Enclosed kitchen garden areas with gentle slope to south giving good uninterrupted aspect to sunshine. House, buildings and hedges protect from cold north-west and north winds

I   Enclosed semi-shaded meadow garden areas

J   Cool, shaded, north walls. Good for ferns

K   Small, very protected garden. Excellent protection from north with oasthouses and farm buildings

L   Warm, sheltered, sunken garden. Full sunshine for most of the area, but good shaded walls also. Heat reflection from buildings, even in winter

Table 2.2: Relationship between wall microclimate and plant selection.

Wall	Microclimate	Plant habitat equivalent	Plant groups
North	Perpetual shade. Cool in summer. Cold or very cold in winter. Good, 'steady' light unless heavily shaded. 'Rain' shadows with high buildings or projecting eaves. Limited evaporation. Shelter from N. winds beneficial.	Woodland or semi-woodland. N. facing cliffs or steep banks. Asiatic, N. American and European species depending on soil pH, moisture content and organic matter.	Woodland and shade-loving species. **Shrubs:** camellia (pH 5-6), garrya, mahonia, cotoneaster, pyracantha. **Climbers:** *Hydrangea petiolaris*, winter jasmine, honeysuckle, *Parthenocissus* sp., also woodland shade herbaceous sp., ferns, hosta, hardy cyclamen, bulbs, etc. **Fruit:** morello cherries, gooseberries, currants.
South	Usually the warmest habitat in a garden given shelter and full sunshine. Favoured mild winter conditions to hot or very warm in summer. Drought or 'sun scorch' can be limiting factors. Exceptionally favourable growing conditions for many sun-loving plants with good soil management.	With good drainage, this offers excellent habitats for plants from the Mediterranean regions, W. United States, S. America, S. Africa, E. Europe and Middle East, parts of China, and Australia and New Zealand.	**Shrubs and woody climbers:** ceanothus, clematis, campsis, callistemon, abutilon, jasmine, hoheria, cestrum, chimonanthus, cistus, *Cytisus battandieri*, hebe, *Leptospermum*, *Robinia hispida*, passiflora, wistaria. **Half-hardy annuals and herbaceous plants:** agapanthus, nerine, gazania, etc., etc. **Fruit:** apples, peaches, pears, plums, apricots, nectarines.

Wall	Microclimate	Plant habitat equivalent	Plant groups
East	Generally cool but variable with considerable extremes in winter and summer: warm, dry in summer to very cold in winter. Wind frost damage to evergreens in severe E.-N.E. wind conditions: protection needed.	An intermediate type between semi-woodland or open scrub to exposed habitat of direct morning sunshine, especially in late spring or summer. Cool desiccating winds can be a limiting factor in E. and N.E. regions particularly in spring.	The **North wall group** plus many hardy **Shrubs** and **Climbers** that can withstand the occasional very cold wintry conditions. Climbing and rambling roses. Shade from early morning sun for camellias and magnolias. Many herbs and bulbs. **Fruit:** plums and hardy pear varieties.
West	Equable, temperate, throughout year. With shelter. A very favourable microclimate for plants that prefer reasonably warm and mild conditions with none of the extremes of the S. or N. walls.	Woodland edge species. W. facing cliffs, slopes. Similar to S. habitat but for plants that prefer indirect sunshine. Shelter from S.W. gales is important.	**Shrubs and climbers:** As for S. Walls until orientation becomes N.W. facing (too cool). Examples: magnolia, azara, actinidia, clematis, honeysuckle, akebia, roses. **Herbaceous perennials:** Very many of these. A range from S. to N.W. habitat. Euphoribia, *Salvia* sp., *Lilium* sp., eremurus, *Viola* sp. **Annuals:** nicotiana. **Fruit:** plums, cherries, apricots, apples.

the surrounding countryside. The figures obtained by Dr T. J. Chandler, director of the London survey, certainly bear this out (table 2.3). The effects on minimum temperatures are especially interesting and of great importance to horticulturists. Cologne in Germany for example, has an average of 34% less days with minimum below 0°C (32°F) than its surrounding area, the corresponding figures for Basle in Switzerland being 25% less. In London, Kew has an average of some seventy-two more days with frost-free screen temperatures than rural Wisley. This means that many sheltered enclosed gardens in Central London are virtually frost free, offering considerable scope for plant selection.

Table 2.3: Air temperatures recorded in the London area (1931-60).

	City	Suburbs	Countryside
Air maximum temp., °C (°F)	14.6 (58.3)	14.2 (57.6)	14.0 (57.2)
Air minimum temp., °C (°F)	7.3 (45.2)	6.2 (43.1)	5.4 (41.8)

Other effects
These are probably less important but all help to determine the characteristics of the plant environment in the city. There is generally slightly more rainfall, and more cloud, reduced wind speeds, apart from the turbulence effect of tall buildings, a higher pollution incidence and, of course, more noise. As regards rainfall and water relationship, the humidity of the town atmosphere is usually lower due to the high evaporation rate, and run-off effects of surface water. Humidities may be as much as 30% less in cities. This means that irrigation or augmented water supplies for plants may be necessary, especially those in raised beds, roof decks and containers. Trees have a remarkable ability to find water beneath the streets and pavements especially thrifty species like plane (*Platanus*) and some maples (*Acer*).

In conclusion therefore, as 90% of the population of West European countries live in towns or suburbs we know that most enjoy a warmer more frost-free climate, but that the atmosphere will not be so clean as the countryside and there may be less sunshine and some localised wind turbulence. The implications for maintenance are associated with these effects. Noise disturbance can be somewhat minimised by thick planting and screening with large-leaved evergreens.

Soils and plant growth

There are plenty of reference books available containing as much as anyone wants to know about soils, that most basic fundamental element of horticulture and agriculture. Therefore to avoid repetition the aim of this section is really to try and determine the relationship between the different types of soils and the expected range of ornamental plants that they will grow, and to offer brief guidelines on the management of such soils for cultivating ornamental plants. I have intentionally avoided the whole business of soil cultivation for vegetable and fruit crops. The objectives are in most cases usually different when producing food crops, especially the short term vegetable crops, the aim being high soil fertility, the replenishment of nutrients removed and the maintenance of a favourable soil structure for easy cultivation and production. There are, of course, a number of ornamental garden plants that respond to such treatment and indeed may demand it for really first-class show plants, like hybrid roses, fuchsias, dahlias, cut flower crops and some annuals like sweet peas and zinnias. In general however, the majority of ornamental hardy plants especially the more natural species and cultivars, do not demand high levels of nutrients, soil cultivation and the like, once established, and it is more important to get the habitat and the soil preparation right at planting. After that, shrubs and trees in particular can exist for many years with limited soil and plant attention.

Soil types

The very different soil types that are derived from the different underlying rocks are a characteristic of the British Isles due to the complex geological origins of these islands, and remarkably different soils can be found within quite small adjacent areas. A particularly good example of this can be found in south-east England. There is likewise an equally interesting range of important gardens on these different soils. Table 2.4 summarises some of the characteristics of the vegetation types and the management of those commonly occurring soil types. All soils, and particularly the top soil layer, need treating with the utmost care and respect. Those blessed with well-drained fertile soils, should nurse them and keep them that way by good common sense management. Those faced with very light or very heavy soils can do much to gradually improve the situation, with patience and good husbandry. Soil structures can be easily damaged or wrecked by compaction in very wet weather by feet or machinery, or disturbance with earth-moving equipment that inverts or disrupts the various horizons. Top soils should always be removed wherever possible on development sites and temporarily stored for future use. The situation is all too common where owners of new houses and gardens in new developments find themselves facing a thin 'veneer' of top soil spread like icing over a very compacted and 'nasty cake' of degraded subsoils mixed with rubble and other debris. Building up a healthy soil profile is a long, but eventually successful process and should begin by breaking up the compacted layers by deep hand digging or for large areas the use of a chisel plough or subsoiler for deep ploughing.

Soil mycorrhiza

Most soils have a complex and variable complement of soil micro-organisms which include minute forms of animal life bacteria, and the important group called mycorrhiza which are usually classified as fungi. Most higher plants in nature develop associations with mycorrhiza of different types on their roots systems which partially substitute for the root systems of these plants under certain conditions. Although much of the original mycorrhizal research has been done with agronomic plants, there is important knowledge being gained with trees and especially forest trees which shows just how important they are. As one research scientist observes:

'It is not really a question of how much better would the trees in a forest grow with mycorrhizae, but rather would the forest exist at all without the mycorrhizae.'

It is known that a very large number of flowering plants and conifers are symbiotic with fungi which are closely associated with their root systems. It seems that their presence is most beneficial in nutrient-deficient situations. Mycorrhizal presence in soil types is thus related to the vegetation and probably the organic matter in the soil. Under difficult or poor soil situations the use of organic matter, mulches or leaf mould might help with the natural inoculation of seedlings or newly transplanted trees or shrubs with the appropriate fungal organism.

Cultivated plants in relation to their maintenance

The fundamentals of the plant environment and the soils in which plants grow have now been reviewed, or at least, some aspects have been examined, and the next and most important fundamental component must surely be the plants themselves.

Table 2.4: Three principal soil types and their associated vegetation and management.

Soil type	Clay	Sandstone	Chalk and limestone
Natural vegetation types			
Upper soil layer or horizon 'top soil'	Oak Ash Hazel — Clay loam, deep tap roots	Pine Birch Gorse heather scrub — Shallow roots, Sandy loam	Beech White beam Yew Rich scrub herb layer — Calcareous loam
Middle/Lower horizon 'sub-soil'			
Soil characteristics and management	pH factor: acidic or alkaline drainage and compaction problems. Use mulches and drainage materials. Avoid deep cultivations.	pH factor: acid to very acid. Drought and low nutrient status with free-draining shallow top horizon. Plentiful and continual mulches, with regular nutrient application.	pH factor: critical high lime levels eliminate calcifuge plants due to low iron and magnesium. Free draining. Frequent mulches. Drought less serious than with sands.
Vegetation growth	Deep-rooting trees and shrubs tolerant of above factors, e.g. roses. Avoid annuals unless soil amelioration good. Thorough soil preparations at planting 'slow start' – long life' for trees and shrubs. 'Cold' soils in spring.	Conifers, ericaceous shrubs, heathers, brooms, etc. Provision of organic matter. Nutrients and water are critical factors, especially at planting. 'Early' soils in spring. 'Hungry' soils.	Avoid calcifuge plants, i.e. lime hating. Once established, good growth of tolerant species, organic matter for establishment and maintenance. Mulches and some nutrients.
Woodland type	Oak woodlands where clays are acidic, rich habitat for exotic trees and shrubs, rhododendrons, magnolias, etc. Also rich herb layer depending on tree canopy control.	Birch–pine woodlands. Usually tend to be dry with more limited plant diversity. Thin ground flora and very dry in summer. Fire hazard. Bracken may be invasive.	Beech woodlands. Dense summer canopy reduces shrub/herb layers, fringes, glades and grassland areas have rich flora including wild orchids, etc. Spring herbs most effective. Bulbs, etc.

A book on the management of gardens is really concerned, for the most part, with the management of cultivated plants and therefore an analysis of the many different categories of such plants is important and also a consideration of the objective or reasons underlying their maintenance and management. Later chapters will look at these aspects in more detail.

Growth cycles and longevity
All cultivated and wild plants have a specific life span which will be shortened or extended by a range of complex ecological factors in the wild, and of cultural maintenance and management factors in gardens and parks.

Annuals and biennials are the most short lived of all plants, but in compensation they rely on prolific seed production to ensure their renewal and perpetuation. In the wild they are usually the pioneer species in disturbed or cleared ground, whereas in gardens and parks they are exploited for their short-term, often colourful displays and rapid growth and maturation in the summer months, e.g. petunia, sweet pea and tagetes. Weed species like groundsel (*Senecio vulgaris*) and bitter cress (*Cardamine hirsuta*) are everywhere abundant. Ornamental biennials like foxglove (*Digitalis*) and mullein (*Verbascum*) can be accommodated in planting schemes with suitable management. They do, however, leave 'holes' in any planting scheme once they have matured and 'passed on', and these have to be allowed for in the planting design.

Non-woody herbaceous perennials including bulbs, corms, and tubers, are all plants that perpetuate themselves by various persistent root or stem structures and under natural conditions it is usually the habitat that determines the success and longevity of such plants. Some are found in grassland or waterside communities, others in woodland glades or alpine habitats, and some, like hardy cyclamen and paeonies can live for very many years. In gardens the same is true to a certain extent but there are many different classes of those herbaceous perennials and their persistence is often related to their habits of growth, and the maintenance treatment. Disturbance and poor habitat location can shorten their lives. Also, cultivars, hybrids and selected seedlings usually need higher levels of cultivation to retain longevity and quality, e.g. delphinium, phlox, and can suffer degeneration and disease if neglected or grown in the same ground for long periods of time. The growth habits of perennials are considered in more detail in Chapter 3.

Turf grasses are very important components of garden vegetation, determining the quality and the character of the swards in which they are found. They also are considered in more detail in Chapter 3.

Woody plants are very diverse in their range of characteristics and very different spans of life. They can be divided broadly into shrubs and trees. In general terms it is the native and wild species that are the longer lived and the more maintenance free. More of these aspects are considered later but in this general summary one can distinguish the short-lived sub-shrubs like rosemary (*Rosmarinus*) and lavender (*Lavandula*) that reproduce easily from cuttings; the fast-growing, moderate-lived brooms, buddleias and heathers, the last responding to clipping annually to keep a compact habit and promote lateral growth; the many medium-term deciduous shrubs like forsythia, weigela and philadelphus that in the wild may sprawl to their hearts content and apparently look none the worse for it, but in cultivation respond to the occasional but necessary discipline of pruning to keep them in good shape and promote longer life. (The difference in the treatment and the longevity of wild and botanical species and garden hybrids is well illustrated with roses in Chapter 3.) Finally, there are the massive tree-like shrubs such as rhododendron and magnolia that may go for years with very little maintenance, provided the habitat has been correctly chosen in the first place. It is more often diseasee or sheer old age that takes these plants, perhaps after fifty or more years of existence. Conifers too, unless used for hedging or topiary can develop to a ripe old age and this may be several centuries in the case of cedars or pines, but perhaps thirty to fifty years with the smaller cypresses and junipers.

Trees as the longest-lived elements in our gardens, parks and forests, also follow the 'rule' that species originating from the wild usually out-live cultivars and hybrids, and certainly require less maintenance as a general rule. A good example in Britain is the common wild cherry (*Prunus avium*) that will grow to a beautiful rugged specimen often well over a century old in our woods and parks. The Japanese hybrid cherries, however, beautiful as they are, seldom live for more than forty to fifty years before succumbing to disease and degeneration.

Maintenance fundamentals of cultivated plants
The basic fundamentals are only outlined at this stage since more specific guidelines and techniques will follow in later chapters. Having reviewed briefly the range of ornamental vegetation on categories that may be grown in gardens, here are some fundamental thoughts on the approaches to maintenance policies.

(a) Maintenance whether it be pruning or mulching or watering should be the result of a sensible course of action based on the needs of the plant or plants and the style or design of the garden. It should not just be because a textbook says so.

(b) Botanical species and cultivars of most hardy plants usually need less maintenance and will usually live longer than hybrids although they may be less striking in appearance and less colourful. The latter may need a higher level of input to encourage the more spectacular qualities for which they were usually bred in the first place, e.g. roses, dahlias and Michaelmas daisies, asters.

(c) Associations, groups or massed assemblages of plants can be surprisingly at home when grown this way. This happens all the time in natural plant communities where slow changes may be happening with the death and renewal of some plants. In the search for rather more low maintenance type planting different associations should be tried and observed. We still know too little of the effects of competition and companionship among cultivated plants.

(d) All garden plants therefore have a finite life and their renewal and replacement should be part of a management policy. This is examined more closely in Chapter 3.

(e) The range of plants grown in any garden or park is essentially according to the tastes and the interests of the owner and the gardener. These can change with fashion and trends, just as the maintenance inputs can be adjusted to suit the resources and the time available. Vegetation welfare and control as the *raison d'être* of most gardens will always swing between intensive sophistication and the more relaxed natural approach, depending on all the factors reviewed briefly in this section and the design style or character of the garden.

Design and maintenance

Today, in almost every sector of landscape activity the maintenance factor is emerging as a key issue. Labour is no longer cheap or skilled as a general rule and designers and managers are now actively aware of the necessity for economical maintenance as far as is possible, to achieve the desired results. Typical examples today are those institutions like public schools, hospitals or business-training centres, many of which are based in large, prestigious country houses with fine gardens and grounds formerly maintained by a full complement of staff in the days when the place was in private hands. Ways and means usually have to be sought of managing such places with a much reduced maintenance force, and apart from investment in machinery and equipment, the original design has to be carefully examined to see what rationalisation is possible to make the whole concern more manageable. This aspect will be examined in more detail in Chapter 4.

Even the owners of smaller private gardens are more maintenance conscious these days, seeking labour-saving designs and planting schemes. For those who have been employing part-time help, attention to design and maintenance may allow for dispensing with such help altogether, while still having a nice garden.

Garden design principles

The qualities that distinguish a good garden from a dull or uninteresting one are invariably those of design, and to achieve a well-designed garden irrespective of size there are certain principles or guidelines to follow. These are as follows: unity and harmony, scale, contrasts of light and shade, enclosure and exposure, colour, tone and texture, and time. These principles are not all directly related to maintenance. Nevertheless, some are of great importance in this respect, and there is no doubt that there is a greater psychological satisfaction and better motivation when looking after a well-designed and interesting garden, than one which is a muddle and a confusion.

Unity and harmony. That great landscape architect and garden designer Dame Sylvia Crowe observed in her excellent book *Garden Design*:

'perhaps the greatest of these (Principles of Design) and the one most lacking in many gardens today is a *sense of unity*. It is a quality found in all great landscapes, based on the rhythm of natural land-form, the domination of one type of vegetation and the fact that human use and buildings have kept in sympathy with their surroundings. When we say that a landscape has been spoilt, we mean that it has lost this unity.'

In gardens, it is usually the strong simple designs that are the most effective, overriding a temptation to overcrowd with too many features and incidents. A good structural skeleton for the design can be found with hedges, or walls or both, and the space divisions and planting composition should be balanced and harmonious with the other principles of scale and contrast all playing their part in the composition. There may be a number of quite different features in the garden, as at

Sissinghurst, or Hidcote, for example, but these should all be related to the design as a whole and connected to it. Hedges, vistas and paths or flowing areas of mown grass all can be used to achieve unity and harmony, and such points as the widths of paths, the heights of hedges and proportions of planted areas will also create the scale of the design (plate 2.1). Maintenance of such design is usually satisfying and less fragmented. It may be labour intensive, but where one is working in a series of ordered spaces, the maintenance tasks will be more logical and fulfilling. Detailing of the design and finish of such features as steps, paths, the shapes of borders and hedges can all contribute to the design, and can also make quite a difference to the maintenance tasks.

Further points about such details and design are considered in Chapter 4.

Plate 2.1 The series of ordered, well proportioned spaces in part of the garden at Sissinghurst, Kent devoted to plants of interest and variety to the gardeners as well as the visitors

Scale is to do with proportion and perspective 'bridging the gap between man's stature and the sky'. Gardens should wherever possible relate to the human scale, and the component parts should be in scale with one another. In respect of maintenance, the effects of excessive height of hedges or disproportionate amounts of planting to grass or great displays of annual colour which may not be in scale or harmony with the design, are also going to be more expensive to maintain. There is, of course, a personal subjective element in all these principles discussed so far.

Contrasts, enclosure and spaces, colour and texture are also principles that are obviously closely related to unity and scale and it is resolving or unifying these themes and ideas in the design that determines the character and quality of the garden. The upkeep aspects should be also borne in mind at the same time. For example, it is possible to create enclosure with massed shrubs that need no regular clipping, rather than hedges, provided the formal effect can be dispensed with.

Colour can also be achieved with a tapestry of shrubs or perennials rather than annuals, again reducing renewal and frequent maintenance, but with the possible sacrifice of brilliant, seasonal splashes of colour.

Time the last principle, is so often overlooked or underestimated. Unlike all other artistic creations, whether buildings, paintings or pieces of music, gardens have to grow to the mature composition foreseen by the designer, and this may take several years, especially where trees and shrubs and hedges are part of the scheme. Thus careful and understanding maintenance and management are needed to help the design to develop and mature.

Maintenance and longer-term management will be infinitely more satisfying and straightforward if a longer-term plan is used as a basis for making or redesigning a garden, resisting temptations to change until the scheme has had a chance to mature. Another possibility is to plan and plant a slow-maturing structure or framework of trees, shelter belts, hedges and the main shrub groups, and while these are maturing, to use 'filler' plants like fast-growing perennials or shrubs like broom and buddleia and annuals. However, one must remember to thin or remove these as the framework matures and takes up more room. The dynamic changes that take place in garden plant associations can also be a fascinating subject for study themselves.

Management in practice

In agriculture and horticulture the use of management and its applied techniques has brought about massive increases in labour productivity and efficiency of crop production so that output in terms of crops has probably never been higher, while at the same time the numbers of personnel employed has never been lower this century. The situation in amenity horticulture and in the world of garden and parks management is, however, changing comparatively slowly and it is worth looking a little more closely into the possible reasons for this.

Firstly, we are concerned in parks and gardens with maintenance for amenity or pleasure as the prime objective, with little or no production aspect or profit motive as an ultimate goal. Without the profit incentive, new techniques or the need for change have less urgency in their application.

Secondly, many owners, and head gardeners and agents, including plantsmen, tend to be somewhat traditional and conventional in their attitudes to garden maintenance and the introduction of new ideas or techniques, and see no reason to change well-tried and successful systems unless forced to do so by circumstances such as drastic labour reduction or financial stringencies.

Thirdly, a highly relevant factor must be the extraordinarily complex and diverse range of styles and sizes of gardens and the even more extraordinary range of plants and plant associations to furnish them, presenting sometimes formidable problems of skilled, careful maintenance with often limited scope for safe and effective application of new machinery, chemicals and other maintenance innovations.

Finally, little or no reliable research has so far been carried out into garden maintenance problems by universities or government agencies, since the necessity has not quite the same priority as that of food crops. Innovations are still mainly by trial and error by gardeners themselves or from the modification of agricultural research and machinery, or as a result of competitive research or development by companies manufacturing or promoting machinery, equipment and chemicals.

Setting the objectives of maintenance and management
The first stage in planning a programme of rational management is to establish the objectives of the maintenance and management programme. Without these objectives as a guide or basis, subsequent decisions or policies can often be very wide of the mark, and non-productive.

The prime objective must be to decide what standards of maintenance are going to be appropriate for a particular garden or park or for the components of the same, consistent with its design and style and the manpower and the resources available. Very careful thought should go into this decision, since there are so many conflicting and interrelated factors that need to be taken into account. For example, almost every aspect of garden and park maintenance depends upon the manpower available either operating hand tools or power-driven equipment, and as labour can absorb up to 70% or more of the total costs of running amenity areas, it is very important to keep a very close watch on the manning levels related to the standards required. In fact the personal whims or tastes of the owner and to a certain extent the aesthetic and pleasurable features of a garden may have to be subordinated to their realistic manning levels if resources to pay for them are limited.

Standards of maintenance
In setting standards of maintenance a number of factors should be taken into account:

(a) In large gardens, particularly, where a fair number of gardeners were once employed, revised standards should be set and implemented as speedily as possible in agreement or collaboration with the existing gardening staff. This may involve simplifying existing designs by reducing flower beds, eliminating ornamental glasshouse crops and the walled-garden activities, and resetting standards for grass mowing and hedge cutting, that will be within the capacity of the staff available.

(b) Standards should also take into account innovations in methods and techniques that may break with tradition or be seen as revolutionary, but having as their objective the realisation of the standards required within new styles or changes in character. Examples might be varied grass cutting zones, ground cover plantings or gravelled and mulched areas combined with the use of new machinery and chemicals.

(c) In the case of gardens that are too large and unmanageable for the owners to cope with, even with some help, a category of standards can be set for different areas. Thus there can be priority or high maintenance areas, usually near the house, receiving the highest possible treatment, grading to progressively lower maintenance areas away from the house, or from functional or pleasure areas to perhaps even wild zones or woodlands or copses where very little maintenance is possible or necessary. The total effect can still be satisfactory in such a compromise and the owner has some objectives to work to, rather than working against impossible odds to keep the whole affair looking 'tidy'.

(d) Standards should incorporate a degree of flexibility to allow for changes that may be necessary, and these standards can be reviewed from time to time.

Manning levels

It could well be, of course, that the exercise of assessing the manning levels one's garden or park requires may appear pointless, but there are nevertheless some good reasons for undertaking the exercise:

(a) As labour costs are by far the greatest item in the garden upkeep budgets, the number of staff employed, and the way they are used are highly critical factors.

(b) The procedures for fixing manning levels to be summarised in the next section, are a way of closely scrutinising the existing maintenance structure and systems in operation.

(b) Maintenance, even in the most beautiful garden or park, can at times be thankless and monotonous for the gardeners employed and the manning levels exercise can often indicate ways of reducing the expensive drudgery of leaf sweeping and it may help in fixing incentive bonuses for satisfactory maintenance standards achieved. Many local authorities do use bonus systems based on agreed standards, manning levels and work completed.

(d) Even the owner who manages his or her own garden may find some revealing facts about the garden being managed and the extent of the tasks being undertaken. This will be amplified later.

Assessing manning levels

Here are some alternative approaches to establishing manning levels:

Manning levels for owner occupiers and single-handed gardeners. The simplest method is to draw up a fairly basic list of all the main areas of the garden or grounds that are being, or are to be maintained, and add to these additional jobs such as replanting and winter pruning, and also 'new works' like patio laying or rock garden construction. Agree on the sort of standards of upkeep that are realistic and/or acceptable and for each area or task listed produce an estimate of the time anticipated to get through all the jobs in the draft schedule. Estimate also any additional help needed to complete the tasks satisfactorily.

Try out this schedule for one full season and if the estimates prove to be moderately accurate this is reassurance that the organisation and manning level is about right for the sort of garden being looked after. If, however, the schedule is badly adrift, perhaps especially after a second season, and, as often happens, one fails to complete many of the target jobs listed, then several things can be done:

(a) Accept the inevitable and alter the standards, accepting a lower one if necessary, or devise different levels of maintenance.

(b) Look closely again at the design of the garden and the methods used to look after this. There may well be ways and means of saving time and effort by simple modifications to the design and layout, or if necessary a more drastic rationalisation can be undertaken. This is discussed more fully in Chapter 4.

(c) Introduce more mechanisation and aids such as herbicides, which in combination with (b) may well bring about really effective results.

(d) Adjust the work programme to spread the load more evenly over the year. For instance, if most of the hedge cutting and the pruning can be done in the winter months, this eases the pressure on the peak summer period.

For gardens where two or three full-time staff are employed. A schedule of maintenance tasks and related work should be drawn up for the full calender year in conjunction with the head gardener and the employer and perhaps clerical staff, if any, employed. The schedule should naturally be based on existing or agreed standards of upkeep.

Table 2.5 gives an example of one type of maintenance schedule. This contains a limited amount of information. More precise details could be given but much depends upon who is to use the schedule and the time available to prepare it. This particularly applies to the man hours in the final column. All sorts of variations of such a schedule are possible to suit the garden and the type of organisation.

Weekly time sheets should be kept as a matter of routine since the information gained from them can be extremely useful in many ways. For instance the actual times taken for most jobs should be shown, to help with work schedules and manning levels, but the integrity and degree of accuracy set down in the time sheets will depend on the attitudes and the consistency of the staff responsible for filling them in.

There should be a column or heading on the time sheet for loss of work due to adverse weather and there is bound to be a considerable amount of time spent in general or miscellaneous duties and tidying up.

Manning levels for gardens, parks and estates employing five or more people. It is usually a matter of routine and indeed a necessity today, certainly in local authority and municipal parks departments, for accurate records to be kept of many aspects of maintenance and management work.

In order to establish manning levels where budgets are critical and economies always being attempted, these authorities have evolved a system of work measurement or work study.

This sort of exercise, perhaps in a simplified form, is worth the consideration of large privately owned establishments employing appreciable numbers of staff (perhaps five or more).

The procedure is briefly as follows:

(a) *Stage I: area measurement.* All areas to be maintained, such as lawns, plant borders, shrub areas, hedges, drives and paths, are measured as carefully as possible using tapes. This sort of work can easily be done by vacation students or school leavers given adequate instructions and some supervision. These measurements may be of extensive areas of grounds and gardens and can be related to an existing plan by a coding or colour key system. Metric measurements are now preferable to avoid confusion. The results of this stage are shown in table 2.6 - an actual working example.

Table 2.5   A garden maintenance schedule (example)

Area	Operations	Time of year	Priority*	Actual man hours (to be filled in)
Front entrance shrubbery	Remove fallen laburnum and dead conifer. Prune some shrubs.	January early March	H.P.	
Peat garden	Hoe when dry enough then simazine spray. Clip callunas. Mulch shredded peat.	February to mid-March	H.P.	
Holly hedge	'Roundup' spray followed by bark mulch and fertiliser.	February	L.P.	
Parkland	Some trimming needed of existing trees and removal of ties/stakes of newly established trees.	January to February	L.P.	
Wild garden	Generally in reasonable condition but still a few roses to prune before bulbs emerge.	January	M.P.	
Tennis courts	Cut holly hedges. Cut Leyland hedges to agreed height. Use new power hedge cutter.	January to March	M.P.	
Pool garden	Thoroughly clean out and replant pool. Mulch beds bark fibre.	March to April	M.P.	

*L.P. = low priority; M.P. = moderate priority; H.P. = high priority.

Table 2.6   Main areas of Withersdane Gardens, Wye College

Description of area	Area (m²)	Percentage of Total Area
Annual bedding	175	0.89
Shrubs	790	4.02
Perennials	271	1.38
Mixed borders	1 127	5.74
Ground cover	65	0.33
Rose borders	12	0.06
Close-mown grass	11 169	56.88
Rough grass	4 642	23.64
Hedges	616 m	3.14
Hard areas	770	3.92

(b) *Stage II: work measurement.* Having determined the actual areas of amenity ground components to be maintained, it is now necessary to produce average figures for the time taken to carry out all the essential operations involved in their upkeep.

These figures can be produced in two ways:

(i) Using the local authority method of work study or work measurement. This means employing specialists or work study officers who will time with stop watches all the operations such as hoeing, spraying, hedge cutting or grass mowing in order to produce mean figures or Standard Minute Values (S.M.V.s) for the normal time taken per unit area. A factor can be built into this figure for stoppages due to breakdown or bad weather or for the time taken to repair equipment or transport it from one site to another. It is important to relate the work being measured to acceptable standards achieved. Examples of a range of man hours and annual labour requirements are given in table 2.7.

(ii) A simpler but less accurate way is to use the time sheets to produce estimates of the time involved in most of the major operations. Often, however, the smaller, but time-consuming tasks such as glasshouse work tend to be lumped under one heading, so that specific analysis becomes difficult. Tidying up is another 'lumped' figure, and in table 2.8 is included in the heading 'All other' work. Much depends on how the time sheets are filled in and the time staff have to do this.

(c) *Stage III: establishing manning levels.* Having assessed how much is to be maintained, and how long the various tasks should take per unit area, it is now possible to calculate manning levels in terms of the number of man hours needed to maintain all such areas and components, provided agreed standards of maintenance have been built into the work measurement exercise. Hastily done work, whether mowing or hoeing, that produces low man hour rates is not acceptable if the standard is well below that required by the senior management staff or head gardeners.

Bonus incentive schemes can be used where large numbers of staff are employed on grounds maintenance work. The calculated manning level figures are used to draw up weekly or monthly schedules of work that allow for agreed standards to be met within the times set. Staff individually, or in teams who consistently meet their target schedules are awarded bonuses as incentives to keep up consistent standards of work. However, the view of John Parker of Kent county council is that 'such schemes are expensive to install and are generally unlikely to be suitable for private gardens'. In these cases it is preferable to find out how long the main routine tasks take by talking to staff and consulting the time sheets. Owners or agents should then work out their own systems of additional payments for high productivity by gardening staff, even if it is only an annual bonus or 'recognition' at Christmas time.

From all this data measurement just described a great deal of useful management information can be extracted and applied, for example, to the easing of seasonal work loads.

It is all too familiar a fact that a summer peak is a very decided characteristic of all garden maintenance work, mainly due to the pressures of controlling vigorous vegetative growth, whether it be grass, weeds or hedges. The size and gradients of the peak will depend on the design and character of the gardens or grounds and the diversity of the components contained in them, and also on the effectiveness of the organisation of staff to carry out the maintenance. An actual example of these summer peaks is shown in table 2.8.

There are several ways of easing the pressures on the summer work load:

(a) *Use of part-time staff.* Where a number of full-time staff are employed it is often a fact that if there are sufficient staff to cope with the summer work load, then there may be too many employed in the off-peak winter months. If there are woodlands attached to the gardens of the estate then in the winter such work as felling, thinning or replanting is a useful occupation for these garden staff. Table 2.8 includes this aspect.

A reduction in the total number of full-time staff with the employment of more casual staff in the peak summer period, May to September, may effect a saving in total wages and also help to cope with the summer work loads.

(b) *Allowing more overtime* by the regular staff in the peak periods. This is not usually favoured by gardening staff who usually have their own gardens to maintain, or other activities, and who feel the extra money is not worth the loss of evening or weekend leisure time. Such overtime can usually only be expected to provide an average additional 10% of the normal working hours.

(c) *More mechanisation* and labour saving techniques may be applied to the summer tasks.

The use of machinery and herbicides can do much to reduce the 'peak' pressures and as John Parker notes 'the use of fairly expensive machinery can be justified in the summer months if it can thereby reduce the man power throughout the whole year'. On the other hand, labour saving machinery in the winter is unlikely to save overall costs unless there are other necessary tasks to be done in the time that is saved.

(d) *Alternative work methods.* A very worthwhile approach, even for the single-handed gardener, is to concentrate on as many jobs as possible in the quieter winter months such as hedge cutting, woodland or shrubbery work, and particularly the

Table 2.7 Annual labour requirements

	Approx. man hours per year	
Landscape/garden category	Small areas	Extensive areas
1. *Fence lines.* Annual weed spray and rotary cut long grass.	3 h/100 m	11 /1000 m
2. *Hedges.* Formal hedge cut four times a year, e.g. privet.		
1.5 m high (approx. 5 ft)	8 h/10 m	50 h/100 m
2.5 m high (approx. 8 ft)	13 h/10 m	95 h/100 m
Hedge cut once a year, e.g. beech		
1.5 m high	2 h/10 m	18 h/100 m
2.5 m high	4 h/10 m	30 h/100 m
3. *Large grass areas.*	up to 0.5 ha	over 1 ha
Playing fields –mown up to once a week (24 cuts/year) with five unit tractor trailed gangmower		
(excluding travelling to and from site).	24 h/ha	14 h/ha
Rough grass cut with a tractor mounted flail four times a year	20 h/ha	17 h/ha
4. *Lawns and grass banks*		
Large lawns cut up to once a week with a 900 mm (approx. 36 in) cylinder mower.	11 h/100 m²	34 h/1000 m²
Ditto with cuttings boxed off.	13 h/100 m²	45 h/1000 m²
Smaller lawns cut up to once a week with a 500 mm (18-20 in) cylinder mower.	14 h/100 m²	70 h/1000 m²
Ditto with cuttings boxed off.	17 h/100 m²	80 h/1000 m²
Rough grass cut up to once a month with a hand-propelled rotary mower up to 500 mm (18-20 in)	4 h/100 m²	25 h/1000 m²
Steep banks cut with a small rotary mower up to once a month.	8 h/100 m²	50 h/1000 m²
Steep bank with grass controlled by one cut and two sprays of maleic hydrazide.	—	24 h/1000 m²

NOTE
The hours shown for the smaller quantities are for isolated amounts and reflect the additional time that is used to prepare and put away equipment and tools for small amounts of work.

	Approx. man hours per year
5. *Shrub borders.* Light digging in winter and sprayed with simazine.	15 h/100 m²
Light digging in winter and hand hoed.	33 h/100 m²
6. *Ground cover* (established). Summer hand-weeding and clip and tidy in winter.	8 h/100 m²
7. Annual bedding. Spring and autumn replanting with hand hoeing in summer (excludes provision of plants	80 h/100 m²

8. *Amenity woodland.* Established (excluding major felling). up to 50 h/ha
   Newly planted (or tree screens). up to 50-100 h/ha

9. *Extensive parkland with woodland.*
   Without grazing animals. 90 h/ha (up to 20 ha/man)
   With grazing animals
   (excluding care of animals). 50 h/ha

10. *Road verges* (grass cutting). Rural roads (four cuts a year with tractor mounted flail). 12 h/km of road (mainly summer work up to 80 km/man)

    Urban roads (twelve cuts per year with pedestrian mower). 75 h (up to 15 km man)

Taken from *Landscape Techniques* (Parker and Wright, Ed. A. E. Weddle, 1979)

Table 2.8   Gardens department, Wye College – labour analysis, 1980

Activities	Seasonal distribution of man hours (five full-time staff)													
	Jan.	Feb.	Mar.	Apr.	May	June	July	Aug.	Sep.	Oct.	Nov.	Dec.	Total	%
Gardens (5 acres)	338	301	303	426	568	845	506	768	448	338	465	392	5698	51.4
Sports Field (4 acres)	99	4	47	73	48	67	74	49	44	82	25	61	673	6.1
Glasshouses	90	38	120	48	28	14	56	36	77	65	51	32	655	6.0
Properties	48	—	2	43	16	28	28	74	29	119	47	—	434	3.9
Teaching Areas	16	13	4	19	—	1	6	7	3	5	8	—	82	0.7
Woodlands (25 acres)	12	92	242	22	—	91	—	—	—	12	206	74	751	6.8
Holiday and sickness	48	56	244	136	128	80	112	360	261	194	96	165	1880	17.0
All other	163	298	45	39	14	56	52	14	18	36	34	123	892	8.1
Total	814	802	1,007	806	802	1,182	834	1,308	880	851	932	849	11065	100.0

Note the peak labour periods or 'humps' referred to earlier.
Also the very significant percentage of time that goes on holidays and sickness.
'All other' refers to cleaning and tidying jobs and miscellaneous work not easily classified.

application of the suitable residual-type herbicides like simazine and 'Casoron' in the late winter or early spring. Such applications can save money and many hours of hand weeding in the very late spring and summer months.

(e) *The addition of extra winter work*. Fencing, forestry, repairs to gates, seats and equipment are all obvious examples of winter tasks. There are also planting and improvement schemes when the weather allows, and the use of glasshouses for raising annuals, pot plants and young plants. One point should be made here about the 'dangers' and the delights of glasshouses and the man hours involved. Table 2.8 includes the total man hours involved in two quite small glasshouses used mainly for raising bedding plants and decorative half-hardy plants. If the cost of these plants was estimated, it is almost certainly the case that it would be cheaper to buy in plants from a reliable source. On the other hand, owners and managers must realise that propagation and glasshouse work is of great satisfaction and importance to most gardeners and can contribute to job satisfaction. To close down glasshouse units on economy grounds alone may not be really justified if the savings so achieved are at the expense of the motivation of the gardening staff. This is a delicate exercise, yet one appreciates so often in large gardens that ranges of once productive glasshouses are now too expensive to run and to maintain, and new roles have to be found for them (see Chapter 7).

(f) *Contract maintenance*. As a complete or partial alternative to all those labour problems, it is quite possible to have one's garden or part of it maintained by contract using a local garden or landscape contractor. More and more people are turning to this solution, particularly elderly people who are finding their gardens a burden and increasingly difficult to maintain and who find reliable part-time gardeners difficult to get. Busy professional people who have insufficient time for their gardens, but who want them to look well cared for, also are turning to the contract system and, of course, many industrial or institutional landscapes are partially or entirely managed in this way. A most important factor here is to find a reliable, responsible and efficient contractor who knows and understands gardens and landscape maintenance. It is also equally important to sign a written agreement or contract with the contractor, in which both sides are quite clear how much is to be done for an agreed sum. It is essential to inspect the garden or grounds with the contractor and preferably itemise areas to be maintained, and tasks to be done, and as most local authorities do, to get quotations or estimates from several firms. As regards costs, one must realise that the rates quoted for particular operations will seem to be high, since the contractor has to cover his own labour costs and his overheads including travelling and wet weather time, in addition to making a percentage profit.

Machinery and equipment

Selecting machinery

Before looking more closely at different types of machinery and equipment it is important to think rather carefully about the sort of aids one really needs for particular situations, and equally, the actual degree of use envisaged, in order to justify the initial or capital cost.

Selection criteria are as follows:

(a) The primary reason for investing in mechanical aids must surely be to get through a range of physical maintenance tasks more speedily, and with less manual and physical effort. As some of the case studies show in Chapter 8 without a range of such machinery, many gardens today would not be maintained at all, or certainly to far lower standards.

(b) The important decision on just how much mechanisation in which to invest depends very much therefore on the size of the garden and the range of tasks that can be mechanised and the extent to which staff are employed whose time can be saved for other activities.

(c) Where staff are employed, machinery can help to reduce the prolonged drudgery of leaf sweeping or hedge cutting as examples. Machinery also, if properly handled, is cheaper than people, and the capital cost of a new mower, for example, may be saved in man hours in less than two mowing seasons.

(d) The important decision as to whether a particular piece of equipment is a luxury or a necessity will depend very much on the situation and the circumstances of the garden or amenity park. This is particularly the case where the garden is of modest size with limited areas of grass to be mown, and lengths of hedge to be cut. Here the investment in mechanical aids needs rather careful thought and should really be dictated by the amount of use to which they will be put. Hedge cutting is a good example here. A run of 20–30 m of established hedge about 1.5 m (5 ft) high can usually be cut with hand shears in 5–6 h or a little longer and, of course, the garden shears are useful for other tasks as well. If one invests £150–£200 in a power-driven hedge cutter this can reduce the time taken to cut the same length of hedge to little more than an hour. These power cutters have limited other uses in the garden.

Time saved could be used for other tasks, but if there were long runs of hedges and topiary, such a machine would be more justified. However, where areas are unsuitable for mechanical aids, one has to think of other reasons than time saved for spending the money on machinery in the first place. This balance is difficult to get right. One either over-equips with aids and gadgets which are then used for a fraction of their working lives, or under-equips with small machines that are not tough enough for the jobs required and wear out prematurely.

An analysis of machinery and equipment
This analysis takes the form of a summary of the essential groups only, with information on performance and guidelines on their selection.

Turf and amenity grass mowing equipment
There are something like 250 different types of mowing machines for turf, excluding the various hand tools and hand-held gadgets, so the choice is wide.
Most of the power machines fall into one of four categories:

(a) cylinder or reel-type mowers
(b) rotary mowers
(c) reciprocating cutter-bar mowers
(d) flail mowers.

Of these four groups, the cylinder and the rotary mower groups are by far the most important and widely used.

Cylinder or reel mowers. The cutting action consists of revolving blades on the cylinder that bear on a fixed blade held at given heights above the grass and usually accompanied by a built-in light roller. A clean, scissor-like cut is therefore affected (if the blades are kept sharp) and the number of blades fixed spirally on the cylinder will determine the quality and the number of cuts per unit length. This number of cuts per metre is a useful gauge of a cylinder mower's performance determined not only by the number of blades in the reel, but also by the revolutions of the cylinder and the forward speed of the mower. Thus top quality mowers may have as many as ten blades per reel and give about one hundred cuts per metre whereas mowers for average lawns will have six blades per reel and sixty-five to eighty cuts per metre. If the cutting rates fall below forty per metre there is a tendency for inferior cutting and a ribbing effect on the grass which incidentally can also happen if one of the blades on the reel becomes distorted or damaged.

The width of cut is also another very important factor, in effect determining the rate of cutting of given areas. Table 2.9 shows this very clearly, as well as the different performance rates for different categories of mowers in the other classes. Width is also related to manoeuvrability. Thus for a series of small lawns with narrow or intimate grass paths around flower beds, and trees, it is better to go for a reliable 30–35 cm (12–14 in) petrol or electric mower with roller. For larger expanses of grass an 45 cm (18 in) hand-propelled or ride-on mower is ideal, and when one has very extensive areas of uncluttered grass to mow the triple-type or gang-type cylinder mowers are fast, manoeuvrable and efficient.

The range of triple mowers now on the market includes some exceptionally versatile machines capable of mowing surprisingly small areas and negotiating obstacles with great efficiency (plate 2.2). Their performance rates are also excellent as tables 2.7 and 2.9 show. Widths of up to 86 in can be cut with such machines.

Plate 2.2 A Jacobsen triple mower demonstrates its versatility and smoothness of cut on the front lawn of an historic house. Note the traditional clipping of lavenders in progress in the background

Table 2.9   Comparison of approximate annual mowing rates for different areas of grass (Kent County Council, 1978)

Grass type	Machine	Annual hourly rate for 1000 m²	Fuel per acre cut (gall.)
Close mown 7-12 mm (¼-½ in) 24 cuts/yr	Gang/triple mowers 1.94-3.45 m (76-125 in)	1.5-3.0 h	0.2-0.6
	900 mm cylinder (36 in) (hand propelled)	35-45 h (box off)	1.2
	500 mm cylinder (20 in) (hand propelled)	70-80 h	1.8
'Paddock' rough 35-100 mm (1½-4 in) 4-6 cuts/yr	Tractor/flail 900 mm (36 in)	5-6 h	1.1
Banks	500 mm (20 in) hand rotary	25 h	2.5
	Ditto steep banks	50 h	10.0
	One cut/1-2 sprays	24 h	—
	Growth retarder		
Hay meadow 1-2 cuts/yr	(1) Cutter bar collect hay	35-45 h	
	(2) Forager harvester	5-20 h	—

Grass collection. The collection of grass cuttings is usually essential for the finest swards used for accurate playing surfaces such as golf or bowls. Otherwise, except in times of vigorous flushes of growth that usually occur in spring and late summer, it is not really necessary, from the point of view of the well being of the turf, to remove the cuttings. Provided the mowing is done regularly at a consistent and not too close a cut, and there are no swathes of clippings left lying on the mown surface, the long-term effects of returning the mowings may be significant. This is discussed in more detail in Chapter 3. Lawn mowings are also useful for compost and mulches and as a general rule it is preferable to collect the first three or four cuts once growth starts in March and April and perhaps again in August or September, depending on the growth factor. 'Boxing off' or collecting the mowings is done by a variety of designs depending on the type of mower but for most cylinder mowers it is usually the standard box in metal or plastic. Collection is not usually possible with triple or gang mowers Boxing off does take additional time as the figures in table 2.7 show.

Power units. Power for cylinder mowers is generated by either the human 'push' petrol engines or electric motors. For small lawns, a well-designed and maintained push mower is cheap and effective.

Petrol engines for mowers are generally very reliable, efficient and long lasting. A good make of engine is the Briggs and Stratton that now powers many mowers. One advantage the petrol engine cylinder mowers have over the rotary types, is that being much slower revolution engines their petrol consumption is usually less than the high 'revving' rotary models.

Electric mowers are, of course, free from possible starting troubles and the maintenance needs of petrol mowers, but in general they do not have the sustaining power, and are best for small lawns and grass areas.

There are also the robust, side-wheel powered cylinder models with flexible blades especially designed for cutting rough or long grass quite successfully, although they do not produce the same quality of finish as the roller-type close-bladed models.

Rotary mowers. These are comparatively modern introductions compared with the cylinder or reel mowers, which really only began to make any impact from the late 1950s onwards. They are now universally popular for all types of grass mowing and their sales have generally exceeded those of other types.

The reason lies in the comparative cheapness and simplicity of design and manufacture, the principle being a rotary plate or disc on which are mounted several flexible blades, or a single propellor-like blade, both types revolving at much higher speeds than the cylinder mowers, cutting the grass by more of a macerating action, than a clean, crisp cut. Even when the blades are blunt their sheer force and speed will remove grass and soft vegetation. (If cylinder mower blades are blunt or badly adjusted, however, they simply will not cut properly.)

There are thus a number of advantages of the rotary mower over the cylinder types:

(a) They are robust, uncomplicated and effective, less easily damaged (stones or metal-like objects, nails or wire can be disastrous to cylinder mower blades) and versatile.

(b) They can usually be used in all weathers, within reason, for quite a wide range of grass heights.

(c) Depending on the machine, they are usually far more versatile, capable of cutting level grass and slopes or banks. The Flymo hover-types are especially useful for many different purposes.
(d) They generally need less regular overhauling and blade adjustments or sharpening, if used properly.
(e) As they tend to macerate or shred the grass, they leave less of a swathe to collect. In this respect they can be used to shred autumn leaves, reducing the bulk to collect or eliminating the need to collect altogether.

Their main disadvantages are as follows:

(a) A close, fine precision cut is seldom possible, due to the very different cutting action, the spacing of the blades, the sweeping macerating cut, and the lack of any rolling action (in most models).
(b) They are usually noisier and thirstier needing more fuel to power the high-speed blades.
(c) Swards cut continually with a rotary mower tends to develop a softer, spongier texture with more moss and weeds. Collection of grass mowings is generally less easy, involving a bag or receptacle slung on behind the mower.

A summary of the main categories of rotary mowers follows.
Wheeled rotary mowers. There are models in which both the wheels and the blades are power driven, or others where only the blades are powered. The latter as typified by the Hayterette are excellent machines, being very light, easy to use and very manoeuvrable, running speedily over quite large areas of paddock length or fairly close-cut grass with surprising ease. Widths range from 35 cm to 45 cm (14 in to 18 in) although some small electrically powered machines may have 30 cm (12 in) width cuts.
Tractor-mounted rotary mowers. These are usually larger, more substantial machines with cutting widths of 1 m (3 ft) or more, the blades either being mounted beneath the body of the tractor in the case of many of the small or mini-tractors, or as a detachable mounting behind, as in the case of the powerful Votex machine for farm-size tractors.
All these mowers are suitable for extensive areas of reasonably short or longer grass such as orchards, among trees in arboreta or woodland or parkland and are simple and easy to operate. The large Votex machines can cope with rough vegetation including brushwood and brambles, etc.
Hover-type mowers. In these a down draft of air or air cushion and a fast rotary propellor blade enable the machine to slide over the surface of the grass, in a remarkably light and flowing action. Flymo have had the monopoly of this type until recently, but there are now other makes of hover mowers. Widths vary from the smaller domestic 35 cm (14 in) models to the larger 90 cm (36 in) professional models, some with supplementary wheels. These mowers are especially suitable for gradients, banks and slopes, and they will also make quite a close and reasonable job of level turf, and will deal with weeds and grass under or among shrubs, hedges and young trees. They can run along grass edges since there are usually no wheels to worry about. They can chop the grass very finely, so there is usually little left to collect or disfigure the grass. For extensive banks the Flymo can be lowered on a rope, the operator standing on the top free from the machine.

Reciprocating cutter-bar mowers (Sicklebar mowers in the U.S.A.). These are much less used and therefore very limited in the range of models available, these cutter-bar mowers are based on the traditional hay cutter design, where a reciprocating blade is forward-mounted on a wheeled machine. They are essentially intended for cutting hay length grass and vegetation and for this purpose there is still nothing better (other than hand scything) since the grass is not flattened or compressed before it is cut. The Allen Auto scythe has been the standard machine for many years, rather heavy, tough and reliable but recently a revival of interest in long-grass management has prompted some manufacturers to introduce lighter models of the same basic design. These reciprocating cutter-bar machines can be hired for occasional use at hay cutting time (see Chapter 3 also) since they generally have little use at other times. The mowings do have to be collected as green matter or dried as hay.

Flail mowers. Developed from agricultural grass cutting and silage-making mowers. Flail mowers consist of a series of free-moving flail-type blades, mounted on a rotary cylinder and rotating at high speeds to macerate the grass and vegetation rather like the rotary mowers. The flail cylinders are well guarded to reduce the risk of flying stones and objects. They are usually intended for farm-scale or estate uses, being mounted at the rear of a tractor (Hayter) or on a flexible arm, the latter now widely used, also for road verges, banks, hedges and scrub. They are too big and expensive for small gardens and limited access area, but have a performance that compares favourably with gang mowers - for rough grass areas.

Other grass cutting equipment.
Brush cutters ('weed eaters'). Recent arrivals to the garden maintenance scene, a wide range of makes and models are now available. In principle, they are rather like miniature flail mowers consisting of a high-speed rotating head disc to which are attached either nylon laces or cord flails, or more robust blades, or even a circular saw. The nylon models are useful for grass and soft vegetation, but the heavier-bladed models will deal with brushwood, brambles and heavy vegetation. Attached to a scythe-like arm these brush cutters are either electrically driven for the small domestic models, or powered with light, chain-saw type engines. The latter are really the robust, ideal models for large gardens and estates. There are many models now available to suit all pockets and purposes. They are especially useful for dealing with small fringes of grass and weeds and trees and shrubs, fence lines, and woodland. Their cutting rate is about four times as fast as hand scything. A recent introduction is the Andrews Auto trimmer, which is a tough wheeled forward - mounted brush cutter, less fatiguing, quieter and very manoeuvrable.

Tree maintenance equipment
When considering equipment to be used for the care of trees and shrubs it becomes apparent that there are two basic categories or levels of operation to be considered:

(a) The professional level of the tree surgeon and the aboriculturalist.
(b) The amateur level with usually a much smaller scale of operations.

Machinery and equipment for tree surgery and arboriculture. The recent emergence of a trained and professional group of people who call themselves arboriculturalists has helped to promote a considerable range of machinery and equipment as well as a more professional approach to tree management. The increasing problems facing the owners of large gardens and parks, and also local authorities and others, of large numbers of mature, or overmature trees or those suffering from diseases have been, to a certain extent met by this comparatively new profession, with excellent work being done by the Arboricultural Association.

The equipment used tends to be specialised and quite sophisticated and for those who want to have a comprehensive guide to such equipment, and to the whole subject of tree surgery, Peter Bridgeman's book on this subject is recommended.

Chain saws. 'The powered chain saws have done more than any other tool to alter methods and to increase efficiency. With the great range of types, sizes and attachments available there are very few cutting jobs that cannot be carried out by this' (Peter Bridgeman). Earlier models were heavy, slow cutting and unsuitable but there are now plenty of newer lighter, faster-cutting models with less vibration. In selecting chain saws there are a number of points to take into account but especially the size in relation to use (weight and engine performance to suit all purposes) the spares and servicing position (breakdown can cause costly delays in time and labour) and the safety factors.

Chain saws are potentially very dangerous tools and accidents occur even with experienced operators. The Agriculture (Field Machinery) Regulations of 1962 apply to professional and regular employers and present such precautions as guards, safety switches, etc. A very useful *Code of Practice for Chain Saw Users* is published by the Power Saw Association of Great Britain.

Hand saws. Still very important for all tree work and when pruning large shrubs. There are three basic types:

The cross cut or bow saw of different sizes with replaceable blades and excellent for small work, especially of green wood (fig. 2.2 (a)).
The pruning saw for intricate work and fruit tree and shrub pruning (fig. 2.2 (b)).
The pole saw - a pruning saw on a long handle for difficult remote cuts.

All saws should be regularly sharpened and set and kept oiled and rust free.

Other cutting tools include axes, mattocks, hooks and secateurs. (There are now over forty different types of secateurs on the market.) A selection of tools used for surgery and pruning is shown in fig. 2.2.

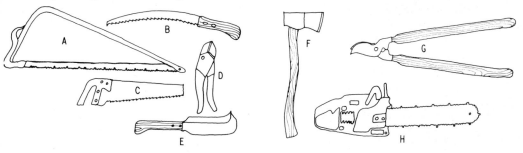

Fig. 2.2 A = Bow saw; B = Pruning saw; C = Hand saw; D = Anvil-type secateurs; E = Bill hook; F = Wood axe; G = Loppers and pruners; H = Chain saw

Hand winches. These portable winches are extremely useful for large tree pulling and stump removal. A particularly useful model, is the Trewhella Monkey winch operated by two men, being moderately mobile and exerting a pull of five tons, sufficient for most tree work. There are also the Tirfor range of light portable hand winches.

Hedge cutting equipment

In reviewing briefly this sort of equipment a distinction is made between farm, estate and countryside hedges; and garden and park hedges. There are obvious differences in the machinery, and equipment used as a general rule, and the standards of finish required.

Farm and countryside hedges. These are mostly composed of native species of woody plants such as hawthorn or quickthorn (*Crataegus*), hedge maple (*Acer campestre*) and many other species. Traditionally many were established as enclosure or stock-proof hedges and the management consisted of hedge laying at infrequent intervals, when hedges had become overgrown, to increase thickness or density with annual or more frequent trimming.

Most farm hedges today are cut by mechanical means. Tractor-mounted cutter bars or saws have now largely been replaced by flails, mounted on a flexible arm, versatile as hedge, scrub and verge cutters. Widespread controversy and some disapproval is generated by certain cutting practices with flails, especially when an overgrown hedge or line of scrub is 'massed' for the first time with a flail. The result is certainly a visual disaster. However, after several years of consistent flailing with a good operator and machine, some very trim hedges can be achieved, in a fraction of the time needed for the hand methods.

Garden hedges. Here we are dealing with essentially more exotic species of hedges and ornamental features, including conifers and many deciduous species (see Chapter 3). The scale of operation is also usually much more restricted, many gardens only having limited lengths of such hedge. The tools therefore are basically of two types: hand tools or mechanical hedge trimmers.

Hand tools for garden hedge cutting are more refined than those for rural work being either variations on the garden shears or secateurs. Reliable, efficient shears are expensive to buy but well worth the additional cost. Modern makes are lighter and less tiring to use, and those with the notch at the base of the blades should be chosen for dealing with the occasional outsize shoots, and also rubber buffers between the handles reduce the jarring and shock on the arm. Stainless steel blades are preferable and frequent oiling prevents the gumming up that can happen when clipping resinous hedges, like cypresses.

Mechanical hedge trimmers. There are now quite a few of these to choose from depending on the amount of hedge to be cut and the cash available. Whether electrically or engine powered most of them work on the principle of the reciprocating cutter bar as an arm whose length varies with the size and design of the model.

Electric cutters operated by mains, generator or battery powered motors are quiet, light and efficient. There are some very light-weight and inexpensive cutters but these can often be false economy if extensive or tough hedges have to be cut. Thus average 1 m (3 ft) high garden hedges of the ubiquitous and effective *Lonicera nitida* and privet (*Ligustrum ovalifolium*) can be trimmed easily with light-weight cutters, provided they are done regularly (four or five times in the growing season) whereas taller, tougher hedges of beech (*Fagus sylvatica*) and holly (*Ilex aquifolium*) really need a more robust longer-bladed model. Just such a machine is the Wolseley Little Wonder 75 cm (30 in) blade machine that may be operated best from the mains or from a generator or battery. It can reduce the time taken by hand shear's cutting by 60-70%.

Petrol engined cutters are increasing in popularity with small powerful two-stroke engines and 45-60 cm (18-24 in) blades. A model like the Japanese Little Arrow can deal swiftly and effectively with all types of hedge and is powerful enough to cut back into overgrown woody hedges. It will cut through woody shoots 2.5 cm (1 in) in thickness. There is a disadvantage of additional weight, especially when held above head height for any length of time, and the fumes and noise are disagreeable. For continuous use with these powered machines, as with chain saws, ear muffs are probably advisable. One also has to be extra careful with such machines to avoid mishaps. Many now have as a regulation fitting a safety 'cut-out' that shuts off the cutter bar as soon as the hand is taken off the accelerator trigger. These powered machines, on average, cut hedges at eight to ten times the rate of hand shears with equally good results if the operator knows what he is doing.

Equipment for soil cultivation

Soil cultivation is usually important (a) at the preparation stage and (b) as a maintenance routine for controlling weeds and maintaining fertility or organic matter levels.

I would add one word of warning to those with heavy clay soils, that using heavy machinery, or even machinery at all, during periods when conditions are too wet, can lead to compaction and clodding.

Routine soil cultivations are usually done in most gardens among shrubs, perennials or annuals to disturb and kill weeds. The use of residual herbicides or mulches is again reducing the need for such surface soil disturbance, especially once the weed population in the soil has been reduced.

The hoe. This is useful for quick mechanical cultivation and weed control. Various models are available from the traditional Dutch, the swan neck (fig. 2.3) to the

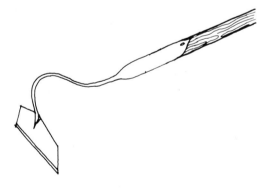

Fig. 2.3 A swan-neck hoe. A design that has not really changed since the days of John Evelyn.

useful Swoe and the unique three-pronged trident used in some French gardens. Admittedly effective use is limited to dry weather conditions, but working with the weather and acting promptly in dry spells, vast quantities of annual weed seeds can be controlled speedily and effectively with the hoe. The action should be a shallow light stirring one, not a deep chop, moving only the top 12-25 mm (½-1 in) of soil. If one has a small fork handy when hoeing, one can also dig out the occasional deep-rooting weeds like docks and dandelions or couch, which really cannot be dealt with by hoeing off. Regular mulches will also produce a friable medium for occasional hoeing.

Spraying and distributing equipment

Although instruments and applicators have been in use for a very long time in gardens, it is only in the last twenty years or so that there has been a 'flow' if that is the right word, of chemicals into horticulture and agriculture and for amateurs and professionals in gardens and parks. There has also been a corresponding array of gadgets and equipment with which to apply them. The chemicals themselves are considered later in this chapter, and some of the case studies give actual examples of the spraying appliances in use today. This is a brief summary:

Sprayers. There are many different categories of these available depending on the scale of the work needed and the frequency of use.

Hand-operated pressure sprayers. Very many models are now available most being of light plastic construction and carried by hand or with a shoulder strap. Capacities are usually 4½-9 litres (1-2 gallons) and the diluted spray is pressurised by a hand pump (which often serves as the handle of the sprayer for carrying). Once pressurised, this is usually sufficient to empty the contents of the plastic container or bottle. Look for robust models with metal nozzles and lances. The pressurised bottle types are very useful for small to medium-sized gardens.

Hand-pumped knapsack sprayers. These have a larger capacity of up to 18 litre (4 gallons), and the pressure is maintained by continuous pumping. One of the best range of models available is produced by Cooper Pegler with a wide range of jets, nozzles, lances and a useful extra lance up to 5 m (15 ft). A hood or shield is also available for herbicide spraying.

Power knapsack sprayers. These are really for commercial use in fruit plantations and nurseries, or where spraying is likely to be a frequent operation. Light, and extremely effective with two-stroke engine units and emitting a fine atomised spray over a wide area. Tractor-mounted sprayers with lances are also available for extensive turf spraying, or for drives and paths.

The controlled droplet applicator: The Micron sprayer. This is a recent development in line with current research and practice that aims to use the minimum of the active chemical (low volume) by a precise placement of very fine droplets. Very small quantities of the chemical therefore are applied, saving in time and materials. One sprayer is battery operated and there is the minimum risk of drift and wastage provided the instructions are followed carefully.

Hand syringes. There is also a range of hand syringes and, of course, watering cans with trickle attachments and sprayers for very local and limited use.

Distribution of granular materials. The application of granular chemicals for weed control or as fertilisers should be done as accurately as possible, and whereas the hand method may be good enough for fertilisers in shrub areas and the like on a small scale, an even, accurate placement is only really possible with some sort of mechanical distributor. There are a number of simple hand-propelled models for treating turf and lawns which are always well advertised, and for granular herbicides, special distributors are available to ensure accurate dosage and placement. Do follow the manufacturer's instructions regarding the rate of application. Adding a little bit more 'to make sure it works' can be disastrous.

Irrigation equipment
Irrigation or watering is one of those activities that depends for the most part on the weather, and unless one is in the propagation or crop raising business, or in charge of intensively used summer sports turf, the occasions when one needs irrigation or watering are as uncertain as the weather itself.

A typical garden or park would need serious watering under one of the following conditions and using the suggested method:

(a) Establishing newly planted trees, shrubs or perennials immediately after planting, and especially following late spring planting in dry weather. Several good 'soaks' are preferable to sprinkles and remember that container-grown plants are less likely to suffer drought effects after planting than bare-root plants. If hoses are not available for watering, cans or containers are the alternative for limited sites, and water tanks for large-scale planting schemes.

(b) Helping all plants through a drought crisis such as occurred in the summer of 1976. If watering is permitted, sprinklers and rotary sprayers attached to the mains supplies are one method, but evaporation is high, and water is wasted with overhead watering. Preferable are the lines of 'lay flat' plastic perforated tubing linked to a low pressure water supply, providing a trickle feed system at the base of the plants. These lengths of tube can be moved freely over an area to be watered. If available a deep mulch of any organic material should follow the soaking.

(c) Turf and lawn irrigation during very dry periods, especially where the turf is in use for sports. There is a whole range of devices for turf irrigation. Remember however, that brown or desiccated lawns are by no means 'dead' lawns and once the rains come, it is amazing to see how quickly the grass will recover. This was the case particularly in 1976. Many of the newer strains of grasses referred to in Chapter 2 are being selected for drought resistance.

Other garden maintenance equipment
Leaf sweepers. Fallen leaves are a problem, mainly in the autumn, but also after storms in the summer months and in the case of a few evergreen trees like holly (*Ilex*) and holm oak (*Quercus ilex*) in May and June when the old leaves are shed in a dried condition.

Large-scale sweepers for large gardens and parks are still not readily available.

There are now petrol engine fan blowers to blow leaves off paths or onto paths into windrows or heaps and the Winro blower has a powerful directional fan to blow leaves into specific areas or heaps. It is also possible to blow the leaves directly into woodland or shrub areas as a mulch without the trouble of collection. It may be used in combination with the Billy Goat vacuum leaf cleaner. This is a purpose-built 'hoover-type' garden vacuum cleaner which is available in various widths (from 65 cm (26 in) to 90 cm (36 in)) engine power units, with a reasonably capacious bag for the leaves, litter or grass clippings. One Billy Goat will do the work of ten persons with brooms. It also has a wandering hose suction attachment for collecting debris etc., in places the machine cannot reach. It is surprisingly effective at picking leaves off loose gravel drives or paths without collecting the gravel. The main limitation is the quantity and area of leaves to be collected. For large gardens and parks it really is not big enough.

There are also various makes of hand-propelled leaf sweepers with rotating brushes to pick up the leaves and flick them into a collecting bag or net. Some mowers have such attachments. These are fine in their way for small areas under dry conditions, but really where leaves have to be collected from large trees like beeches or planes, a good spring steel lawn rake or the 'Grabber rake' and a 'Donkey' or large lay-flat collecting sheet can be even quicker. Transport to the nearest compost heap or bonfire is the main factor. If a central compost heap is a long way from the source of the leaves, try making one or more secondary leaf compost heaps. Four corner posts and fine mesh Netlon netting can quickly make an enclosure for the leaves, grass clippings, etc., saving hours of tramping backwards and forwards especially if only a small barrow is available for transport and not a sizeable tractor or trailer. Leaves may also be deposited among shrubs and trees.

Light-weight barrows and trucks are now available in many different sizes and designs and the latter can also be used in conjunction with small tractors to haul the heavier loads. The type of barrow or truck should be related to the design of the garden and its accessibility, widths of paths and gates, the location of steps and steep slopes.

For off-the-ground work there are excellent sturdy light-weight alloy steps and extending ladders that take some of the effort out of hedge cutting, and to reach even higher to cut occasional overhanging branches or damaged shoots, the extending long-arm secateurs are also very useful.

For edging lawns and borders in turf, long-handled edging shears are still favoured by most practical gardeners using robust, well-sharpened, light-weight models. There are also a few powered edging models particularly the Spin Trim (see p. 174) but these really work best in stone-free soils and with well-defined edges.

Some principles of weed control

Weeds are often defined in terms of horticulture and in gardens, as plants that are out of place, or that do not belong in the planting scheme or design. Despite the fact that many are quite attractive and decorative (the majority are British native plants) their invasive or competitive qualities in the wrong place can impair the visual qualities of a garden and in fact physically affect the successful establishment and growth of recently planted subjects. This can be an especially serious matter with commercial crops. A series of interesting experiments carried out by the Agriculture Research Council on weeds in woody nursery stock showed that newly planted shrubs of different species that were allowed to become weed infested suffered a reduction in growth and size by as much as 50%. The critical months for weed control in these experiments were May and June. Similar batches of plants that were kept weed free until the end of June and then allowed to become weedy suffered far less check in growth.

Weed biology. The concept of weediness is really not easy to define satisfactorily since to some people weediness can be said to be a subjective thing in the eye of the beholder. Further, with today's move towards conservation and more natural plantings, the inclusion of British native plants with some accepted weed species in planting schemes and seed mixtures is certainly likely to be an increasing trend in the future. Nevertheless there are many situations in gardens and parks where weeds must be controlled, if agreed standards of maintenance of plant associations and plant welfare are to be kept up, and on this assumption some understanding of the biology and life cycles of garden weeds will be helpful in considering various alternatives available today for their control. The *Weed Control Handbooks* issued by the Weed Research Organisation offers a useful basis for the definition of such weed species.

'These species establish themselves without deliberate action by man, and when present are difficult to eradicate. They tend to be aggressive, competitive and adaptable, capable of exploiting habitats created or modified by man, and of forming extensive populations that interfere with agricultural and other activities. Their most important attributes are efficient reproduction combined with mechanisms that permit survival under temporary unfavourable conditions.'

The weed population of a particular area is determined by a number of interrelated factors of which climate, soil and the natural ecology all play a part.

However, the most important factor is undoubtedly the use to which the land is being, or has been, put. Thus arable cropping and market gardening if efficiently done with frequent cultivations, discourage deep-rooting perennial weeds, but often allow quick-maturing, shallow-rooted annual species like groundsel (*Senecio vulgaris*) and shepherd's-purse (*Capsella bursa pastoris*) to gain a foothold. On the other hand, permanent or semi-permanent planted areas of shrubs, perennials and rock plants, for example, unless regularly weeded can become invaded by annual and perennial species, the latter becoming an especial problem when their vigorous and invasive root and shoot system become intermingled with those of herbaceous perennials and rock plants.

The majority of garden weeds therefore will be either annuals, (a few biennials) or perennials, and in the latter case they can be non-woody herbaceous plants or less commonly shrubs. To reduce populations of any of these in the soil has been the practice of gardeners for many centuries using for the most part, well-tried techniques or hand tools, already discussed, to control them.

Annual weeds are capable, as many know only too well, of building up large populations of seeds in the soil. For example one individual plant of shepherd's-purse will produce up to 4000 seeds in its short life span of a few months and the figure for the corn poppy (*Papaver rhoeus*) is about 17000.

Professor E. H. Roberts of Reading University gives some quite dramatic figures of weed seed populations in cultivated land. The average population of weed seeds in weedy ground is around 50 000/m² in the upper 15 mm (½ in) of soil, or 500 000 000/ha. If the soil is undisturbed but no further seeding occurs, the number decreases by about 22% per year. However, if the soil is dug twice yearly the rate of depletion may increase to 30% and with frequent cultivations as in traditional intensive horticulture, the population may fall as rapidly as 45% each year. However, it is almost impossible to remove weed seeds entirely, but a population of about 100 seeds/m² is acceptable as almost weed free. It can take up to eleven years of frequent cultivation to reach this figure in practice, and only one year of poor weed control can undo all the good work of many years. Any weed control programme, whether by manual or chemical methods, should aim to kill annual weeds before they seed, or preferably to prevent their emerging through the soil.

Prompt action with the hoe or the sprayer or applicator at the appropriate time can save hours and hours of hand weeding, not counting the competitive effect on the plants being weeded. Remember also the A.R.C. trials quoted earlier which showed that the May or June weeds can be the most competitive and harmful to crops or ornamental plants.

Another point with annual weed seeds is that some have a remarkable persistence and viable life in soils from a few years to records of more than fifty years with some vetches and leguminous plants.

Perennial weed species with creeping stems either as rhizomes (usually below soil level) or stolons (usually at soil level) increase often rapidly by a series of these stems, each stem having a series of nodes or joints along its length from which new shoots can arise. Roots can also arise at these nodes if the stems are severed or damaged. For example, with couch grass (*Agropyron repens*) in undisturbed grassland, it is estimated that 95% of the lateral buds of the rhizome system do not need to grow at all. Control aims at either continuous cultivation under favourable weather conditions to desiccate and weaken the stems and roots, or careful removal from the soil or chemical control.

The same goes for the deep-rooted perennial weeds, which are even more difficult to control or eradicate. It has been recorded that in a single year, the root spread of creeping thistle (*Cirsium arvense*) was about 12 m (40 ft) across in agricultural land. An interesting point with this weed is the fact that in permanent grassland its root spread is much more restricted due to the competition from grasses and a state of near dormancy can be reached in light swards, which when broken by ploughing can result in a forest of thistle shoots. However, when flowering shoots are produced there is a considerable reduction of food reserves in the roots.

Weed control measures in gardens and parks

The following alternatives should be considered:

(a) Hand tools and mechanical cultivators, forking, etc.
(b) Mulches and ground covers
(c) Chemicals as herbicides.

Hand tool methods and mechanised cultivations
From the brief insight into the biology of weeds therefore, control methods should now be more clearly understood. Hand methods using hoes, forks, or mechanised cultivation with plough, harrow discs and rotary cultivators should all aim to disturb weeds as frequently as possible. Hoeing or hand weeding already described can be a successful and precise method of weed control among mixed borders and special plant collections provided the operator is skilled in using the hoe and knowledgeable about the plants being weeded. In dry periods and dry areas, routine light hoeing three or four times in the growing season will disturb or destroy most annual weeds. Deep-rooted perennials like docks (*Rumex* sp.), dandelions (*Taraxacum*) and creeping species like buttercups (*Ranunculus*) and the inevitable ground elder (*Aegopodium*) really need forking out of planted areas. In support of chemical control of weeds Dr Robinson of the Kinsealy Research Institute, Dublin, has shown convincing evidence that surface cultivations can damage the roots of woody plants with a possible reduction in growth and vigour. Flame guns

have limited use on drives and paths now that effective herbicides are available. Fuel is now too expensive also.

Kitchen gardens or other more extensive areas with a high population of perennial weeds. like ground elder and couch, can be cleaned up without chemicals in dry seasons and naturally low rainfall areas, by continuous cultivations throughout one full growing season, by a process of disturbance and desiccation. Most weeds can be removed this way, but the weather is a critical factor. Thus chemicals will be an invaluable aid in this respect during wet summers or in high rainfall areas, or where quick results are desired.

Mulches and ground covers

There is a renewed interest in mulches in all aspects of horticulture, and especially for gardens and ornamental areas. It is perhaps misleading to place this short section on mulches under weed control since it must be emphasised that in general mulches alone will not control weeds under very weedy conditions. If used in conjunction with other techniques they can be of great help, and, of course, plastic film sheeting, used as a mulch in crop production certainly does reduce weed growth considerably. If mulching materials (summarised below) are used thickly enough, they can also smother annual weed growth, but perennial weeds will usually grow through the mulch unless deterred in other ways, i.e. by chemicals. The cost factor does, however, have to be considered.

Also when mulches have a high carbon to nitrogen ratio, e.g. sawdust or straw, bacterial breakdown causes loss of nitrogen from the soil and compensating dressings are needed to allow for this (see table 2.10). Ratios above 1:30 normally need this nitrogen.

Table 2.10 Nitrogen content of organic materials and carbon to nitrogen ratio

Material	Nitrogen (%)	C:N Ratio
Sewage sludge	5-6	1:6
Young grass clippings	4.0	1:12
Grass clippings (average, mixed)	2.4	1:19
Farmyard manure	2.15	1:14
Seaweed	1.9	1:19
Potato haulms	1.5	1:25
Garden compost	1.0	1:25
Combined refuse	1.05	1:34
Wheat/barley straws	0.4-0.5	1:100
Fresh sawdust	0.11	1:500

Organic mulches and weed control. The best materials to use are those that are weed free, normally containing no weed seeds or fragments of perennial weed. Here are some to choose from depending on availability and costs:

Peat is widely used in limited quantities, since it is usually too expensive for large-scale mulching. Varying grades and types of horticultural peat are available but sometimes rougher, coarser peat can be bought in bulk at a lower price. Peat is not too persistent as a mulch and needs applying as a 50 mm (2 in) layer to be effective. Especially beneficial on ericaceous plantings, rose beds and for special shrubs.

Another cheaper source of peat, can be from the spent 'Gro bags' used mainly by commercial glasshouse growers, usually discarded after one season. There is a slightly greater risk of some weed infestation, but the lower price is well worth the risk. Contact your local grower to see if he has any of these.

Shredded or pulverised bark. Now a more expensive material since its promotion by one of the big chemical companies, nevertheless for a general-purpose, persistent and effective mulch, this material has much to recommend it. Well-matured, and shredded grades are better than too much dry, chippy wood, and for those living near large forestry plantations, the Forestry Commission or private timber companies should be approached to see if a limited supply is available. Apply at thickness of 50-75 mm (2-3 in). For large gardens and parks there is the possibility of investing in a chipping or shredding machine which can convert prunings, woody debris, large branches and stumps into chippings which are very useful as a mulch.

Sawdust is usually very limited in availability but is certainly a very useful material for shrub beds or mixed borders. Apply at 50 mm (2 in) thickness.

Lawn clippings. Usually weed free, although annual meadow grass, that most invasive and insidious weed often found in lawns can be spread as seed heads in clippings; but allowing for this, these clippings are useful as a mulch direct on to shrub borders, rose beds and the like. It also saves a walk to the compost heap if the borders are beside the lawn being mown.

Some experts find that a mulch of lawn clippings on rose beds 75-100 mm (3-4 in) thick reduces black spot disease of roses.

Spent hops and mushroom compost and other materials may be available locally, or in limited quantities and are very useful. Chopped or shredded straw is also another very useful material, if one can get a few bales from a local farm source. Additional nitrogen should be applied (see table 2.10).

Plate 2.3 A gravel garden two years after planting. The limestone chippings were laid as a 50 mm (2 in) layer directly over a site known to be weed free and well drained

Farmyard manure and garden composts are of considerable benefit for soil conditioning and nutrient supply as regards texture and organic matter.

Inert mulches. Plastic film has been used for sometime now by fruit growers, but it has limitations for informal garden areas used as a surface material. However, it can be used with some success in conjunction with gravel. The film is laid direct on the ground after treating the soil with a residual herbicide. 500-600 gauge film can be used, black or opaque and some allowance should be made for water percolation by pricking small holes or slots but not too large or the weeds will grow through. Then a 25-50 mm (1-2 in) thick layer of gravel or chippings is spread over the plastic assuming the site is reasonably level. This can either be left as an inert gravel area or, much more interesting, made into a gravel garden by planting through the gravel and film into the soil beneath (plate 2.3).

Gravel, chippings or cobbles can also be used as a mulch as such laid over hard core or direct on soil surface, followed by regular herbicide treatment.

Chemical herbicides
To quote Dr Robinson of the Kinsealy Research Institute Dublin, Eire:

'For centuries weeds have been controlled laboriously by manual and mechanical means. These methods can be highly inefficient particularly in the milder, wetter areas of Britain where the potential for planting a wide range of interesting trees and shrubs is greatest. Today, effective, relatively cheap herbicides are available which can suppress the development of seedling weeds for prolonged periods and give better control of many perennial weeds than soil tillage. In contrast to traditional soil cultivations, many soil-acting herbicides are more effective in the high rainfall areas.'

Although this statement was made in 1976 at the start of an important lecture to the Royal Horticultural Society its implications are even more important today as the problems of manpower and economics increase.

A recent personal survey carried out into the maintenance and management aspects of a range of the larger privately owned gardens and parks shows that chemical herbicides are now generally being used by most establishments, in many cases as a sheer necessity to complete maintenance programmes. On the other hand the widespread use of a range of chemicals, despite Dr Robinson's views, for weed control in amenity areas still does not compare with the very great use of such materials in commercial horticulture. There are a number of reasons to account for this:

Research up to now has concentrated on evolving herbicides for commercial crops such as a soft fruit and vegetables, where the chemicals are developed for their safe selective use, for weed control in these crops.

The very wide range of ornamental plants grown in gardens may have an equally wide range of tolerances or susceptibilities to herbicides and until these are fully known or understood there is bound to be some mistrust or doubts about using herbicides except in situations where they are known to be safe and effective.

There is a public sensitivity, not without cause and perhaps due to prejudice or misinformation, on the subject of using chemical sprays (and granules) in pleasure grounds, and the safety of children and dogs is usually one of the main concerns.

The somewhat cautious, and traditional attitudes among gardeners and garden owners when introducing a chemical weed maintenance programme in their gardens, where there may also be the necessary lack of motivation or skills that are essential to ensure the full success of such a programme.

The implications underlying these four points are well summed up by Dr John Davison of the Weed Research Organisation, Oxford

'There is no reason why herbicides should not be equally as effective in amenity plantings as in commercial horticulture.

Herbicides offer amenity horticulture a cheap and effective form of weed control that requires less labour than traditional methods. The full potential of herbicides cannot be developed if they are merely seen as alternatives to the hoe. They enable and indeed require a complete re-appraisal of land management.'

Herbicides for use in landscape and garden planting can be divided broadly into two categories:

(a) Leaf acting (L.A.)
(b) Soil acting (S.A.)

Leaf-acting herbicides. These may be further subdivided into two subgroups:

 (i) Contact (L.A.C.)
(ii) Translocated (L.A.T.)

Contact herbicides kill only those parts of the plant that they touch. They are used mainly as directed sprays for controlling seedling or annual weeds, and do not really control or eradicate deep-rooted perennial weeds at a single application. **Their effect is a rapid scorch and kill of actively growing green tissues a matter of days after application. Examples: paraquat/diquat.**

Translocated herbicides are absorbed through the leaves and green tissues of the plant during periods of active growth into the sap-conducting tissue (phloem) where they are carried or translocated to all regions of active growth including storage (roots) and reproduction (flowering shoots). They then proceed over a period of time to interfere with the fundamental processes of the plant cells with the eventual breakdown and death or damage to the plant. It may take ten to fourteen days for this effect to be seen, or even longer. Examples of translocated contact **herbicides: M.C.P.A., dalapon and 'Roundup'.**

Soil-acting herbicides. These may also be approximately subdivided into:

 (i) Residual (S.A.R.)
(ii) Translocated (S.A.T.)

Residual herbicides are those that are normally applied to surfaces of soil or paths and drives in a weed-free condition where they remain active in the upper few millimetres of the soil and prevent the germination and growth of seedling weeds. They work best when the soils are moist and undisturbed, and on drives and paths. On very light soils they can be leached away after periods of prolonged rainfall. Hoeing or forking ground treated with a residual herbicide can shatter the protective layer allowing seeds to grow. Note they do not normally kill actively **growing or deep-rooted weeds. Examples: simazine, atrazine.**

Translocated herbicides operate through the soil by being taken up by the roots of established or establishing weeds. They may have considerable persistence in the soil and are not normally used among newly planted stock. Their effect may not be seen for several weeks after application. Examples: 'Casoron G', 'Roundup'.

It should be remembered that there are quite a number of herbicides available and that some may fall into more than one of the categories above. Also some may be offered as 'a cocktail' mixture for a more all-round effect and can be applied as such.

Total herbicides (T.O.T.). The term total herbicides is often used to denote those that are both soil acting and leaf acting in their mode of action.

Soil sterilisation. For weed control, rather than pest and disease control, it is possible to use chemicals as powder or liquid applications. However, materials such as 'Dazomet' or 'Basomid' are normally applied as a total treatment to control weeds, harmful organisms and pests and diseases to local areas such as infected planting borders or vegetable and fruit gardens, if on a reasonable scale. For very small areas, such materials are not recommended.

A Guide to herbicides in current use in gardens and amenity areas. Table 2.11 summarises the main herbicides currently being used, with some indication of their season of use and the approximate costs involved. It is important to realise that this is a guide only. There are other chemicals available which are used less frequently as a general rule and some which should not be used at all (sodium chlorate has been suspended now). New compounds are also beginning to appear, but until their use is proved, they should be used on a trial basis. Two of these are oxadiazon which looks to be a promising bindweed control and alloxydimsodium ('CLOUT') for the suppression of perennial grasses growing through ground cover.

A full list of these chemicals and all those normally used in agriculture and horticulture is published annually in the Ministry of Agriculture's Approved Products for Growers.

The use of herbicides. It should be obvious that most chemicals of this nature are potentially dangerous to plants and man so do not ignore the plea, repeated many times on makers' packs and leaflets, for all managers, head gardeners and operators to be quite sure that the correct dosage is being applied, in the recommended manner and at the right time of year, by the right appliance and by an operator who knows what he or she is doing and who is wearing the right protective clothing while doing it. Chemicals must be stored out of the reach of children, animals or intruders, and all sprayers etc. must be washed out after use.

The safety factor of all chemicals used in agriculture and horticulture is covered in the Approved Products publication already referred to together with some advice on their safe use.

Application. The survey referred to at the beginning of this section confirms the almost universal practice of using a reliable knapsack sprayer for the application of most of these materials. An 18 litre (4 gallon) capacity model like the Cooper Pegler is adequate for quite large gardens. The pressurised bottle types are also surprisingly effective for smaller areas.

Table 2.11 Herbicides

Area of use	Chemical name and category	Proprietary Name	Time of year of application	Approx. cost material per 1000 m²	Comments
Weedy ground clearance brushwood/dense vegetation away from young trees, shrubs, etc.	Glyphosate (L.A.T.)	'Tumble weed' 'Roundup'	May–July (spray)	£5–10	Most effective herbicide for controlling perennial weeds.
Fence lines, woodland edges for initial weed control. (Avoid bulbs, natural flora.)	Dichlobenil (S.A.T.)	'Casoron G'	Jan.–Mar. (granules)	£30–40	Very effective for annuals and perennials. Expensive.
	2,4,5-T (L.A.T.)	'Brushwood killer'	Apr.–July (spray)	£1.0–1.50	Effective woody scrub. Drift dangers.
Hard surface areas. Drives, paths, cobbles, gravel, etc. Paving.	Simazine (S.A.R.)	'Herbazin 50' 'Gesatop' 'Weedex'	Feb.–Mar. Sep.–Nov. (spray)	£1–1.50	Residual effect. Avoid use near susceptible woody species. Best on weed-free surfaces.
	Paraquat (L.A.C.) Paraquat/diquat (L.A.C.)	'Gramoxone' 'Weedol'	Mar.–May or when young weeds growing actively throughout season. Winter also. (spray)	£2.50–10	Excellent for eliminating ephemeral annuals before they mature and seed. Rapid effects.
	Dichlobenil (S.A.T.)	'Casoron G'	Jan.–Mar. (as granules)	£30–40	Expensive form of residual for this purpose but useful if drives and paths infested with persistent perennial weeds, i.e. clovers, etc.
Established shrub borders, rose beds, woody ground cover.	Simazine (S.A.R.)	'Herbazin 50' 'Gesatop' 'Weedex'	Feb.–Mar. in moist soil conditions (spray)	£1–1.50	Prevents germinating weeds. Note susceptible woody species especially on very light soils.
	Atrazine (S.A.R.)	'Gesaprim 50' 'Weedex 50 WP'	All year round, best spring months. Effective on dry soils (spray)	£1–1.50	Total spectrum if used with care on seedling weeds.

Situation	Chemical	Trade names	Timing/application	Cost	Comments
	Paraquat (L.A.C.)	'Gramoxone'	Spot treatment as weeds appear (spray)	£2.50-10	Careful application with spray guard or dribble bar or watering can.
	Glyphosate (L.A.T.)	'Tumble weed' 'Roundup'	May-July (granules)	£5-10	Both need using with care where weeds are a real problem.
	Dichlobenil (S.A.T.)	'Casoron G'	Jan.-Mar. (granules)	£30-40	
Herbaceous borders non-woody perennials.	Lenacil (S.A.R.)	'Venzar'	Autumn Feb.-Mar. (spray)	£6-12	Some herbaceous perennials are unfortunately susceptible. Needs using with care.
Newly planted trees and shrubs especially in turf and grassland.	Paraquat (L.A.C.)	'Gramoxone'	Annual application Mar.-June to reduce competitive growth. A 24 in diameter control zone (spray) is sufficient.	£2-50-10	Avoid spray contact on stems, leaves, of new stock.
Lawns and amenity turf	M.C.P.A. (L.A.T.) Mecoprop (L.A.T.) 2,4,-D (L.A.T.)	'Clovatox' 'Lornox plus' 'Supertox' 'Verdone'	April-June (Aug.-Sep.) Active growing periods of turf weeds (spray)	75p-£1.50	Most broad-leaved turf weeds controlled. Care with spray drift especially in hot weather.
Ponds, lakes and water courses	Although herbicides like dichlobenil ('Casoron') are recommended by the distributors as being 'safe to use' in such places to control vigorous aquatic growth, they are not recommended here. Further advice should be sought, or trial treatments made in this very delicate area!				

Larger sprayers are available, of course, and these become important if extensive areas of turf or drives and car parks need treating.

Pests and diseases in gardens and parks

Incidences of serious pest infestations and disease epidemics of plants, mainly occur where large-scale production of mono-crops has been in practice for a considerable period of time.

In the agricultural and horticultural industries there is a continual need to carry out regular pest and disease control programmes on crop plants for these reasons.

Chemicals are normally used for such control although there is increasing interest in using natural predators and organisms to achieve what is termed biological control.

In landscape and garden maintenance, where mature or established plantings are usually of a very diverse age and species structure, there is much less likelihood of a build-up of series pest or disease problems. A notable exception has been the Dutch elm disease outbreak which has been disastrous in some areas. Also, in extensive forestry plantations and woodlands, grey squirrels can sometimes cause serious damage and plagues of leaf-eating larvae of some moth and sawfly species can occasionally defoliate areas of woodland plantations.

It is strongly recommended that a specialist from the Ministry of Agricultural Development Advisory Service be approached in the first instance where any serious plant pest or disease problems occur, or one could contact the county or local council forestry officer, or staff of the regional horticultural colleges for more specific problems. Table 2.12 summarises the more commonly occurring types of pests likely to be met in gardens and parks with brief notes on control measures.

Bullfinches

These attractive garden birds have, in fact, had a price on their heads ever since the time of Queen Elizabeth I. Records at that time note that 'one penny reward' was an offer for 'everie bulfynche or other byrde that devoureth the blowthe of fruit'.

Recent research at East Malling Research Station in Kent is studying the yearly life cycle of these birds in order to arrive at more successful control measures. Major food sources in the summer and autumn are seeds of nettles, docks and brambles, and it is only in the late winter and early spring that they turn their attentions to the swelling buds of flowering or fruiting trees and shrubs.

Repellent chemicals seem to be the most hopeful line of research at present. Bullfinches seem to operate in 'pools' of between 100 and 200 birds, very few of which will move more than 2-3 km (1.2-1.9 miles) away. The potential destructive powers of one pool are frightening. In the case of an orchard of 2 ha (5 acres) of pears, the crop was devastated by only ten or twelve birds from this pool, working at amazing speeds. In practice damage is characteristically sporadic and seasonal. The answers are still being sought, and in the meanwhile the various protective measures suggested are still all that can be advised.

Diseases of gardens and ornamental plants

By comparison with the many other more pressing maintenance problems already

Table 2.12 Pests in gardens and parks

Pest group	Damage	Control
Deer	Increasing problem near commons, woodlands, etc. Roaming herds can invade gardens and damage roses, shrubs, etc.	Human hair in balls and reflective plastic strips suspended from trees may control deer! Contact local Deer Control Society.
Grey squirrels	Occasional damage to young and establishing trees.	Consult Forestry Commission. Trapping and shooting are unpleasant but perhaps essential.
Rabbits/hares	Barking of young trees, winter damage to newly planted trees/shrubs.	Tree guards, repellent paints, trapping, shooting, electric fences.
Bullfinches/small birds (see page 58)	Usually widespread stripping of flower buds. Rosaceous trees and shrubs and wide range woody, amenity plants. Damage often late winter, or early spring.	Difficult on large scale. Protective netting, or cotton, or repellent sprays. Fruit cages really the only answer where soft fruit is regularly attacked.
Mice, voles	can be a nuisance eating crocus corms etc.	Traps or keep a cat or two!
Moles	Disruptive tunnelling in lawns and cultivated areas.	Traps, cartridges, repellents.
Leaf-eating larvae Caterpillars	Occasionally extensive defoliation of some trees - oak, willow, and shrubs, roses, etc.	Not usually economic to control on a large scale. Natural predators usually take control in due course.
Leaf-sucking pests	Seasonal and localised 'build-up' of aphids on trees, especially some species of lime, (sticky honeydew effect), Plum trees, and serious on honeysuckle and amenity and crop plants. Red spider can cause yellowing and premature defoliation of some trees especially Limes and shrubs in dry, warm summers.	Natural predators such as birds, ladybirds, hover fly larvae usually efficient control in large-scale landscape areas. Use systematic insecticides in gardens and small-scale areas especially on roses where feasible and the infestation severe enough. Plant aphid-resistant limes.
Soil-borne pests - Chafer grubs, Wireworms, Leather jackets, Cut-worm, Slugs, snails	Occasionally serious on newly planted annuals and softer plants and in lawn areas, sports turf, etc.	Soil-applied pesticides only where situations really demand this.

covered in this book, the likelihood of serious and widespread diseases breaking out
and affecting whole populations of plants in a garden is not very great. The reasons
have been briefly referred to at the beginning of this section.

Nevertheless there are some diseases that are quite likely to be a problem in gardens
and plant collections and these will be summarised briefly here.

Honey fungus or bootlace fungus (caused by the fungus *Armillaria mellea*)
This root pathogen is one of the commonest causes of the death of trees, shrubs and
even non-woody plants in Britain and indeed virtually throughout the world. It is a
very common fungus of woodlands where it can occur as a saprophyte living on dead
wood, but the disease is much more of a widespread and serious problem in parks,
gardens and arboreta. Most woody plants are susceptible to some degree, although
there is a range of more resistant species (see table 2.13).

Table 2.13 Susceptibility to honey fungus

Some susceptible species	
Apple	*Malus*
Birch	*Betula*
Lilac	*Syringa*
Maple	*Acer* (some species)
Privet	*Ligustrum*
Willow	*Salix*
Some more resistant species	
Ash	*Fraxinus*
Bamboos	Several species
Beech	*Fagus*
Elder	*Sambucus*
Holly	*Ilex*
Ivy	*Hedera*
Lime	*Tilia*
—	*Mahonia*
Oak	*Quercus*
Sumach	*Rhus*
Thorns	*Crataegus*
Tamarisk	*Tamarix*

The fungus gets its popular name from the clusters of honey-coloured toadstools
produced in the autumn around infected trees or stumps, and its other popular name
bootlace fungus from the subterranean strands of black, stringy rhizomorphs that
spread through the soil as a principal means of infection. Fig. 2.4 shows the life cycle
of this disease and the characteristic stages when its presence usually becomes
obvious.

Control. This essentially depends on the removal of the main sources of infection
such as stumps, old posts or buried logs, or old roots. This may well be difficult or
impracticable in many cases. (See also Chapter 3 stump removal.) When a hedge is
being progressively killed several plants ahead of the infected area should be
removed.

Another alternative where the removal of the sources of the infection is difficult, is

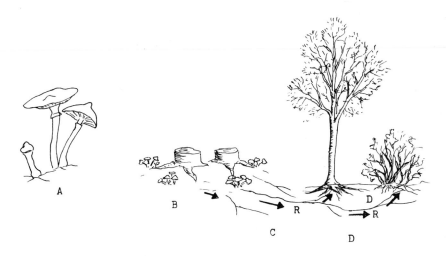

Fig. 2.4 The life cycle of honey fungus (*Armillaria mellea*)
A   Honey coloured fruiting bodies or toadstools appear in early autumn. Note presence of annulus or ring beneath the cap, and the shape of the cap
B   Spores from the 'toadstools' infect dead or decaying stumps, fallen timber, etc. Eventually clusters of fruiting bodies appear round these 'host centres'
C   Subterranean rhizomorphs or black root-like mycelial strands ('boot laces') (**R**) radiate from sources of infection to affect adjacent healthy plants (**D**)

to isolate the fungus, or prevent its further spread into planted areas by sinking a vertical barrier to a depth of at least 1 m (3 ft) of heavy gauge plastic sheeting, or asbestos sheeting. This is really only practicable with localised outbreaks.

Chemical treatments have not really been found to be predictably effective. A proprietary creosote-based liquid 'Armillatox' may save valuable infected, but still living, plants from being killed, and recently a treatment with copper carbonate seems to have been successful, as a preventive. A teaspoonful of the crystals is mixed with the soil, leaf mould or peat when planting or in a trench around important plants, where infection is threatening.

Bacterial canker and canker diseases
These can be widespread and occasionally serious on such trees as ornamental cherries, willows and poplars. Canker can be removed by cutting out the infected parts or branches, but in the case of cherries and the balsam group of poplars the disease is eventually fatal or very disfiguring due to continual loss or dieback of main branches. There is usually no real control.

Diseases of roses
The great popularity of hybrid roses for over a century has brought its accompanying problems, with the incidence of a number of pests and diseases that are all too familiar to most gardeners. The National Rose Society has produced excellent literature on these and their control, especially on Rose Black Spot and Rose Mildew as two very prevalent diseases which usually need some measure of control. Remedies can lie in the choice of more resistant varieties or in using different cultural techniques or in the use of the fungicide 'Benlate' and others. Planting sites and weather factors are also important.

Other diseases and disorders

Turf diseases may occasionally be serious and further reference is made to these in Chapter 3. Virus diseases, widespread and serious in commercial crops, are also found in woody and non-woody ornamental plants, but their incidence and effects are usually not serious enough to cause marked adverse effects on growth or performance.

Replant diseases, causing poor growth or other effects, with woody plants planted back on land that has been used for certain types like roses or fruit trees have been the subject of fairly extensive research. Rotation, the use of soil sterilants or additional nutrition may be some ways of dealing with this phenomena.

   Finally, one must not forget the various agencies that produce disease-like damage such as frosts, salt winds and atmospheric pollution.

3
Specific Vegetation Maintenance and Management

Introduction

In many respects this chapter and its contents lie at the very heart of garden maintenance. Controlling vegetation in one form or another must take up the greater part of a gardener's time, certainly in the growing season, whether it is maximising a short prolific life in the case of vegetables, regularly disciplining and training fruit trees, or working on the longer-term management of tree and shrub communities, and by no means least, the incessant beheading of leaf blades on mown lawns and of the continually regrowing hedges.

The plant range

Dr Gren Lucas of the Royal Botanic Gardens, Kew, estimates that over 30 000 different plants have been introduced to English gardens since the sixteenth century and although many of these have been lost, new cultivars, hybrids and seedling forms are coming forward all the time. Thus the potential range from which to select hardy or near-hardy plants for amenity use in the British Isles is quite unique.

Woody plants

Woody plants in cultivation in most gardens and parks usually comprise trees and shrubs and occasionally subshrubs. They normally develop a permanent or semi-permanent framework of branches with or without a basal trunk. The trunk in the case of trees, can assume massive proportions and persist for a great many years. Shorter-lived woody plants like the hybrid roses or buddleias usually need a constant renewal of branches to perpetuate a reasonable life.

General principles of maintenance
The objectives here are to maintain for as long a period as possible healthy, effective growth with some regulation or control of the shape and size of the plant as and when considered necessary. These are usually achieved by various inputs of pruning, nutrient treatments and pest and disease control. Renewal is the ultimate stage.

Pruning. This may occur as a succession of treatments in the life of the woody plant. The first takes the form of formative pruning, or training the tree or shrub in its early nursery or post-nursery years to form a well-shaped framework or stem and branch structure. The second is usually regulation or routine pruning if necessary, to maintain the plant in good health and shape, and to promote flowering and fruiting. Finally, remedial or surgical pruning may be necessary in the case of disease, damage, decay or old age in order to maintain effective life towards the end of the plant's normal life span. The input of each stage depends very much on the species or kind of woody plant.

Nutrient application. Woody ornamental plants are generally less demanding of nutrients and fertiliser than those grown to produce regular crops. However, there is no doubt that some shrubs, rather than trees, tend to be what the garden books call 'gross feeders'. These include magnolias, hybrid roses and walnuts. Further, where woody plants are being established on poor thin soils they will certainly respond to some nutrient applications.

Protection and pest and disease control. Woody plants may be vulnerable in their early years to attacks by rabbits and hares and locally, by deer, either during very cold winters or where sufficient numbers of such grazers are about. There are, of course, a number of other pest and disease problems summarised in Chapter 2.

Renewal. Management implies longer-term planning of current plantings, and this should allow for the eventual renewal by replacement of overmature, decaying or senescent woody plants as a positive decision. One should not be too timid or hesitant over such decisions even if one's favourite tree or shrub really is reaching the end of the road. If it is an extreme rarity or really outstanding specimen, every attempt should naturally be made to keep it going on as long as possible, and certainly one should take as much seed, cuttings or grafts from it as is possible. A good local nursery might be glad of these, perhaps in part exchange for more plants.

Trees
Stimulated by the dramatic losses of trees now occurring from the two serious tree epidemics of Dutch elm disease and beech bark disease and the prolonged effects of the great 1976 drought, there has been a limited, but nation-wide programme of tree planting, promoted by the Countryside Commission, Tree Council and Men of the Trees and regional and local authorities. Large gardens and designed parks, and particularly the eighteenth century landscape parks of Brown and Repton tend to have populations of mature or overmature trees as belts, clumps, specimens or avenues, and many of these are due for renewal now or certainly in the next few decades. This, of course, is a serious and expensive business to be covered in more detail in Chapters 6 and 8.

The following are the main operations involved in tree maintenance work.

Pruning. The need for pruning or tree surgery depends very much on the age and health of a tree, its location, growth habit and its species or variety. Trees as we all know, have a remarkable adaptability and tenacity for life, and will live for many years without especial attention, and in many cases little or no pruning is needed, except under the conditions or situations now described.

Table 3.1 gives an outline timetable for tree pruning or tree work throughout the calendar year.

Formative pruning. Most broad-leaved deciduous tree species will eventually develop a single leader, and lateral or side branches, so that in the young and formative years a tapering silhouette should be encouraged. If the tree develops this form naturally, even in the nursery, one can leave well alone, but sometimes a forked or double leader develops, or one lateral grows too vigorously at the expense of the others, and in such cases formative pruning should take place before the tree becomes too large or misshapen (fig.3.1). Damaged leaders (eaten by deer, cattle or snapped off by vandals) should be cut off cleanly at the next side branch or lateral

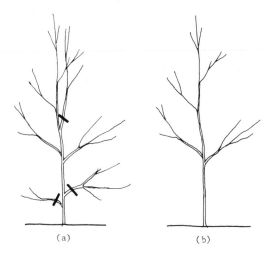

Fig. 3.1 Formative pruning of a young tree. Where a straight main leader and clear stem are required, some pruning in the nursery or establishment years of the tree may be necessary. Pruning cuts shown in (a) should produce the desired effect (b)

which should eventually become the new leading shoot. Trimming up or renewing laterals from the lower trunks of young or establishing trees should not be done too

Table 3.1 A timetable of tree pruning and tree work

Operation	Season	Seasonal Exceptions
Pruning and cutting work	All year round	Maples (*Acer*), and birches (*Betula*) should not be cut during the period of active sap growth usually Feb. - May otherwise severe 'bleeding' may result. Members of the plum group of the *Prunus* family should be pruned in early summer to avoid risk of 'silver leaf' infection.
Cavity cleaning and removal of dead wood	All the year round but dead wood is easier to see when the tree is in leaf	
Bark wounds and other cavity work	All the year round	Avoid work in severe frosty weather where tissues may be exposed to possible frost damage.
Tree felling and stump removal	All the year round	Possible damage to under planting or the herb layer if done in the growing season. Also damage to soil structure in excessively wet weather.

Adapted from *Tree Surgery* by P. Bridgeman

prematurely since all these growths are important in building up the strength of the tree in general, and the girth of the trunk in particular. Stakes or supports alongside the tree (plate 3.1) can normally be removed after four or five years but, of course, protective permanent guards will be essential in grazed paddocks or parkland.

Plate 3.1 This commemorative tree is now well established six years after planting. The stake is unnecessary and should be removed

Flowering trees which are normally budded or grafted on to various related rootstocks are usually trained in the nursery as round-headed trees without a leader. Examples here are flowering cherries and ornamental crab apples. The only formative pruning is to keep the crown of even shape, especially if damaged in any way, and to remove any suckers from the understocks that may arise. Note that apple trees are different in this respect and although usually round headed, special pruning systems are practised to promote fruiting and required frameworks.
Regulation or routine pruning. Once the shape and the structure of the tree are established, usually between five and ten years after planting, then the need for pruning, if any is needed at all, depends on:

The need to remove lower branches in the way of people or vehicles, or when casting too much shade for under planting or light penetration.

Repair of damaged or diseased branches.

Thinning of the crown due to excessive dense growth of laterals. This is more likely to become necessary with trees reaching early maturity and in urban or housing areas, rather than in gardens and parks.

Remedial pruning and tree surgery. Reference has already been made to the advisability of calling in reliable specialists for work on large, overmature or very inaccesible trees, together with the fact that where staff are employed, the Health and Safety at Work Acts now impose considerable regulations and restrictions on potentially dangerous work of this kind.

Dangerous or dying trees must be attended to as soon as possible, particularly where they are liable to be a danger to the public, and it is important to know the law in this respect or the owner's liabilities.

Cavity treatment normally involves removal or cutting out of the diseased or rotting tissue back to the clean surface, followed by treatment with an antiseptic paint such as Arbrex, Santar or Lac-Balsam. Cavities are not usually filled or plugged (see fig. 3.2). However, recent research by the Forestry Commission now

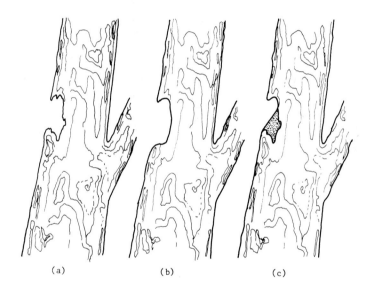

(a)   (b)   (c)

Fig. 3.2. Cavity and limb treatments. Current research and practice now suggests that cavities (a) are cleaned of rotting or diseased tissue and shaped to avoid water cupping (b) and left open and unpainted, or as in (c) the cavity is plugged with a suitable flexible filler.

suggests that even protective paints may be unnecessary or at times harmful in the case of clean cuts with healthy trees. Sealing may hinder the process of healing. Deep cavities, however, may need draining. The first signs of a tree in distress are usually yellowing of the normally green foliage during the growing season and premature leaf fall and a possible die back of the extremities of branches, a phenomenon known as 'stag-heading' by tree specialists. Remember that such materials as excess herbicides, sump oil and road salt deposited round the base of trees can cause similar stress symptoms due to root injury.

Trees and the law

Ownership of trees. The owner of the land on which the tree is growing is accepted by law, as being responsible for the safety and maintenance of the tree. There is one exception - in the case of tenancy, depending on the terms of the agreement between landlord and tenant.

Trees overhanging boundaries. The owner of a tree whose branches overhang the boundary and encroach upon neighbouring property is not responsible for the removal of the overhanging branches of the tree. He only becomes liable if actual damage is caused. The law allows the neighbour to cut or remove the overhanging parts of the tree provided he does not cross the boundary in so doing, and that he realises that the prunings or even fruit so detached belong to the owner of the tree.

Roots that encroach onto adjoining property are again not the liability of the owner, unless damage by the roots can be proved.

Dangerous trees. Trees known to be dangerous that overhang or threaten public highways and thoroughfares are the responsibility of the owner. If he is in the process of taking reasonable precautions to deal with the trees and they fall, he may not be liable. However, negligence can be proved if no apparent action has been taken to deal with such trees.

Tree preservation orders (T.P.O.s). Under the Town and Country Planning Acts the government is empowered to make orders to protect trees from mutilation and irresponsible felling. The local planning authority normally makes the orders on trees, usually growing on private rather than public land, and covering healthy trees or groups of trees above a certain size or maturity. For all advice on these T.P.O.s one should contact the local authority forestry officer or a tree specialist.

Stump removal and treatment. Stumps of large trees, in particular, always present a problem when it comes to deciding what is to be done about them. They should of course, wherever possible, be removed, since apart from possibly being unsightly unless covered with climbing plants they do represent a considerable disease hazard especially from the dreaded honey fungus already described in Chapter 2. The following are some methods of treatment or removal:

Hand grubbing. Stumps of limited size, and where access is difficult, can be removed without too much difficulty if a hand winch or block and tackle is used. A monkey winch or the lighter Tirfor winches can be hired for these occasions. Hand tools like a sharp mattock, a good axe and a tough spade will also be essential.

Mechanical grubbing. There are now several stump grubbing or stump cutting or chipping machines available for large tree roots. Some are mounted on the rear of a farm tractor, while others can be towed by a land rover or similar vehicle. There is a small Vermeer machine operated by two men for removing stumps in gardens and awkward places.

Chemicals may be used to kill stumps of newly felled trees, to prevent sprouting and regrowth. One recommended treatment is to spray the stumps immediately after felling with a solution of 1.8 kg ammonium sulphamate dissolved in 4.5 litres of water (4 lb in 1 gallon). The stump should be thoroughly wetted with the solution, and this should be done within forty-eight hours of felling the live tree, and during dry weather. When trees have been cut down for more than two days notches should be made as low down the stump as possible to expose living tissue, and this should be filled with neat ammonium sulphamate crystals or with the solution. An alternative to this is to use 2,4,5-T, 'Brushwood killer' (see table 2.11).

For stump burning where semi-decay is already beginning, a slow and not always effective method is using saltpetre (potassium nitrate) and paraffin poured into slots or holes in the stump surface and once soaked, ignited.

Protection. Far too many trees are lost or seriously damaged due to thoughtlessness or deliberate damage. Some sort of protection is advisable to prevent one or more of the following types of damage:

Physical damage to the bark and vital living tissues above ground caused by careless use of machinery, especially grass mowers or by vandals' penknives or worse, or much more commonly by hares, rabbits and deer on younger trees, or cattle and horses on older trees in grazed pastures or parkland. The effect of all this damage is to girdle the tree, with usually fatal or serious results. The remedy is really some sort of tree protection and some alternatives are shown in fig. 3.3. Costs of these vary considerably from a few pounds to over £25 per tree for permanent cattle-proof guards.

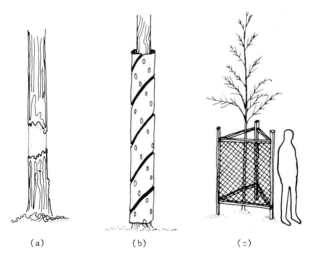

(a)   (b)   (c)

Fig. 3.3 Tree protection. Serious damage as in (a) by animals or vandals can be fatal. Young newly planted trees can be fitted with spiral guards (b). Parkland trees must be protected from animals and people and one version of a strong, simple guard is shown in (c)

Root damage due to deposition of soils or waste materials above the trunk. If the boles are buried in such materials at depths greater than 500 mm (20-24 in) for periods of several months, the effects on the tree can be very serious. The remedy is to avoid all dumping of such materials around the bases of trees, where changes of level have to take place or for other reasons (plate 3.2).

Deposition of chemicals. Toxic materials like road salt have already been referred to. The most likely risk of damage in this category is from an excessive dose of herbicides.

Nutrient application. The feeding of garden or parkland trees is seldom necessary unless the soils are exceptionally poor and deficient, or the trees are clearly suffering

Plate 3.2 Trees suffering from soil deposition. Depth here of 30-40 cm (12-16 in) **of soil or debris** can be sufficient to damage or kill trees

from stress factors due to drought, malnutrition or damage from one or more of the 'agencies' already described. A 'tonic' in the form of a judicious fertiliser application can often help the tree to recover, or at least maintain life for a longer period. Nutrients may be applied to trees in several ways:

As a slow-release compound fertiliser applied as a granular formulation mixed with an organic mulch around the base of the tree. Trees respond to leaf litter and 'natural' dressings and where growing in grass and all leaves are regularly swept up, some compensation as above may be necessary.

The alternative is a shallow forking of the area of application - a 3 m (10 ft) wide band approximately 100 mm (4 in) deep - and incorporation of the fertiliser with a suitable mulch.

Quick results can be achieved by injecting concentrated fertilisers into the root area of the tree by means of holes drilled 300-600 mm (1-2 ft) deep and 37-50 mm (1½-2 in) in diameter, and about 450-600 mm (1½-2 ft) apart, using a power auger or bulb planting tool to drill the holes. A guide to the amount of fertiliser to use is on the basis of 0.5-2 kg (1-4 lb) per 25 mm (1 in) of trunk diameter 1 m (3 ft) from the ground. Thus a tree with a trunk diameter of 900 mm (3 ft) would need 72 kg (158 lb) of fertiliser as a balanced concentration.

A recent development has been the 'Green Pile' concentrate fertiliser sticks driven into the ground like cricket stumps at intervals beneath and around the tree. Each 'pile' contains nutrients and trace elements held in layers of waxed paper, which gradually break down in the soil, releasing the nutrients over a considerable interval.

Renewal. When mature or overmature trees finally have to be removed, it is preferable to avoid planting back similar species in the same or near the same site due in some instances to what research scientists call 'replant disease' (Chapter 2). This mainly affects members of the Rosacease family. A resting period with some soil treatments, perhaps using a local soil sterilisation, is advisable before replanting. Stumps should be removed for important amenity tree groups. In the case of historic or important avenues, tree roundels, clumps and specimens in designed parklands, it is obviously desirable to renew these features or choose an alternative as close as possible to the original location (see Chapter 6).

Conifers

General pruning. Except in the case of those coniferous species used for clipped hedges or for ornamental features such as topiary, this important group of predominantly evergreen woody plants normally needs little or no pruning once the formative nursery stage is over. In fact, the majority of conifers intended for specimens are best left well alone to form shapely specimens with branches clothed to the ground. In forestry practice where close planting is usual to create clean straight stems, there is a progressive removal of lower branches ('brashing') to lift the canopy. Such removal of lower branches can be done, of course, in gardens and parks, particularly where coniferous species are used to screen or enclose and where space and excessive shading are a problem. This work is best done in late spring if possible or in the summer months. A very important point to note in connection with pruning conifers is that very few species, when mature, are capable of regeneration if the leaders or tops of the trees are drastically headed back or removed. Two notable exceptions, however, are the yew (*Taxus baccata*) and the Californian redwood (*Sequoia sempervirens*). The latter can even regenerate from stumps in its native habitats, and in gardens.

Root compaction. Some conifers are sensitive to root compaction and poor soil aeration often caused by excessive trampling by visitors. Such compaction can cause a reduction in growth or die back of branches, with the complete death of the plant in serious cases. Speciments with unusual bark, like the redwoods whose spongy texture visitors cannot resist feeling or punching, can suffer in this way and in heavily visited gardens like Sheffield Park in Sussex there is now concern for the health of some of the most visited specimen trees. It may become necessary to protect such trees with rails or fencing or to use ground-cover shrubs like 'Shallon' (*Gaultheria*) in a heavy mulch. The famous *Juniperus chinensis aurea* that was a golden columnar landmark for so long by the lower lake at Sheffield Park in Sussex died in 1979 probably due to root compaction from visitors

Snow damage. This is a particular problem with some conifers and those few evergreen trees whose habit is naturally ovoid, umbrella shaped or horizontally branched, and where such species orginate from warm temperate regions where snow fall is rare. During periods of heavy snowfall, especially if the snow is wet and bulky these conifers tend to hold the snow on account of their shape, and the sheer

weight can be disfiguring or damaging unless the snow can be shaken off as
speedily as possible (see fig. 3.4). Cedars are prone to damage in this way and the
great snowfalls in the late winter of 1979 did considerable damage to many fine

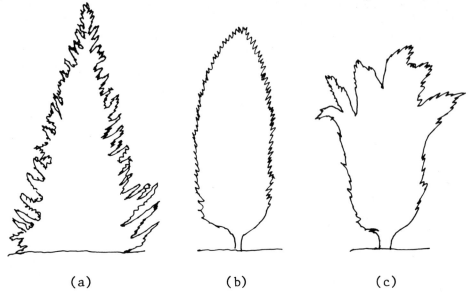

(a)   (b)   (c)

Fig. 3.4 Conifers and snow damage. The natural conical or pyramidal form of species like
Norway spruce, *Picea* (a) and flexible branching sheds heavy snowfall without damage.
Ovoid or columnar conifers need clipping or tying-in at intervals to maintain their shape (b)
since heavy snowfall can cause disfigurement (c)

conifers in the West Country where the blizzards were particularly severe. With
large mature trees the aftermath of such a phenomenon can mean expensive repair
and surgery work. Conifers of more moderate size that can suffer in this way are the
Irish yew (*Taxus baccata* 'Fastigiata') *Chamaecyparis lawsoniana* 'Erecta' and the
related *Chamaecyparis lawsoniana* 'Ellwoodii'. Snow is more likely to spoil the
shape of these if they are tending to become 'loose in the head' so to speak, and it is
advisable to keep them compact by regular tying in with black or dark green nylon
wire or Netlon netting.

Shrubs
The British Standards Institution defines a shrub as 'a woody plant usually of less
height than a tree with many stems arising at, or near ground level'.
    Such a definition covers in fact a pretty large and very variable range of wood
plants, from tree-like rhododendrons to the many middle-sized shrubs, like
forsythia, weigela or roses, to the low-growing species like heathers and hebes.
There is an equally large range of maintenance inputs depending on the different
characteristics of these shrubs, which can lead to considerable confusion and
uncertainty for those who are unfamiliar with the different pruning systems.
    It will be helpful to subdivide shrubs into three main categories for this purpose:

(a) Shrubs
(b) Roses (shrubs, of course, but kept separate here)
(c) Woody climbers and wall plants.

Shrubs. The three main stages in pruning already discussed at the beginning of this chapter may be applicable to many shrubs, namely formative, regulation and remedial pruning, with the emphasis tending to be on the regulation and remedial operations. There is, in fact, as in most gardening techniques, a fair amount of applied common sense in such pruning, but there should always be a very good reason for all pruning work.

All shrubs, like trees, will develop their own characteristic shape and size modified of course by the climate, soils and maintenance aspects, and with native species there is often a very good case for the minimum of pruning over a very long period. However, with garden forms, hybrids and seedlings, bred or selected for special effects such as flowers or fruits there may be a need for regular pruning to promote those qualities. Hybrid roses are a good example here.

Pruning in relation to shrub species. With over 14 000 woody plants in cultivation from many very different climatic and ecological habitats and countries, clearly no blue print can be laid down for pruning shrubs. However, table 3.2 does give some guidelines to pruning and also relates this to the longevity and the normal life expectancy of a range of shrubs.

Timing or the season of year one prunes shrubs is important to understand. The guidelines to remember are the time of year the shrub flowers and the maturity of the growth that produces the flowers. Winter or early-spring flowering shrubs like forsythia will form their flowering shoots the previous season and clearly excessive winter or spring pruning would remove flower buds. Thus any necessary pruning is normally done after flowering which is usually spring or early summer. Mid-summer or late-summer and autumn flowering shrubs usually flower on the new season's flowering shrub shoots (e.g. garden roses). Pruning of this group is normally done in autumn, winter or early spring depending on the species, locality and risk of severe winters. Some dead-heading or light pruning may also be done after flowering.

Formative pruning Shrub nurseries should really be sending out plants with the framework and bushy habit already developing that will become the characteristic of many in the years ahead. Regrettably still too many nurseries sell such plants prematurely before this initial training stage has been begun, or else poorly shaped, due to lack of care in the nursery itself. Very simply, to create bushy growth in the early stages, excessive leading shoots should be headed back by half or two-thirds, and very weak or misshapen growth removed altogether. This is more often the case with vigorous deciduous shrubs, and more care and experience is needed with expensive or slow-growing shrubs like rhododendron, or magnolia which tend to be naturally bushy in habit, perhaps need little early pruning at all.

Regulation and remedial pruning. Most experts and most books on this subject generally agree that there are three essential reasons normally put forward for shrub pruning:

(a) To limit or correct or improve the overall shape and size.
(b) To remove diseased, damaged or dead wood.
(c) To encourage or promote rejuvenation of new wood, flowering and fruiting.

Whatever the main reason for pruning, the aim should always be to maintain a natural and informal shape, leaving aside, of course, topiary and sculptural forms.

To achieve this natural look, careful, thoughtful pruning is essential, perhaps the absolute minimum in some cases (see table 3.2), and taking into account the site, situation and species of shrub involved. Sharp secateurs or a pruning knife should be used unless it is a clipping job with shears (fig. 3.5)

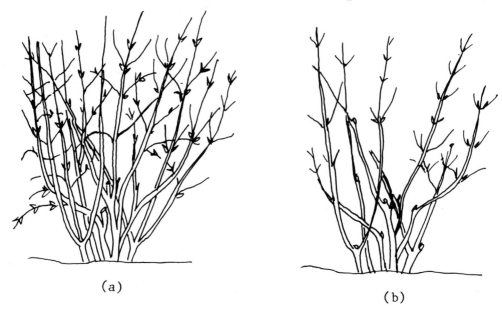

(a)

(b)

Fig. 3.5 Thinning and pruning a dense overgrown shrub such as forsythia (a) to open up the centre and promote new basal growth (b)

Table 3.2 A guide to shrub pruning

Group 1

These normally require little or no annual or regular pruning and attention. Many evergreens are included in this category. Grafted plants may cause suckering problems (Su) and in very hard winter those marked (W) may be cut back by frosts. See 'Pruning notes'.

Examples of genera* and effective life or longevity†	Pruning notes
Arbutus (E) L	
Aucuba (E) L	
Berberis (D) (E) M	
Camellia (E) M/L	W
Choisya (E) S/M	Die-back problems.
Cistus (E) S	W
Corylopsis (D) M	W
Cotinus (D) S/M	Hard pruning encourages leaf effects with purple-leaved cultivars.
Cotoneaster (E) M	Thinning and shaping advisable.
Daphne (D) (E) S	
Enkianthus (D) M	
Escallonia (E) M	W. Light clipping after flowering.
Fothergilla (D) M	
Hamamelis (D) M	Su
Hibiscus (D) M	
Kalmia (E) M/L	

Magnolia (D) (E) L	Su. Some occasional thinning. Heading back encourages bushiness.
Mahonia (E) M	
Osmanthus (E) M	Light clipping after flowering
Prunus laurocerasus (E) M/L	
Rhododendron (*Azalea*) (E) (D) L	Dead heading after flowering. Su
Skimmia (E) M	
Styrax (D) M/L	
Syringa (D) M/L	Dead heading some thinning and size reduction. Su
Viburnum (D) (E) M	Su

Group 2

Shrubs normally needing some annual regulation pruning. Pruning may be by thinning and cutting back (Cu) or clipping over with shears (Cl). W indicates winter damage.

Examples of genera* and effective life or longevity†	Pruning notes
Abelia (E) M	(Cu) depending on occasional winter damage, vigour, etc.
Buddleia (D) S/M	(Cu) Hard pruning winter early spring, normal.
Calluna/Erica (E) S/M	(Cl) after flowering. Remember winter effect of 'dead' flower heads.
Ceanothus (E) S/M	(Cu) careful thinning after flowering. W. (Cu)
Chaenomeles (D) M/L	after flowering Su.
Chimonanthus (D) M	(Cu) occasional thinning, etc.
Cytisus (E) S	(Cl) after flowering
Deutzia (D) M	(Cu) after flowering
Forsythia (D) M	(Cu) after flowering
Hydrangea (D) M/L	(Cu) light pruning early spring.
Indigofera (D) M	(Cu) early spring. W.
Kolkwitzia (D) M/L	(Cu) light regulation pruning every two/three years, winter/early spring.
Philadelphus (D) M/L	(Cu) thinning winter dead heading.
Ribes (D) M/L	(Cu) occasional thinning after flowering.
Rosa see next section	
Salix (D) M/L	(Cu) shrubby species for winter stem colour. Stool back annually early spring.
Spiraea (D) M/L	(Cu) regular thinning and occasional cutting back winter or after flowering.
Weigela (D) M	(Cu) thinning, etc., winter early spring.

Group 3

Dwarf shrubs or sub-shrubs normally pruned back hard in early spring to maintain good shape and vigour. Pruning or clipping depends on the species and the winter factor

Examples of genera* and effective life or longevity†	Pruning notes
Calluna/Erica (E) S/M	(Cl) after flowering
Caryopteris (D) S	(Cu)
Ceratostigma (D) S	(Cu) (Cl)
Fuchsia (D) M/L	(Cu) W.

Helichrysum (E) S	(Cu) or (Cl)
Lavandula (E) S	(Cl)
Olearia (E) S	(Cl) W
Potentilla (shrubby) types (D) S/M	(Cl) or (Cu)
Rosmarinus (E) S/M	(Cl) W
Santolina (E) S	(Cl)
Senecio (E) S/M	(Cl) or (Cu) after flowering

*E = evergreen; D = deciduous.
†L = long lived (25-50 yr); M = Medium life (10-25 yr); S = short lived (5-10 yr).

Effects of pruning. It is essential to remember that the one main effect of pruning most woody plants is to stimulate more vigorous basal or lateral growth which will affect the proportion of younger vegetative growth wood to more mature fruiting or flowering wood. Excessive pruning can upset this balance for a time by generating too much young wood, whereas no pruning at all, may lead to plenty of flowering wood but at the expense of a densely crowded and thicket-like shrub. Thus results of leaving well alone may in fact be the answer for shrubs growing in wild gardens, and is to be preferred to over-pruned restricted specimens, but this really depends on the site and the space available and the species.

Roses and their pruning. It is quite impossible to do full justice or give comprehensive recommendations on this complex group of plants and George Brown's book - *The Pruning of Trees, Shrubs and Conifers* or some of the National Rose Society's excellent publications are recommended.

Hybrid roses. A very large group of mixed and complex origin, including the most popular of the garden roses such as hybrid teas, floribundas and grandifloras. They are in effect summer and late summer flowering shrubs, and therefore normally flower on new lateral growth made earlier in the same season. If little or no pruning is done at all, and the bushes are left to grow from year to year without much attention, they generally make massive, tall, leggy, impenetrable thickets with flowers, apart from needing step ladders to admire, reduced in size and quality and a fair amount of die back of older growth. Pruning may be done in late winter or early spring depending on the locality and risk of late frosts, and the operation can conveniently be considered in three stages:

First operation (fig. 3.6. (a)). Remove any dead, diseased or frosted wood. Sharp loppers or a pruning saw may be needed for the thickest growths.

Second operation (Fig. 3.6 (b)). Remove very old branch systems and weak or straggly growths and basal suckers.

Third operation (fig. 3.6 (c)). Shorten all previous season's growths as an essential rejuvenation process. The extent of the shortening back depends on the vigour of the variety, the condition of the bush generally, and the aim of having a balance of new and older wood. Cuts should always be back to good dormant buds.

Later in the growing season some summer pruning and dead heading is important to promote continuity of flowering.

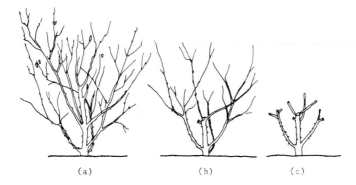

(a) (b) (c)

Fig. 3.6 Stages in the pruning of a hybrid tea rose

Floribunda and grandiflora roses have similar treatment except that in general pruning is less vigorous and a more permanent framework is encouraged to create what really are shrub roses in form and habit. Hedges can also be made of some of these with light regulation pruning and training.

Shrub and species roses. Another very large category including many species (botanical roses), cultivars, seedlings and hybrids which all broadly speaking can be grown as specimens or flowering shrubs with much less regular attention than the first group. Hence their increasing popularity at the present time together with the fact that many have historical associations (a current romantic appeal) and many are sweetly scented too!

In essence, the aim of pruning these shrub roses is to keep a permanent framework of branches for as long as possible with the occasional removal of dead, diseased or very old wood, and when shape and size needs control, to shorten back very vigorous growth. In practice such roses can often be left for years at a time with little or no attention at all.

Suckering is, however, one tiresome but essential job that cannot be ignored due to the fact that most of the shrub and botanical roses sold today in nurseries are propagated by budding or grafting on to understocks of dog roses or similar vigorous species. These inevitably throw up suckers and are not always distinguishable from the main scion growth, since so many of the botanical roses have more compound leaves than the hybrids. Suckers, however, can be identified by close observation, and they should be removed at ground level as soon as they appear. Hopefully rose producers will aim to produce such shrub roses on their own roots in the future to save this maintenance item.

Support. Some of the larger and more bulky single-stemmed shrub roses are not very stable, and tend to 'rock' especially in winter or on wet soils. Some permanent support is advisable by means of short discreet posts or suitable framework.

Woody climbers and wall plants. In a book that is mainly concerned with maintenance and management of vegetation, this group of woody climbers and wall plants, as traditionally grown, must involve a fair amount of ongoing maintenance work if they are to achieve their main object. The very fact of exploiting walls or supports on which to grow a variety of often vigorous rampant or specialist plants will usually mean at least two main maintenance inputs: the provision of support for the plants and their training and control after planting. In many large gardens and parks today, this is one group of plants that cannot be grown to the standards achieved in the days of plentiful skilled gardeners. This applies especially to wall fruit which is really beyond the scope of this section. Climbing and rambling roses are another group that may not always get the attention they really need.

Nevertheless, there are less fastidious and less labour-intensive systems or techniques for growing many ornamental plants in this group, and often a break with tradition, necessitated initially by labour and resources may point to new ways of growing plants that would previously not have been explored.

Table 3.3 summarises the main categories of woody climbing and wall plants and their training and management. A fine example of well-maintained wall plants at Sissinghurst Castle garden is shown in plate 3.3.

Plate 3.3 A range of well-managed climbing and wall shrubs at Sissinghurst Castle garden in Kent

In addition to the selection of climbing plants given in the tables, there are also a number of shrubs which benefit from being grown against walls, either for the microclimate effect (see Chapter 1) or because they need additional structural support. Examples here would include ceanothus, magnolia, and carpentaria for warm sunny walls, and garrya, jasminem and pyracantha for shaded walls.

Trellis, wires or masonry nails are needed to hold such shrubs against walls, and pruning is usually regulation cutting back or thinning depending on the species; in winter, or early spring, or after flowering.

Pests and diseases of wall plants. Chapter 2 broadly summarises the main pests and diseases of ornamental plants, but it should be pointed out again that a separate book could be written on this subject. Aphids or greenfly are the most likely pests to

Table 3.3 Woody climbing and wall plants, their pruning and maintenance
(See also table 2.2)

Group 1 - Self-clinging by adhesive sucker-like appendages or similar

---

Examples, siting and effective life*
Campsis tecoma, 'Trumpet vine' (M). Full sun
Hedera sp., 'Ivies' (L). Sun or full shade
Hydrangea petiolaris, 'Climbing hydrangea' (M/L). Shade
Parthenocissus tricuspidata, 'Boston ivy' (L).
P. quinquefolia, 'Virginia creeper'.
P. henryana (L/M)
Pileosteagia viburnoides (M/L). Evergreen, shade
Trachelospermum sp. (M/L). Sun/shelter. Not cold areas. Scented

Sun or part shade

Training
Any vertical surface or vertical support which may be either constructed: walls, fences,
pergolas, posts, central heating tanks, or natural: old trees, or dead or dying trees, provided
they are stable and not dangerous, large deciduous shrubs, etc. Beware of excessive growth
behind or up drainage pipes, gutters and tiles. They may do damage if left to explore on their
own.

Pruning
Trellis or wires not usually needed. Once the climber has covered the allotted spaces or
volume, some annual cutting back or clipping as required - done in winter for deciduous
species, and early spring for evergreens, with shears or secateurs.
Note: many of these may also be used for ground cover.

Group 2 - Twining, trailing or tendrils

Examples, siting and effective life*
Actinidia sp., 'Kiwi fruit' (M/L). Sun/shade
Akebia sp. (M). Sun/shade
Clematis sp. and hybrids etc. (S/M). Sun/part shade. (See Pruning below)
Lonicera sp. etc., 'Honeysuckles' (M). Sun/shade
Passiflora sp., 'Passion flower' (M/L). Sun
Polygonum baldschuanicum, 'Russian vine' (M). Sun/shade. Very invasive but effective
Rosa sp. and hybrids etc., 'Climbing and rambling roses' (M/L). Sun/part shade.
(see Pruning below)
Solanum sp., 'Climbing potatoes' (S/M). Sun
Vitis sp., 'Ornamental/fruiting vines' (L). Sun/part shade
Wistaria sp. (L). Sun. (See Pruning below)

Training
Trellis, walls wired with supports, pergolas, fences, posts. Can be trained over stumps, tree
trunks or associated with other suitable types, e.g. roses and clematis.

Pruning
Some exceptionally vigorous types in this group, e.g. polygonum, wistaria and some roses.
In general, once the plant has covered the area or volume allotted, cutting back or tying-in
new or vigorous extensive/growth is essential, in winter or early spring. Specific examples
needing more specialised treatment are:

Clematis. Two main groups as regards pruning:
(a) Species and hybrids flowering spring or early summer on previous season's wood, e.g. C.
    montana, little pruning except to remove dead wood and restrict excessive growth. After
    flowering, if overtangled cut really hard back and start again!

(b) Species and hybrids flowering summer/early autumn on current season's wood, i.e. large flowered hybrids and *C. jackmanii*. Cut back hard to strong living buds removing at least one-third to a half of last year's growths. Prune in spring. Treated in this way they can be used for bedding displays and ground cover.
Note: Clematis in general are not very long-lived plants and are liable to sudden collapse due to wilt and other causes.

Climbing/rambling roses. In general a policy of renewal or replacement should be aimed at once a framework is established by tying in the more vigorous extension growths and cutting out a proportion of the older or dead wood in March. Otherwise many vigorous climbers like 'Albertine' can be actually cut back with shears in late winter or early spring or after the first flowering flush in summer. Climbing varieties of well-known hybrid teas varieties should generally not be cut back in the early years after planting as this may cause them to revert.

Wistaria. Once established, the normal pruning of wistarias is in two or three operations:

(a) Summer pruning of the laterals or long trailing growths back to 15 cm (6 in) in July.
(b) In December or January, shorten these laterals back to two buds.
(c) Training in new growths as required, and removal of old or dead wood.

---

*L = long lived, (25-50 yr); M = medium life (10-20 yr); S = short life (5-10 yr).

infest some woody wall plants, especially honeysuckles (*Lonicera*) and roses. The favourable sheltered microclimate allows these pests to overwinter and to begin multiplying and feeding quite early in the year, so any spraying that is done should be as early in the season as possible to prevent a build up and damage to the flowering shoots.

Black spot disease of roses can be persistent on some climbers and ramblers especially on varieties that may tend to be almost evergreen on sheltered walls. Some fungicidal spray is usually necessary such as 'Benlate'.

Clematis wilt is occasionally a serious and fatal disease, attacking young plants which suddenly collapse during the growing season. There is no real control, and such a calamity with newly purchased clematis should be reported to the nursery or supplier immediately. Older, established plants are less likely to be infected.
Nutrient application. As has already been noted, woody plants grown for ornamental effects usually require less feeding than those grown for crop production. However, the soils often found at the base of walls of houses and buildings may be impoverished, dry and of poor structure, usually as a result of the building operations, and most climbers, particularly the more vigorous types, like clematis and roses, do benefit from a combined mulch and light balanced fertiliser application in late winter, when the soils are probably still moist. The mulch will help to conserve soil moisture in any case.

Herbaceous non-woody perennials

There are probably more than 1500 introduced herbaceous plants in cultivation to which must be added very many attractive native plants. It was the writings and examples of John Loudon and Mrs Loudon in the mid-nineteenth century, later to be joined by those two garden and plant lovers, William Robinson and Gertrude Jekyll, that really established 'perennials' as they came to be called, as important elements of the floral displays in late-Victorian and Edwardian gardens. Gertrude

Jekyll also noted the more simple kinds including herbs in cottage gardens. During the 1920s and 1930s majestic and spectacular herbaceous borders became the *pièce de résistance* of many large gardens, and in a humbler, more modest way, of countless smaller gardens also. However, the 1939-45 war meant the inevitable neglect of many of these fine features and while battles raged across Europe the ground elder and couch invaded the phlox and lupins! Since then the traditional herbaceous borders have never really staged a general comeback, the simple reason being that such features are expensive in time and labour, they have peaks and troughs of visual impact, and the newer introduction of less labour-intensive shrubs are more attractive for many people.

However, new ways of growing perennials were being advocated in the 1950s and 1960s, the great pioneers here being Alan Bloom with his island borders of shorter-growing (no-staking) varieties of perennials and Christopher Lloyd with his idea of mixed borders. Margery Fish and Beth Chatto have also helped promote the cause of these plants and another great advocate is Graham Stuart Thomas who has been responsible for some magnificent planting schemes in National Trust gardens as well as for prolific writings. His book *Perennial Garden Plants* is now the standard work on these plants. There have always been reasons, for not being able to use many good garden perennials in public plantings, such as vulnerability to damage and trampling, the problems of poor visual winter effects and the labour involved with their upkeep. A number are also susceptible to some herbicides in common use

Plate 3.4 *Bergenia cordifolia purpurea* makes a fine foliage plant throughout the year. It will grow in difficult shaded sites and is remarkably maintenance free

in shrub areas. These problems, are, however, not insuperable and these plants have so many good qualities and uses to be analysed shortly, that more widespread appearances in gardens and parks should be encouraged.

Maintenance requirements

Growth habit and renewal. To really understand the maintenance and management of these plants, it will be helpful to appreciate their different growth habits. Non-woody, herbaceous perennials, by definition, are plants that persist for a few or many years by means of subterranean root systems or structures. From these are produced the aerial leaves and flowering stems during the course of one growing season which then die away after flowering to the dormant root structure in the soil. A few non-woody plants may be termed 'winter green' in that they have evergreen or persistent rosettes or stem leaves throughout the winter, examples being bergenia (plate 3.4), helleborus and some arums.

The majority however, are completely herbaceous and a range of these plants and their related maintenance follows.

Rootstock (fig. 3.7)

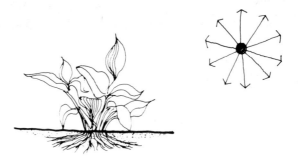

Fig. 3.7 Rootstock, e.g. hosta, Michaelmas daisy

Examples – Aster, Delphinium, Helenium, Hosta (plate 3.5).
Maintenance – The original or parent clumps normally need periodic lifting every three to five years due to decay of the old central nucleus and gradual shift of new vigorous growths to the perimeter. These new growths can be divided up and form the basis for rooted plants for replanting programmes. Perennial weeds should be carefully dissected out of these divisions before planting.

Runners and stolons (creeping stems with little storage capacity) (fig. 3.8).
Examples - Ajuga, Fragaria, Lamiastrum, Vinca.
Maintenance - Usually very maintenance free and commonly used for ground cover under trees and shrubs. The main 'intervention' necessary is to curb the growth of the more vigorous or invasive species by chopping out with a spade or hoe. Propagation is simple and the persistence of this group is usually good due to continual self-renewal by new runners, etc.

Plate 3.5 Hosta 'Royal Standard'. A fine example of this extemely valuable group of perennials

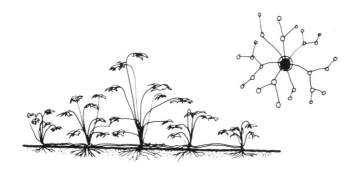

Fig. 3.8 Runners/stolons, e.g. geranium

Rhizomes (creeping stems with considerable storage) (fig. 3.9.).

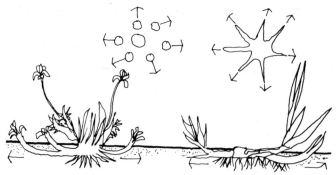

Fig. 3.9 Rhizomes

Examples - *Alchemilla mollis, Anemone hupenensis, Geranium, Iris, Lysimachia.*
Maintenance - There are different growth habits in this group: flag irises have
fleshy surface-growing rhizomes that slowly spread from the original parent plant.
Reasonably maintenance free renewal is usually necessary every five to eight years
depending on disease incidence and general condition of the plants.

Creeping rhizomes, as in geranium, present little regular maintenance
requirement, lifting and division should be done at intervals depending on the
condition of the plant.

Fleshy tap rooted plants (fig. 3.10).

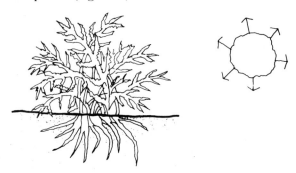

Fig. 3.10 Tap rooted, e.g. *Acanthus spinosa* etc.

Examples - *Anchusa, Eryngium, Gypsophila, Lupinus, Paeonia.*
Maintenance - Very persistent and long lived as a rule with low maintenance
requirements for many years. Plants do not move easily and propagation in some
cases is less prolific than with the other categories. Minimal disturbance until
necessary should be the rule.

Note: Some perennials may grow by means of a combination of some of these
categories. Good examples are *Echinops* the globe thistle, which produces deep
running roots, *Acanthus* and, of course, the very invasive butterbur (*Petasites*). All
these may become over-luxuriant in confined areas, and unless herbicides are used
can be quite difficult to eradicate.

Support or staking. For those interested in the origins of cultivated plants, it is intriguing to remember that many herbaceous perennials grown in gardens today are derived from species in their native countries found in meadowland or woodland edge or waterside communities. The competition from other species makes them shorter and sturdier than their cultivated relations, and the close companionship with many other plants must help to some extent in keeping the flowering stems upright, at least for most of their flowering period. Breeding, plant selection and intensive cultivation have conferred the benefits of bigger, brighter and more spectacular flowers, and also of taller, softer growths, and as many perennials flower in the summer months when the weather can be quite treacherous, staking or support have become almost a necessity for traditional means of cultivation. This is essential for example with delphiniums and the taller campanulas and lilies. There are various ways of providing support, from individual stakes or canes, to netting or pea sticks or twigs, but all are inevitably time consuming, although well worth the effort.

Where staking is used, the means of support should be put in place in good time, usually late March or early April, before the plants have grown too high.

Cutting down. The eventual cutting down and removal of dead leaves and flower stems is usually done from November onwards, but there is a case for leaving the job until late winter, or early spring, since there are some visual effects of flower heads and seed capsules, especially when they have frost on them, and they may give some protection from frost.

Pests and diseases. Snails and slugs are probably the most serious pests, particularly with newly established plants and also with certain groups like delphiniums and hostas. Regular application of granular slug bait will help to reduce the population.

Nematode eelworms may be serious in phlox varieties often disseminated by infected stock from nurseries, causing stunting and poor growth.

Verticillium wilt and mildew have had drastic effects on the once popular and very numerous varieties of Michaelmas daisies. Resistant species and varieties are now mostly grown.

Nutrient application. Good organic matter and fairly high nutrient levels are needed to produce the best quality herbaceous groups, particularly with genera like delphinium, lupin, and phlox and many others. Mulching plus a top dressing layer greatly helps with hoeing or hand weeding, both of which are almost inevitable practices with many herbaceous plants. Herbicides can be used, but with care (see Chapter 2) where these plants are grown in wild garden associations, no nutrition is necessary as a rule.

Bulbs, corms and tubers

Growth habit. In many respects this group collectively put together under this heading, are really herbaceous perennials whose aerial parts die down to a more definable and compact dormant storage organ. They are also among the more fragile and vulnerable groups of garden plants, many needing rather special habitats and cultivation to survive.

Bulbs have fleshy scale leaves and aerial flowering stems arising from a flat plate-like stem. Under most conditions, bulbs have a remarkable persistence especially when used for naturalising and left undisturbed. Narcissi and tulips are typical examples. They increase naturally by seed, or by a division of the parent bulb into smaller side bulbs.

Corms are really swollen, fleshy root-like structures, rather like beetroot and carrot, with stems and aerial shoots born on the upper part and the fibrous roots beneath. Gladioli generally need lifting regularly to produce the floral effects, but hardy cyclamen should be left undisturbed when they may make enormous plate-like woody corms. Crocus also will naturalise happily for long periods of time with little attention needed.

Tubers are swollen, storage stems (as in potato or dahlia) and are in many respects similar to corms. Hardy orchids generally have tubers which may persist for many years in the ground.

Maintenance and planting habitats. There are so many fragile, very beautiful and varied species and varieties in this large group of herbaceous perennials that only brief guidelines can be given, but important maintenance aspects should allow for the prolonged dormant period that most of them need, when little or no aerial parts are visible. This means therefore that cultivation is often in very special habitats in the garden, where the location and life cycle of each is carefully noted, or else with the more adaptable and tolerant species, a more flexible method is by naturalising in turf or permanent ground cover. The following are some suggested habitats for bulbs, corms and tubers.

Naturalising. This is by far the safest and most effective way of ensuring the continuity of many bulbous or similar plants, provided they are ecologically suitable for naturalising in the first place, and also that the maintenance or management afterwards is adjusted to the growth cycles of the bulbs and other species in the ground-cover plantings. Species most suitable for naturalising are those from temperate climates and would include many of the more common genera such as narcissus, crocus, snowdrop (*Galanthus*), anemone and colchicum. Less satisfactory or reliable are those from drier, hotter regions like gladiolus, tulip, or bulbous iris which prefer more specialised cultivation as a general rule. When naturalising in grass a critical management factor is the timing of mowing the grass. Once the bulbs have flowered in the grass an adequate period of time should be left to allow any seeding to take place (*Crocus tomasinianus* will seed very freely in thin turf, for example), but more important, for the foliage to die away. For early-flowering species like snowdrop and crocus, it should be safe to cut the grass by the middle of May, but for narcissus, it may well be late June before this should be done.

Premature mowing can result in poor flowering and the gradual decline of the bulb communities.

Woodland gardens and mixed borders. Here the more exotic genera like *Lilium, Eremurus, Galtonia* and *Gladioli* usually prefer rich soils and higher levels of cultivation and maintenance, to thrive. This can be achieved in mixed borders or on specially prepared areas for *Liliums* perhaps in woodland glades and borders. Staking, careful weeding and pest and disease control may all be needed with these beautiful but rather specialised plants. Bark and leaf-litter mulches, and shallow hoeing in the dormant season (usually September to March) are infinitely preferable to indiscriminate forking. Herbicides need very special care if used at all.

Weed control. Herbicides have to be used with the greatest care on bulbs, and although used in a commercial production, in gardens and parks, I would suggest the alternative as referred to above, of mulching and hand weeding or hand hoeing.

Pests and diseases. Slugs and snails are the most serious pests. Mice can sometimes consume crocus and other corms and small bulbs.

Virus diseases are becoming a problem in some lilies.

Alpines and rock plants
In the great days of Reginald Farrer the vogue started for building rock gardens, as a habitat for alpine and rock plants, and with plentiful supplies of stone and of cheap labour, and the examples of Farrer pointing the way, some magnificent creations came into being with enormous populations of suitable plants. The great era of rock garden building continued into the 1930s with a number of nursery and landscape firms developing an expertise in this. Examples of great rock gardens built in those days, and since extended or modified, are still to be seen in botanic gardens such as Kew, Cambridge and Edinburgh, and in some public parks.

There are a fascinating and remarkable range of hardy alpines and rock plants, which given the right habitat to start with, can be remarkably maintenance free and effective. In fact a former President of the Alpine Society, Dr Lionel Bacon, writing in *The Garden* in March 1980 poses the question 'Rock gardening - a dying art' and proceeds to show that there are indeed many ways of growing such plants in the smaller gardens of today without the space or resources of the 'great days'.

Cultivation of alpines and rock plants.
Alpine plants by definition grow in the high places of the world, and have developed compact habits and a tolerance of most weather extremes, except for water-logged conditions around the roots. Their natural mountain soils tend to be stony and free draining. Deep shade is another habitat disliked by most alpine and rock plants.
Rock plants. A looser term, may include plants from sub-alpine regions or stony lowland or coastal habitats but they too share the general dislike of wet soils and poor drainage.

Planting habitats. Bearing in mind the dislike of wet soils, the following structures or systems are suggested for growing these plants, all having the common aim of providing raised levels for good drainage and planting for exposure to sunshine. Very limited maintenance may also follow, if the planting habitat has been successful.
Raised beds and terraces and rock walls (fig. 3.11). Constructed over well-drained parent soil, or over hard core or rubble. Use weed-free compost of about two equal parts sand and gravel to one part peat and one part loam. Cover afterwards with about 25 cm (10 in) of coarse grit. Select dwarf spreading alpines, reliable cushion-forming types, dwarf shrubs etc. Plant small bulbs before cover is complete. Pounce

Fig. 3.11 A raised bed offering dry stone wall habitats as well as a free-draining surface for many different plants

on any weeds, especially in the first few years. Such a feature can be very low maintenance indeed once established.

Sinks and troughs. Glazed sinks suitably treated, or the all too scarce stone troughs are ideal places for specialised alpines and rock plants and can be placed on terraces or paved areas near the house (fig. 3.12).

Fig. 3.12 The right selection of specialised plants in a sink like this can provide an attractive and remarkably maintenance-free feature for many years

An informal area with the minimum of rocks or stones (plate 3.6.). Sometimes termed a 'rock bank'. Site away from trees or overhanging branches preferably where there may be a natural change of level. Drainage materials and a gritty soil are important on heavy soils as a basis for the successful rock bank. Avoid steep gradients. Many close-growing mat or hummock-forming plants including shrubs and conifers can be selected and maintenance can be remarkably simple once established.

A small rock garden (fig.3.13). Many excellent books have been written on the building of rock gardens and miniature stone outcrops. A good rock garden should have most of the stone well buried and be richly scattered with plants.

Fig. 3.13 A small rock garden showing restrained use and layout of stones. Siting and careful choice of plants will also determine the success or failure of a rock garden

Plate 3.6 A rock bank showing an attractive range of well-established plants. Very few stones were used here

Maintenance of alpines and rock plants. Since these groups may include dwarf shrubs, conifers, evergreens or herbaceous perennials, cushion-forming and carpeting plants and bulbs, no real blue print can be put forward for their maintenance, the real answer lying in the site, the habitat, and the plant selection being right in the first place. After that, hand weeding is essential, especially removing promptly any perennial weeds. A mulch of grit or chippings will help to reduce weed invasions. Occasional renewal, clipping over, or control of invasive species are also necessary from time to time. Slugs, snails and pecking birds may be a nuisance. If the plant selection is restricted to the dwarfer, shrubs and woody sub-shrubs. It is possible to use a herbicide like simazine as a residual-acting weed killer especially if the plants are growing in gravel.

Annuals, biennials or half-hardy display plants

Annuals are naturally short-lived plants that complete their growth cycle from seeding to flowering and death, within one growing season. Examples: lobelia, clarkia, and sweet pea (*Lathyrus*).

Biennials have a life cycle extended over two years with overwintered seedlings from the first year, flowering and seeding in the second. Examples: foxglove (*Digitalis*), *Verbascum* and ornamental thistle (*Onopordon*).

Half-hardy display plants may be non-woody or woody perennial plants that will not normally overwinter in the open, outside in Britain but are valuable for summer display. They are usually overwintered under glass or rooted cuttings. Others may be raised from seed each year. Examples: dahlias (*Helichrysum*) and geraniums (*Pelargonium*). They are often used for tub and container planting.

Utilisation and maintenance

As the emphasis is on maintenance throughout this book, this group of colourful and attractive plants by virtue of their ephemeral character and constant need of renewal, are considered of high maintenance requirement to be effective and should therefore be considered with this disadvantage in mind. Many private gardens rely on annuals for their main show of the summer but more use could be made of the easier group of annuals like *Nigella, Eschscholzias, Nasturtiums* and others by direct seeding into suitable areas of well-drained soils where perhaps such colourful species could be used as temporary displays between more permanent shrubs. Much depends on the weed content of the soil and the type of annuals used. Annuals do give generous and speedy floral displays. Traditional bedding schemes will always find a place, even though now more limited, in large gardens and public parks, and there is considerable scope and ingenuity for the many possible associations and combinations of colours and textures. Children too often begin their gardening interest with colourful annuals so always allow a space for these in any garden. More schools should encourage gardens as a general revival of a once excellent practice. In Holland, children and young people's gardens are a normal practice in most large towns.

For the wilder gardens, biennials like foxglove, honesty, mulleins (*Verbascum*), poppies and others can be seeded into suitable places with very pleasant effects. Robinson and Jekyll advocated such ideas. *Heracleum mantegazzianum*, the giant hogweed, is a magnificent biennial plant for wild gardens and damp places.

Plant communities and their management

So far, this chapter on vegetation management has been mainly concerned with the principles and practices of maintaining individual or specific groups of plants, and it is usually this approach that is followed in most of the reference works on the subject. This section looks at policies and some broad guidelines for ornamental plant community management. A number of categories are defined here.

Woodlands, copses, arboreta and pineta

Without getting too much involved with commercial forestry and woodland management, there is nevertheless much relevant information that can be drawn from the foresters' systems of planting and management, even though the longer-term objectives are rather different.

Maintenance and management aspects. To ecologists, a woodland represents a climax community composed of a complex association of flora and fauna, with the dominant layers or vegetation category being trees. As most trees are long lived and of very low maintenance requirement, once established, it follows that a woodland community may be one of the lowest and most economical vegetation associations to manage (see table 2.7 for man hour figures). Using the ecologists' term 'layers' for these different vegetation types as a maintenance guide the following are the essential management inputs one would expect to carry out, once woodlands or arboreta are established. Table 3.4 illustrates these points also.

Tree layers. The species range, age, health and planting density are all obvious factors. In arboreta and pineta where a heterogenous and often very mixed range of species are usually grown, competition will be inevitable between widely differing genera and species with quite different growth rates and habitat not normally growing together in association. This may lead to overcrowding and eventual stunting of growth. Where collections are associated in botanical groups, this may be less of a problem.

If considered as ornamental or woodlands designed for pleasure and botanical or horticultural study, the potential for design and management is enormous. Westonbirt arboretum in Gloucestershire is an example in its century old maturity and makes an interesting comparison with the younger Pinetum at Bedgebury in Kent.

On the other hand, the most recent Hillier arboretum in Hampshire although planted with an incredible range of hardy woody plants and valuable for this reason alone, is less successful as a designed, visual woodland of the future.

The aim should be for groups and drifts of well-spaced trees of similar habitat, contrasting with other groups of different character and forms, with generous glades and rides as viewing areas and 'breathing spaces' and to show off carefully selected specimens allotted special clearings of their own.

It is all too easy, and very tempting, especially if space is limited, to over-plant or plant up glades and clearings with insufficient thought for the future. Overcrowded arboreta and woodlands can soon become claustrophobic for visitors and are often more difficult to maintain. Extraction or removal of dead, dying or overmature trees is more of a problem.

When renewal becomes necessary, it is seldom successful to attempt to interplant new young specimens among old mature trees, since unless the former are exceptionally shade tolerant the competition for light and nutrients can produce weak, deformed specimens. Far better to take a longer-term forester's view and clear fell blocks or compartments of overmature trees and use these new glades for planting and clearings (see table 3.4). Stump removal has already been referred to.

In extensive woodland areas it is probably best to leave the stumps and interplant as a general policy, only removing stumps in future glade areas or where expensive or rare trees are to be planted.

The canopy will help determine the character and the plant diversity of particular woodlands and canopy control can be used to create a balance between light and shade areas. The soil and topography will also be important to decide on

Table 3.4 Woodland garden maintenance

MATURE TREE ZONE

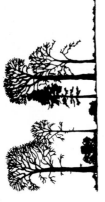

Trees. Check for disease, obvious senescence and decay. Where appropriate leave a few dead or decaying specimens for bird life and conservation. Retain canopy as long as possible.

Shrubs. Introduce groupings of shade-tolerant species such as viburnum, holly, rhododendron depending on light and pH factor. This layer is important for enclosure and shelter, visual diversity and all year round interest. Honey fungus may be a problem (see Chapter 2).

Herb layer. Encourage woodland flora after controlling or removing excessive weed competition where nutrient-rich species like *Urtica* (nettles), *Rumex* (docks) and *Rubus* (brambles) are invasive, using judicious herbicide regimes. Introduce or encourage seeds/plants as appropriate. Light rotary mowing, only never closer than 50 mm (2 in) of areas of grass or herb swards not before late June, to encourage primroses, bluebells, wood anemones, etc. The herb layer will be also determined by the soil and pH characteristics.

GLADE ZONE

Glades are important to contrast with the denser tree canopy zones and will provide contrasts in design and atmosphere and visual experience, and for the plants 'edge' habitats and clearings.

Trees. Carefully select or plant really suitable outstanding single specimens, e.g. *Picea omorika* the Serbian spruce, unusual birches (*Betula*), cedars (*Cedrus*), maples (*Acer*). Do not overplant the glades. Clearings are of great importance.

Shrubs. Strategically group where space and design allow related to the ecology and the character of the woodland. Drifts, groups and enclosures of similar or contrasting species are preferable to a scattered diversity of single species.

Herb layer. Lightly mow to 4 cm (1.5 in) paths and informal grass herb areas with long grass zones for herb species, bulbs, etc. These can be flail or rotary cut in late June. Judiciously spot treat with herbicides vigorous colonies of nettles and thistles, if really competitive. Introduce new species as plants or seed.

YOUNG TREE ZONE (RENEWAL)

Trees. Groups and compartments of new trees should be planned as replacements for felled areas. Retain framework of *native species* to keep character of the wood. Use a forester's system of planting suitable species among old 'treated' stumps unless resources are available to remove these. Control vigorous scrub and 'weed growth' around newly planted trees for at least three years while establishing. Mow paths or areas between compartments with a Votex rotary mower, or similar, leave some scrub, or introduce nurse species to protect young trees in the early years. Later, thinning and some felling may be needed to maintain diversity.

Shrub / herb layer. There are opportunities for manipulating or encouraging existing woodland scrub and herb flora after the initial flush of growth that usually follows felling. Introduce new plantings before the canopy becomes too closed. Maintain balance of native and introduced species, if possible.

the range of species grown. Thus there will be a great difference between dry shaded beech woodlands overlying chalky soils and damp more open oak woodlands on moist clay.

Shrub and herb layers in woodlands. Table 3.4 includes some of the main guidelines to be followed when introducing or managing shrubs in woodland areas.

Shrubs are important for many reasons in such communities. Apart from giving visual contrasts and interests at human eye level, they can break up extensive tracts of even-aged plantations by creating enclosures, and helping to reduce through draughts and internal wind turbulence that can be an unpleasant feature of thin belts of mature canopy trees. They may also have important wildlife conservation values.

Shrubs can be planted as specimens or in groups and may be native or exotic, but in all cases one should select those appropriate or adapted to the woodland type being managed. Soil pH and type will be critical factors as will shade and aspect.

Canopy density can be misleading in the winter months for any one unfamiliar with woodland planting, especially where beeches (*Fagus*) and sweet chestnut (*Castanea*) are dominant species. Light values that seem good in winter or early spring can be very different indeed by mid-summer and good indicators are the natural herb layers that develop under these species. Early bulbous and herb layer species like anemones and bluebells and some grasses, complete their growth cycles before the shade becomes too dense. There is also a drought factor to consider here. A gardenesque example can be quoted in the case of a large, spreading copper beech in a garden which in January, March or April has a delightful ground carpet of aconites (*Eranthis*), crocus, narcissi and anemones beneath it, in the grass. By late May when the tree is in full leaf, the shade effect has become the dominant factor, the spring display reverts to a thin grass cover in deep shade mown occasionally from June onwards. If a desirable herb layer is lacking in more open woodland, and there are drifts of brambles, nettles and less desirable woodland species, a combination of mowing or brush cutting (see Chapter 2) and very careful herbicide application may be the basis for a 'clean slate' from which to begin more appropriate planting.

Leaves. An essential component of the ecology of woodlands is the layer of leaf litter or leaf mould that is normally present in varying depths depending on the species and the type of woodland. In managed ornamental woodlands, leaves should be allowed to remain wherever possible as a mulch beneath trees or shrubs, by blowing or raking off the grass areas and depositing among the woody plants, or they should be collected from the grass areas, paths and drives and converted into mulch or compost in some central or convenient place. Leaf harvesting is considered in Chapter 2.

Forestry and woodland. Many larger estates may have extensive areas of woodlands and forests managed for sporting or timber purposes and they are beyond the scope of this section. Advice can be obtained from the Forestry Commission and Timber Growers Organisation.

Shrub borders and shrubberies
The shrub or scrub layer in natural or semi-natural communities makes an

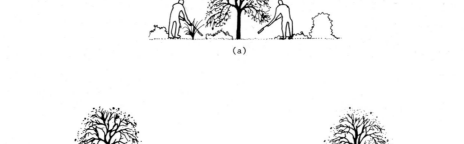

Fig. 3.14 Three alternative maintenance systems for shrub areas:

(a) Hand hoeing or forking bare soil regimes between shrubs or trees. A traditional system requiring about thirty-three man hours per 100 m² per year
(b) Use of residual herbicide and/or mulch layer. Man hour figures may be reduced to five hours per 100 m² per year
(c) Use of ground cover as a total closed community among shrubs and beneath trees. Once established the occasional clipping or hand weeding of the ground cover amounts to about eight man hours per 100 m² per year

interesting basis from which to consider the design and management of such areas in gardens and parks. Examples in nature are the Maquis or Garigue zones of southern Europe, where the tree layer is missing for a number of reasons.

Close masses or groups of many different species, but of generally similar growth habit, form compact associations with intervening zones of grassy or herb layer communities. As such therefore they are essentially low maintenance associations. One can see similar communities but of quite different species in the heathlands and moorlands of Britain. However, one must appreciate the fact that it is a combination of climate, soil and management that has produced these dense shrub communities.

In more general terms of maintenance and management the following alternatives can be considered:

Traditional shrub borders and shrubberies. Often seen in gardens and municipal parks. Collections of shrubs are used as specimens or for background screening (*Aucuba, Euonymus, Viburnum tinus*, etc.). The annual clipping over these are sometimes subjected to is in most cases an unnecessary tradition, apart from the labour costs involved. The ground surface treatment is often of bare soil with winter forking and summer hoeing (fig. 3.14). Richer more effective associations can be achieved with bolder contrasting shrub masses and contrasting bays of low ground cover of perennials or low shrubs and bulbs planted in a mulch which will then be weeded by hand or with careful herbicide use (see plates 3.7 and 3.8). The latter treatments are far more economic to maintain.

Plate 3.7 Low ground cover (*Lamium galeobdolon*) a shrub and woodland fungus at Hidcote, Gloucestershire, a property of the National Trust

The Maquis approach of mixed shrub associations for texture, contrast and seasonal interest and low maintenance, may be used in conjunction with herbicides and mulches. Conifers can also be introduced and specimen trees and some perennials. There is endless scope for experimentation with such associations (plate 3.9).

Renewal. The shrub pruning table (see table 3.2) indicates the considerable variation in the longevity and life spans of some shrubs and these should be taken into account when planning extensive shrub associations. 'The plantsman's collections' style of shrub gardening allows for replacement, but where extensive

Plate 3.8 High shrub ground cover of azaleas (rhododendrons) at Leonardslee, Sussex

Plate 3.9 Attractive massed associations of shrubs and perennials at Killerton, Devon, a property of the National Trust

groups of the same species are used, one must allow for their eventual replacement on something similar to the forester's compartment basis. There are alternatives even here:

(a) *Phased planting*. Shrub areas or borders can be deliberately planned to include groups or a framework for longer-term structural shrubs or even trees, with intervening spaces used for fast growing filler shrubs such as brooms (*Cytisus*), buddleias or even fast-growing perennials. As the longer-term shrubs establish, then the 'fillers' should be progressively reduced or removed.
(b) *Phased replacement* of complete shrub groups as this becomes necessary.
(c) *The cottage garden approach* with a mixture of shrubs, perennials and annuals, presenting little serious disturbance when one or two shrubs have eventually to be removed, unless very large or of special value. An individual style and discerning plant knowledge and maintenance approach are really necessary to make this alternative a success.

Mixed borders

These have already been referred to several times and are really developed from the cottage garden style above and concepts put forward by William Robinson and Gertrude Jekyll in the late-Victorian and Edwardian eras, and since developed by such successful exponents as Christopher Lloyd and Alan Bloom.

The main object in designing a mixed border is to explore all the ecological layers and adapt them to specific situations using the relative advantages of foliage trees, shrubs (flowering and foliage), perennials, bulbs and annuals depending on the space available, the soil and the tastes of the design. A blend of these will determine the ultimate selection and effects.

Visual effects can be spread throughout most of the year, with careful plant selections, and likewise the maintenance although moderately skilled or intensive at times, can also be spread over a longer period. This is particularly important where more shrubs than perennials are used in the blend, and indeed the selection can be adjusted to suit the time available for maintenance.

Hedges and screens

Hedges may be defined as:

linear and continuous communities of one or more species of woody plants, which by reasons of their dense bushy growth and regular clipping or pruning, form effective living barriers, screens and enclosures.

Hedges for protection and enclosure have been very traditional and historical features of gardens (and farmsteads) from medieval times (see Chapter 1). The complexities of hedged enclosures and clipped boundary and ornamental features reached incredible levels in the great Renaissance formal gardens of France and one restored garden of that era at Villandry in the Loire Valley still has about 30 km (18.75 miles) of box hedges to be clipped annually, apart from well over 1000 limes to be pleached or pruned by hand each winter.

Hedges are very important as space division in the newer gardens designed this century, such as Hidcote in Gloucestershire, and Sissinghurst in Kent, when clipped yews, hornbeams and other species create the sequence of outdoor rooms that have now become a popular concept for many much smaller gardens. With a wide variety of hedging species of different growth rates, and an array of mechanical tools to cut them quickly and effectively, the place of the hedge is an important one in gardens and parks today.

Maintenance of hedges. There is a regular maintenance commitment with all hedges but the frequency of cutting and the methods used will vary considerably with the species used, and the purpose of the hedge. This can best be demonstrated in table 3.5.

Table 3.5 Hedge maintenance

Hedge species	Usual no. of cuts per year	Seasons of cutting	Average range of height (m)	Rate of growth
1. *Deciduous foliage hedges*				
Acer campestre 'Field/hedge maple'	One	Sep.-Mar.	1.5-3	Moderate
Carpinus betulus* 'Hornbeam'	One	Sep.-Mar.	1.5-3	Moderate
Crataegus spp. 'Hawthorn'	Two	July Nov.-Mar.	1.5-3	Moderate to fast
Fagus sylvatica* 'Beech' also purple and copper-leaved cultivars	One	Sep.-Mar.	1.5-3	Moderate to slow
Prunus cerasifera 'Myrobolan plum' and purple-leaved forms	Two	June/July Nov.-Dec.	1.5-3	Fast
Rosa rubiginosa 'Sweet briar'	Two	July Nov.-Mar.	0.75-1.5 1.0-1.5	Fast
Rosa rugosa	Two	July Nov.-Mar.	0.75-1.0	Moderate
Viburnum lantana 'Wayfaring tree'	One	Nov.-Mar.	1.0-2	Moderate
2. *Flowering deciduous hedges*				
Chaenomeles. 'Japonica'	Two	May Dec.-Mar.	1.0-1.5	All quite fast. Discerning pruning to avoid cutting out all flowering wood.
Cornus mas 'Cornelian cherry'	Two	June Nov.-Dec.	1.0-2.0	
Cotoneaster simonsii	Two	June Dec.-Mar.	1.0-1.5	
Forsythia spectabilis	Two	May Dec.-Mar.	1.0-1.5	

Hedge species	Usual no. of cuts per year	Seasons of cutting	Average range of height (m)	Rate of growth
Gooseberry	Two	June Dec.-Mar.	0.75-1	Produce fruit but picking is tricky within the hedge!
Red currant	One	Nov.-Mar.	0.75-1	

3. Evergreen hedges

Hedge species	Usual no. of cuts per year	Seasons of cutting	Average range of height (m)	Rate of growth
Buxus sempervirens 'Common box'	Three/four	June-Sep.	0.15-1	Slow
Chamaecyparis lawsoniana 'Lawson's cypress' and cultivars	One	Feb.-Mar.	1.5-3	Moderate. Avoid excess hard cutting into old wood.
Cupresso-cyparis leylandii 'Leyland cypress'	One/two	July-Apr.	2-10	Very fast – one cut in March may be adequate for tall hedges.
Eleagnus sp.	One	Aug.	2-3	Moderate informal hedge.
Euonymus japonicus	Two	June-Sep.	1.5-2	Moderate coastal areas
Ilex aquifolium 'Holly' and cultivars	One	July/Aug.	2-5	Slow
Ligustrum ovalifolium 'Privet'	Four	May-Sep.	1-3	Fast. Frequent clipping to keep in shape.
Lonicera nitida	Four/five	May-Sep.	0.5-1.5	Fast, needs regular clipping.
Pittosporum tenuifolium	One	Aug.-Sep.	1.5-3.0	Milder and south south-west areas. Cut foliage value. Moderate/fast.
Prunus laurocerasus 'Common laurel'	One	May-June	2-5	Careful hand pruning with secateurs. Shears can disfigure. Slow.
Phillyrea augustifolia	One	May-June	2-4	Slow. Ditto.
Prunus lusitanica 'Portuguese laurel'	One	May-June	2-5	Ditto. Not in cold areas. Slow.
Quercus ilex	One/two	Apr.-Aug.	1.5-5	Slow. Not very cold areas.
Thuya plicata	One	Mar.	2-5	Moderate. Excellent hedge

Hedge species	Usual no. of cuts per year	Seasons of cutting	Average range of height (m)	Rate of growth
Taxus baccata 'Yew'	One	Aug.-Sep.	1.5-4	Moderate. The best architectural hedge.
Berberis darwinii	One	May-June	0.75-1.5	Orange yellow flowers. Lacks density. Slow.
Berberis julianae	One	June-July	1-2.0	Spiny barrier. Moderate.
Cotoneaster lacteus	One	June-July	1-1.5	Berries/flowers. Moderate.
Escallonia macrantha and others	One/two	Apr.-Aug.	1-2	Seaside hedge. Red flowers. Fast.
Fuchsia 'Riccartonii'	One	Mar.	1-2	Milder S.W. areas. Fast.
Olearia *Osmanthus delavayi*	One/two	May-Aug.	0.5-1.5	Scented white flowers. Slow.
Osmarea burkwoodii	One/two	May-Aug.	1.0-2.0	Scented white flowers. Slow.
Rhododendron ponticum	One	July-Aug.	2-4	Acid soils. Purple flowers. Moderate.
Viburnum tinus 'Laurustinus'	One	Apr.-May	1.5-3	Winter flowering. Pollution resistant. Moderate.
Olearia macrodonta	One	Mar.	1.5-2	Seaside berries. White flowers. Fast.

*Retain dried leaves in winter.

Newly established hedges should generally be allowed to grow up to their ultimate intended height, unless exceptionally tall, without heading back the leading shoots. The laterals or side growths should certainly be trimmed, however.

Very old or overgrown hedges of certain species only, can be restored to their original shape, or completely rejuvenated by splitting or cutting back to the original trunk or trunks and then allowing new growth to develop. This is possible with deciduous hedges such as thorns, hornbeam and beech, and evergreens like holly and laurel. Yew is really the only conifer to be treated in this way. With *Thuya* or *Cupressus* hedges it would be disastrous. To reduce the impact on the hedge, it is preferable to take out one side at a time with an interval of a year or more, at the same time feed the hedge with a mulch and fertiliser dressing. Figure 3.15 shows the procedure.

Flowering hedges need some care and understanding of the precise time to clip or prune. Table 3.4 does give some rather arbitrary times as a guide, but in general the

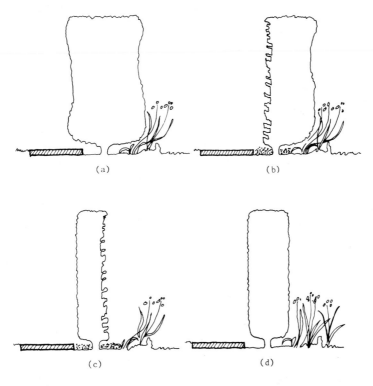

Fig. 3.15 Stages in the thinning and renovation of a yew hedge.

(a) Overgrown hedge reducing path width and stifling plant borders
(b) One side cut back hard to main trunks. Follow with organic fertiliser and mulch
(c) Repeat process with the remaining one or two years later
(d) The hedge after four to five years restored to its original dimensions

best time for most of these is after flowering. If berries are also aimed at, the early spring is the alternative, e.g. *Cotoneaster lacteus*.

Hedge cutting in relation to height and species and man hours is important as table 3.6 shows.

Table 3.6 Hedge cutting in relation to height and species

Hedge	Height of hedge (m)	No. of cuts per year	Total man hours per year per 100 m lengths
Ligustrum ovalifolium 'Privet'*	1.5	Four	50- 80
(*Lonicera nitida* is similar)	2.5	Four	100-130
Fagus sylvatica 'Beech' (Hornbeam and yew	1.5	One	18- 20
are similar; holly may take a little longer	2.5	One	30- 40
due to the prickles)			

*Privet hedges are very susceptible to honey fungus, *Armillaria mellea*.

Maintenance of screens and shelter belts. The maintenance of most of these is usually much less intensive and frequent, since the majority are single or double rows of woody plants - often tree species allowed to grow naturally for much of their existence with the periodic cutting of laterals and topping of the leaders. Even this may not be necessary for large, farm-scale windbreaks. Species used may be the deciduous beeches, sycamore, birches and alders with poplars and willows for quick effects and evergreens would include Austrian and Corsican pines and possibly Leyland cypress.

Nutrition of hedges and screens. Garden hedges, which are having a constant removal of green matter over the years may become impoverished and although generally not high in nutrient demands, some replacement is advisable by applying a light dressing of a balanced slow-acting fertiliser every two to three years with mulches of well-rotted farmyard manure or suitable organic matter.

Pests and diseases of hedges. Not usually a serious problem, but the most likely one to be met in gardens is honey fungus, already referred to which is particularly partial to privet hedges (*Ligustrum*), slowly killing a few plants each year. Removal of dead and infected plants should be followed by local soil sterilisation if possible, or the planting of a more resistant species such as holly in its place. Yew scale can also be occasionally serious.

Herbaceous perennials have already been dealt with in some detail, and some suggestions have been given regarding maintenance and utilisation. Associations of entirely non-woody herbaceous perennials are not normally found in natural systems except meadow and grasslands since shrub and trees are usually also present. Thus the mixed border is an excellent way of including perennials.

Aquatic and waterside plant associations
Aquatic or freshwater habitats are familiar to most of us from childhood with our primary school introduction to pond and stream life and the plants and animals found therein. The introduction of such features or habitats into gardens, whether as small ponds or larger pools or lakes creates the opportunity for cultivating yet another range of fascinating plants including British native and exotic species and the associated fish and freshwater fauna.

As regards upkeep and management, water and wetland features, if properly sited and created can be amongst the most maintenance free of all elements. In summarising the basic maintenance of such features, a brief analysis of their components follows.

Figure 3.16 shows a diagramatic section of a 'natural' pond with its associated wetland zones, and the vegetation of these habitats, with some notes on management.

Garden pools. Water gardens and water features in historic gardens concentrated on the design elements and the use of water for reflection, movement and inspiration. In recent years there has been a great renewal of interest in the more horticultural and ecological values of water in gardens. Francis Perry in her excellent book - *Water Gardens* - attributes this revival to three main reasons.

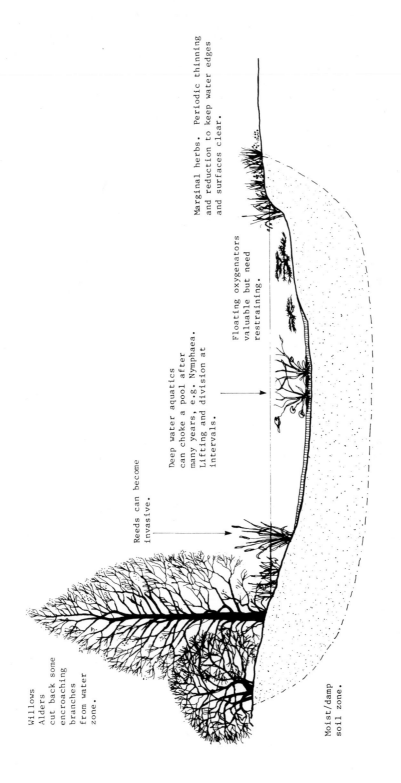

Willows
Alders
cut back some
encroaching
branches
from water
zone.

Reeds can become
invasive.

Deep water aquatics
can choke a pool after
many years, e.g. Nymphaea.
Lifting and division at
intervals.

Floating oxygenators
valuable but need
restraining.

Marginal herbs. Periodic thinning
and reduction to keep water edges
and surfaces clear.

Moist/damp
soil zone.

Fig. 3.16 Some maintenance aspects of a natural pool

(a) The development of concrete and more recently of plastic and fibre glass for quick pool construction.

(b) The work of the famous French breeder of waterlilies Marliac.

(c) Biological and ecological research and education.

Constructed garden ponds will, of course, usually have a different cross-section with steeper walls or shelving, but the general conformation and ecology should be the same.

One should aim for a balance between clear water areas and the marginal or floating plants by controlling the growth of the plants where necessary. This may be by hand pulling or cutting, and in most ponds there is an inevitable process towards the gradual choking of the pond with vegetation and organic matter. Eventually unless this process is arrested a complete engulfing of the water areas will lead to the next stage of a march or bog. Every three or four years or so, depending on the depth of the pond and its maintenance, a fairly major clearance of the vegetation is usually necessary by lifting out most of the tougher rootstock types of plants such as waterlilies, bulrushes and reeds and dividing and replanting with healthy divisions. This operation is best done in the late spring.

A summary of the maintenance jobs of a typical constructed garden pool is given in fig. 3.17.

Periodic problems will arise of excessive growth of such floating plants as duckweeds (*Lemna*) or milfoil (*Myriophyllum*). Hand pulling and skimming are really the best methods, if fish and other pond animals cannot cope with these. Avoid the use of herbicides in garden pools. Maintain at least 30-50% of the surface area of water clear of plants, in order to encourage the fishes. This operation can be done in the summer when the weather is usually more suitable for playing with water, but be careful not to remove too many submerged plants that give protection to small fish at this time of the year.

The clarity of water in pools is frequently a problem, since cloudiness may be due to a number of complex causes; but usually to the presence of masses of single-celled algae thriving on mineral salts in the water and sunshine. Larger pools eventually reach a balance as mineral salts are absorbed by plants and animals, but very small ponds can remain obstinately murky. There are chemical clearing agents that are effective in these circumstances, e.g. Algizin and Acurel 'E'.

Lakes can be comparatively maintenance free for many years.

Silting up and invasion by marginal reed beds or massive islands of waterlilies are nevertheless common problems with such features. If the water depth becomes too shallow, there is a danger of eutrophication in dry summers and a loss of fish and animal life. Ornamental wildfowl can help to control excessive aquatic vegetation. Herbicides should be used with care.

Dredging lakes may be expensive, but if it is possible to drain the lake and hire mechanical diggers once the bed has dried out the job may be done perhaps less expensively. Allowance has to be made for depositing the mud and silt not too far from the source and 'conservation interests' and anglers may be concerned by the fish and bird life that will be temporarily disrupted by the dredging.

Reed bed invasions can be dealt with by mechanical cutting up of the rafts - not too easy - or judicious use of herbicides for this purpose (see Chapter 2).

If partial areas of the lake are silted up and dredging is too expensive, an attractive

Trees
Avoid large-
leaved species.
Remove over-
hanging
branches
causing
shade effect
and excessive
leaf drop
in autumn.

Keep 30-50 % of water surface
clear of aquatic plants.

Waterproof liners
or concrete
construction.
No moist soil zone
as with natural
pond. Grow
marginals in
submerged
containers.

Water lilies are less
rampant if grown in
restrictive baskets.
In pool substrate they
will gradually enlarge
to form massive rootstocks.
Lift and divide every
four to five years.

Oxygenators can
multiply rapidly
and choke pond.
Thin and remove
after fish breeding
season. Select less
invasive species.

Marginals will
encroach across
water (raft effect).
Limit spread by
dividing every two
to three years.

Pool surface should
receive minimum
of half a day's
sunshine hours.

Fig. 3.17 Some maintenance aspects of a constructed pool

habitat can be made for wetland species of plants, birds and other animals. As such areas are becoming scarce in the British countryside the conservation value of such a feature may be very considerable and it may become an additional source of visitor attraction. Planting with exotic and native species is also possible along lake margins (plate 3.10).

Plate 3.10 Natural planting of native and exotic species along a lake margin. Such planting is also excellent for wildlife conservation

Amenity grasses, lawns and turf

There must be little doubt that the 'great British lawn' represents to foreign visitors and the British public alike, the very essence of the English garden.

From its early beginnings in the sixteenth century as the 'laund' and bowling green of Tudor and Elizabethan gardens, as modest pieces of maintained turf, the lawn became expanded into the spacious rolling pastures and grazed parkland of the great eighteenth century landscape gardens, where only the ha-ha or sunken fence prevented the animals from reaching the smooth-scythed lawns immediately around the mansion.

It was the introduction of Dr Budding's mechanical lawn mower in the 1830s coinciding with the population explosion and the coming into being of thousands of new villas with gardens attached, that really marked the rise of the English lawn, and all classes then, as today, regarded the lawn as the green carpet and centrepiece of the garden. Today, visitors to the great Chelsea Show in London every May cannot miss the array of mechanical aids and gadgets now available for lawn care, to which must be added the products of the chemical companies tempting one with fertilisers and weed killers. Some of these have already been referred to in Chapter 2.

From the maintenance point of view, lawns and amenity grass areas are the one feature of gardens and parks that absorb more national man hours in the growing season than any other activity. Figures to show this follow in the next section.

In recent years the 'umbrella' phrase 'Amenity grasslands' has become popular to cover all these types of pleasure or recreation swards or areas of turf like domestic lawns, as well as the more extensive, less intimately managed open spaces of country parks and golf courses. This collective phrase distinguishes these grasslands from the agricultural types used for animal and crop production.

The first National Survey of amenity grasslands was commissioned in 1973 by the National Environment Research Council, the Sports Turf Research Institute and the Department of the Environment, and in two years a survey was compiled of most of the areas of managed turf in Britain, from the lawns of private gardens and stately homes to the important areas of sports and recreation turf and the more extensive tracts of commons, airfields, cemeteries and highway verges.

Much of the findings of the survey go well beyond the scope of this book, but a selection of some of the survey results are given in table 3.7. to illustrate the scope and the complexity of the world of amenity turf, and the overall costs involved in its maintenance.

Table 3.7 The amenity grassland survey of Britain 1973-1974 (Adapted from the N.E.R.C. Survey)

Type of turf	Area, km² (sq. miles)
Intensively managed, e.g. bowling greens, golf courses, etc.	1100 (429)
Man-made trampled – usually less intensively managed but heavily used. Sports turf, domestic lawns.	2700 (1053)
Untrampled with limited maintenance, e.g. road verges, cemeteries, etc.	600 (234)
Semi-natural grasslands of country parks, National parks not used for agricultural purposes.	4100 (1599)
Total	8500 (3315)

Areas
The total area of all amenity grasslands in Britain in 1973-74 was estimated to be 8500 km² (3315 sq. miles) or 3.7% of the total U.K. land surface.
The total area of domestic lawns was estimated to be 90 000 ha (222 390 acres).

Costs
The total annual expenditure to maintain these 8500 km² (3315 sq miles) was assessed at £140 million, representing £57 millions on the intensively managed turf, £79 million on domestic lawns and municipal parks, etc. and the remainder on the untrampled category grasslands.

Use of amenity turf
It was estimated that in 1974 some 2.5 million people (4% of the U.K. population) engaged in various activities specifically depending on amenity turf.

Composition of turf. The fact that grass normally grows everywhere in 'England's green and pleasant land' is only too evident from the figures just quoted and perhaps it is this familiarity that leads to an all too common lack of appreciation of the fascinating and very significant diversity of grass (and sometimes other) species that make up any area of so-called 'turf'. It is, of course, this variation in the species composition that can have such important effects on wear, colour, mowing frequency and disease and drought resistance of turf.

There is also a steadily increasing range of new, and very effective strains of the more familiar species of turf grasses available now, and gardeners and managers should keep themselves up to date with these introductions. One of the best sources of reference in this respect is the Sports Turf Research Institute and some reliable grass seed companies. Not only are some of these newer strains and mixtures more wear resistant, but they can also save considerably on mowing frequencies and maintenance.

There are in fact about 10 000 species of grasses in the great botanical family *Graminae*, but only about 160 are native to Britain, and of these, six main species groups have been selected for turf grasses. A comprehensive 'at a glance' guide is reproduced in table 3.9 to help those unfamiliar with the range of species and strains to find their way through them. It does also give much other useful information on establishment, growth habits and wear tolerances.

Mowing. To make a point that really must be obvious to many, the N.E.R.C. survey produced an analysis or breakdown of the costs involved with grass maintenance in the British Isles in 1974 table 3.8.

Table 3.8 Analysis of cost involved with grass maintenance in the British Isles in 1974

Operation	Percent total cost
Mowing (man hour/machinery)	59.00
Fertilising	14.00
Weed control	5.00
All others aerating, rolling top dressings, etc.	22.00
	100.00

This really emphasises the fact that mowing far exceeds all other maintenance operations in turf management. As such therefore it is worthy of perhaps more care and attention than sometimes happens. That great pioneering authority of turf grass culture and management R. B. Dawson observed:

'Mowing is not the simple operation of removing excess growth as many imagine but a process having far-reaching effects and therefore worthy of more careful study and control.'

Mowing heights and frequencies. A most valuable long-term trial is in progress at Reading Univerity investigating these two important aspects of grass maintenance with the aim of providing answers to a number of challenging questions now being asked about traditional practices.

Table 3.9 A guide to turf grasses

Relative proportion of turf grass seed sales per annum (1980)	Turfgrass species		Average number of seeds/g	Rate of establishment	Habit of growth and leaf width (mm)	Minimum height of cut (mm)	Wear tolerance (trampling)	Conditions - adapted to or more tolerant of (including pH range)	Diseases of turfgrass species
7 %	**Bentgrasses** Brown bent	*Agrostis* *canina* ssp. *montana*		Slow	Rhizomes 1-3	Medium 13	Very poor	Acid. Damp. poverty 3-7.5	*Corticium* (Red thread)
	Brown top (or Highland)	*tenuis* (*castellana*)	15000 Range 12–20/000	Slow	Stolons and rhizomes 1.5	Very low 5	Very poor	Acidic, dry poverty 3-7.6	*Fusarium* (Patch)
	Creeping bent	*stolonifera*	12000	Slow	Stolons 0.5-5	Very low 5	Very poor	Acidic/alkaline, damp/dry 5.4-7.6	*Ophiobolus* (Take-all patch)
	Red top	*gigantea*	11000	Slow	Rhizomes 2-8	High 50	Very poor	Dry, poverty 5-7.6	*Pythium* (Snow mould)
	Velvet bent	*canina* ssp. *canina*	12000	Slow	Stolons 1-3	Very low 5	Very poor	Damp 5-7	
2%*	**Crested Dogstail**	*Cynosurus cristatus*	2000	medium	Tufted 1-4	Medium 13	Poor	Acidic/alkaline, damp/dry 4-8	*LMV* (*Lolium mottle virus*)
40 %	**Fescues** Fine-leaved sheeps	*Festuca* *tenuifolia*	1200	Slow	Tufted 0.2-4	Medium 13	Very poor	Acidic, poverty, dry/damp	
	Hard	*longifolia*	950	Slow	Tufted 0.5-1	Low 8	Very poor	Acidic/alkaline, poverty, dry	*Corticium* (Red thread)
	Red fescue Chewings (hexaploid) 42 chromosomes	*rubra* spp. *commutata*	1200	Medium	Tufted 0.5-1	Very low 5	Poor	Acidic/alkaline, dry 4-8	*Erysiphe* (Mildew)
	Dwarf creeping (hexaploid 42 chromosomes	*rubra* ssp. *litoralis*	1000	Medium	Rhizomes 0.5-1	Very low 5	Poor	Acidic/alkaline, dry 4-8	*Fusarium* (Patch)
	Normal creeping (octoploid 56 chromosomes)	*rubra* ssp. *rubra*	960 Range (7-12500)	Medium	Rhizomes 0.5-3	Low 8	Poor	Acidic/alkaline, dry 4-8	*Sclerotinia* (Dollar spot)
	Sheeps	*ovina*	1200	Slow	Tufted 0.3-6	Medium 13	Very poor	Acidic/alkaline poverty, dry 3-8	

Table 3.9 (contd)

Relative proportion of turf grass seed sales per annum (1980)	Turfgrass species		Average number of seeds/g	Rate of establishment	Habit of growth and leaf width (mm)	Minimum height of cut (mm)	Wear tolerance (trampling)	Conditions - adapted to or more tolerant of (including PH range)	Diseases of turf grass species
40%*	**Perennial Ryegrass** Turf varieties	*Lolium perenne* for winter wear for summer wear for ornamental use	600	Very rapid	Tufted 1-2	Medium 13	Excellent	Fertile drought free —	*Corticium* (Red thread) *Erysiphe* Mildew
	Other varieties	early flowering, hay types intermediate types late flowering, pasture types dual purpose (pasture/sportsfield) types	500 Range (450-700)	Very rapid	Tufted 2-6	Medium 19	Good	Fertile, drought free 5-8	*Puccinia* sp. (Rusts)
1%*	**Timothy** Common (hexaploid)	*Phleum pratense*	3000 Range (3-5000)	Medium	Tufted 3-9	Medium 13	Moderate	Damp 5-8	*Mastigiosporum* (Leaf spot)
	Turf (diploid)	*bertolonii*	4000	Medium	Stolons 2-5	High 25	Good	Acidic/alkaline, dry	
8%*	**Meadow Grasses** Annual	*Poa annua*	4000	Medium	Tufted 1-5	Very low 5	Very poor	5-8	
	Rough stalked	*trivialis*	4300	Medium	Stolons 1.5-6	Medium 13	Very poor	Damp, shade 4-8	*Drechslera* (Melting-out)
	Smooth stalked	*pratensis*	2600 Range (2-5000)	Very slow	Rhizomes 2-4 (6)	Medium 13	Very good	Dry 3-8	*Erysiphe* (Mildew)
	Swamp	*palustris*		Slow	Tufted 2-4	Medium 13	Very poor	Damp	
	Wood	*nemoralis*	4350	Very slow	Tufted 1-3	High 25	Very poor	Shade	*Puccinia* sp. (Rusts)

N.B. Cultivars invariably possess individual tolerances less than the species range.
*Signifies an estimated figure.

Briefly the treatments involve weekly, monthly or annual cuts at different heights and times. The two significant heights of special relevance to most gardeners and managers are: a close cut at 10 mm (½ in) the lowest setting for many domestic mowers, and a cut of 15 mm. (¾ in).

After six years of those treatments some most interesting results are emerging which are summarised briefly here.

(a) For intensively managed turf frequent mowing is better than erratic or infrequent treatment. There is nothing new in this finding, but the experiements do show that weekly and more frequent cuts are essential for the finest lawns. Plots at Reading, for example, cut closely, but at monthly intervals, became very uneven and looked bare immediately after the monthly cut.

(b) The higher and longer grass cut gives a better looking turf over a longer period especially in winter and during periods of drought. Very close cutting of turf or 'scalping' as so often seen in excessively well-groomed gardens has been shown in research elsewhere to be damaging to the root system of turf grass. The effect is to produce shallower rooting patterns with less drought resistance. Such close cutting as is practised on golf or bowling greens to be successful has to be compensated for by higher levels of nutrient and irrigation and other treatments.

(c) A longer grass cut needs less frequent cutting. This is a most important and interesting result. A comparison with the close mown (10 mm-½ in) monthly and the 15 mm (¾ in) monthly cuts, for instance, shows the latter to be a reasonable uniform and acceptable turf, and the indications are that one might be able to reduce mowing of average lawns to a monthly cut at 25 mm (1 in). If this became accepted on a nationwide basis the savings in fuel, and man hours would be quite dramatic! See the figures in table 3.6.

(d) Mowings left on the grass produce a better turf than plots where mowings are regularly removed. This can be explained by the recycling of nutrients and the invigorating effect on the grass. The recommendation therefore for all but intensively managed sports turf such as golf or bowling greens, is to remove mowings only during periods of excessive growth such as spring and possibly late summer, depending on the nature of the swards and provided the mowing is done regularly to cut at the 15 mm (¾ in) height.

Mowing frequencies and species composition. Mowing frequencies are also influenced by the species composition of swards, and research now in progress at the Sports Turf Research Institute shows the relationships between species and strains of grasses and mowing.

The so called low maintenance mixtures should include predominately bent grasses (*Agrostis*), smooth-stalked meadow grass (*Poa pratensis*) and dwarf creeping red fescue (*Festuca rubra*), to reduce the mowing frequencies in particular. *Zones of mowing heights.* Considerable savings may be achieved and some interesting contrasts in grass textures and overall effects realised, if different mowing heights or regimes are adopted especially in larger gardens and parks. There is no doubt, however, that for large grass areas the very fast and manoeuvrable triple-type mowers do enable quick close cuts to be made at comparatively low man hour levels, whereas longer grass may present more of a problem if suitable machinery is not available to deal with it efficiently. This was discussed in Chapter 2. Another look at table 2.9 showing the comparative rates for mowing with different types of machinery, and the approximate fuel consumption, which is now a factor to take into account, will also be useful at this stage.

The following zones of cutting heights are suggested depending on the size, style and design of the garden or park and the particular tastes of the owner or manager:

(a) *Close mown turf* 10-15 mm (½-¾ in). As described in the Reading experiments, the normal regime for most mown turf with closer cuts for the more intensively used areas. Regular cuts with cylinder and rotary mowers with clippings removed at the stages suggested, should be the procedure here.

(b) *'Paddock' length grass* 35-100 mm (1¼-4 in). This zone corresponds approximately to the 'rough' areas of golf courses or for non-golfers, to heights normally used for road verges, country car parks and orchards under grass and grazed paddocks. Rotary or flail mowers are best for this height of cut, preferably at the lower heights since there are still few machines to top grass at 100 mm.

The differentiation of close mown to rougher grass may help with reducing maintenance costs.

Swards of arboreta, woodland and wild gardens may also come into this regime. Banks and slopes when the gradient does not exceed 1:3 can be cut by rotary machines to this height. Unless treated with a selective herbicide, the flora of these longer swards can become quite varied under certain soil and consistent management regimes.

(c) Long grass/hay meadows. The key to successful meadow-like areas of grass is primarily one of soil nutrition and the species composition. High nutrient-status soils will encourage the vigorous, coarser grasses with little diversity or attractive mixture of meadow flowers, and such areas of long grass can look rather dull, and be quite a problem to cut. The lower the nutrient status of the soil, and usually the higher the pH, the more varied and interesting the flora becomes, and the less competitive and vigorous the grass species also.

However, there may be a number of other objectives of long grass areas other than the meadow grass culture and whatever they are, the method of mowing is important and still very much a critical factor when any question of saving mowing time and money are concerned. The following methods may be used:

(i) Hand scything. Using the short bladed Turk scythe intended for hay grass gives a very effective cut with practice, and the exercise is excellent for the waist-line depending on how much there is to be mown, and how much time is available. A method very useful for small inaccessible places.

(ii) Brush cutters. Mechanical hand scythes are efficient (see Chapter 2) and much faster. No hay-length grass is produced since the effect is like a miniature flail.

(iii) Reciprocating cutter-bar machines. These have already been referred to in Chapter 2 and they are certainly the best machines for achieving a hay-type cut. Unless large areas are to be mown, the most sensible procedure is to hire one of these cutters for the few days it will usually be needed. Mowings do have to be removed at some stage after cutting as fresh green material or as hay for the ponies or the pet rabbits!

(iv) Forage harvesters. For large accessible areas of reasonably level terrain, the agricultural forage harvester often used for silage making is a fast, effective way of dealing with long grass as can be seen by the man hour rates in table 2.9. A number of the larger gardens and parks now deal with formerly close mown turf by allowing them to grow long and then making arrangements with the local farmer to use them for grass or hay. This can be very economical.

(v) Flail mowing. This is already included in Chapter 2 and is of limited application in all but the largest gardens. The forage harvester above often uses flail mowers as the cutting principle.

(vi) Grazing animals. An alternative to mechanical mowing is to use the time-honoured practice of letting appropriate herbivorous animals do the mowing. Cattle and horses usually need extensive areas of pasture or grazing and are more suitable for large parks and associated farming land. Fencing needs to be very effective and all trees of whatever age normally need some sort of protection. Many mature park trees have been damaged by horses, in particular, gnawing the bark at certain times of the year.

Deer are useful in large parkland areas, they are excellent and thrifty grazers, and traditionally have been used for centuries for historic parks like Petworth and Powderham Castle. Visitors like to see them and there may be additional income from the venison. However, fencing has to be at least 2.5 m (8 ft) high unless the animals are docile. Mature trees do not usually need fencing.

Sheep are the most placid and the most even grazers, and are compatible with smaller areas. Normal 1.5 m (5 ft) fencing is adequate for most sheep and ha-ha's can be used for these and other grazing animals. Some of the more ornamental breeds like the Jacob or Soay, can add a touch of rural charm to the park and visitors like to see these. Mature trees are seldom damaged.

Goats/Donkeys are rough and uneven grazers, best for wild scrub areas, but not really even or consistent in their eating habits.

Geese are excellent grass mowers for quite small areas, in the right places. They will not damage trees or shrubs and provided the perimeter fences are sound, geese will live thriftily, but noisily from quite poor grass. Well worth considering, and the eggs and meat are an extra bonus even though their droppings can be a nuisance.

Other turf maintenance operations.

Drainage and aeration. Drainage is, of course, a subject in itself and it is especially important with intensively used turf grown for winter sports like rugby, soccer and hockey. It is a specialised subject and rather beyond the scope of this book.

In gardens and parks, drainage and aeration of turf areas tend to fall into two categories - sub-surface and surface aeration - and indeed except where large numbers of visitors are involved, and turf intensively used, and where time and money exist for remedial treatments, these operations have a fairly low priority for most lawns and grass areas.

(a) *Sub-surface aeration* really means getting the water away from the upper 250-450 mm (10-18 in) in areas where there are perpetual wet spots. This may be due to springs or seepage from a local spring or naturally high water table. One immediate remedy is to consider the area for alternative vegetation cover, instead of grass by converting it to a willow/alder group for example, or use moisture-loving perennials as a feature. A few birch, alder and willow incidentally can take up sufficient water in the growing season to locally dry out such wet spots quite effectively. If the areas lie in an important visitor access route, then drainage is important and one has to consider sub-surface pipe systems or local piping to a nearby drain.

(b) *Surface aeration* is much more feasible and at times necessary to maintain the health and vigour of turf. Continual use of mowers and equipment and the passage of many feet can compact the turf and upper soil layers reducing the penetration of water, nutrients and air, and causing a 'dead' thatch of fibre to accumulate around the grass roots. Remedial techniques involve the creation of slots, slits or narrow plugs in the upper 5-10 cm (2-4 in) of the profile using a range of different equipment or machinery, and/or also scarifying or raking out the dead roots and thatch to provide healthy grass growth. Hollow-tined forks or hand forks can be used for small areas, but for larger areas of turf particularly where the soils are inclined to be heavy and large numbers of visitors can cause frequent compaction, it is worth investing in one of the power propelled slotters or slitters as produced by such firms as Sisis and Hayter. Alternatively one can hire such machines or use a contractor to carry out the operation. The Sisis auto-rake is an excellent scarifying machine for removing 'thatch', moss and the like from neglected turf. The frequency of the operation, and indeed whether it is really a problem at all, depends on the nature, and function of the turf, and also the attitude of the owner to his or her lawn, and the degree of priority attached to such attentions. In practical terms, it is often as much as many large garden owners can do to keep the grass mown regularly without any other treatments.

Top dressing fertilisers and irrigation. The long-term trials of mowing already described, show that by continually returning the mowings to regularly cut turf the nutrient levels will not fall substantially and hence the need for continual replenishment of nutrients is less important. One would therefore only expect to feed lawns and turf for normal use under the following conditions:

(a) To compensate for excessive wear and tear, or where prestige areas are continually mown and the mowings removed (boxed off).
(b) To enable turf to recover from excessive drought or adverse weather conditions.
(c) Turf on very thin, hungry soils may need occasional nutrient applications.

Top dressings are very useful and beneficial to turf that has been treated for aeration and scarification by applying 0.9 kg/m² (2 lb/sq. yd) of a sand, peat, loam mix (free of stones, of course,) in the autumn or winter. A fertiliser can be incorporated in this dressing to promote root and tiller (side growth) activity of the grasses. Fertilisers that apply the main elements nitrogen (N), Phosphorus (P) and Potassium (K) to turf should only be used as suggested and not as a matter of routine, unless one likes to see a deep-green vigorous lawn that may need very frequent mowing. This is the essential difference between sports and intensively managed turf and the lawns of large gardens and parks. Fertilisers are expensive, so is labour and fuel for mowing, and to undertake a programme of feeding and mowing for grass that has only the lightest use is really an expensive luxury. For bowling greens and golf greens that is quite a different matter.

Irrigation has already been referred to in Chapter 2. Few people with large gardens these days can afford the time and the water to irrigate grass unless it is used for a specific purpose. It is preferable to reconsider mowing heights, the grass mixtures in the turf and other aspects that can influence the drought-resistance qualities of turf. The 'gadget people' of course, offer all manner of watering aids for the great British lawn, but irrigation of lawns in the British climate is not normally necessary.

Rolling is unnecessary. Sports turf requirements are different, being compact, level playing surfaces, but otherwise most lawns get quite enough compaction without rolling. Also, many of the newer grass strains tend to be more compact and prostrate growing with less need for flattening by the roller, than the earlier, coarser strains. Cylinder mowers in any case incorporate a light roller behind the cutters, but where swards are continually cut with a rotary mower, there may be a case for the occasional light rolling in early spring.

Weed control. Intensively managed turf for precision ball games like golf and bowling must consist of mono-cultures of tightly mown grass species to ensure accurate play. Regular herbicide treatment is essential here but for the 2700 km² (1053 sq. miles) of other managed turf in Britain how much of this needs treating and for what reasons?

For most pleasure lawns the main reason is the visual one of smooth green expanses undotted by daisies or plantains or the dark mats of clover in the dry periods, but is this really a convention we have grown to accept or demand, and could we not accept mown turf made more interesting with a confetti of small flowers among the grass. The costs of chemicals, and the labour and equipment to apply them are rising all the time.

Pests and diseases of lawns. It is the sports' turf people who are more likely to encounter the various diseases that can effect turf grasses and there are various remedies for these. There is one disease of turf, however, that appears periodically in many gardens and areas of extensive turf. This is 'Red thread disease' caused by the fungus *Corticium fuciforme* and the symptoms are brownish bleached patches of turf like persistent dead grass clippings. On close examination one finds tiny pink branched threads of the fungus on the dead or dying grass blades giving this pinkish brown effect. Red thread disease is usually not serious and is seasonal in its appearance, being most likely in prolonged, damp, mild, humid weather, and particularly in the south of England, and in the summer or early autumn period.

Fungicides can be used, but only if essential. The disease usually disappears after a few weeks with a change of weather.

Earthworms should be encouraged in garden lawns, as natural drainage agents, whereas they may have to be eradicated for the sports' turf entusiasts.

Moles are a spasmodic problem, due to season, locality, the presence of earthworms (their main diet) and perhaps other factors. Trapping is probably the most successful method of control, otherwise one has to resort to such discouragements as smoke cartridges, gorse spines in the main run, and other devices, to persuade the little diggers to move to fresh pastures. Incidentally the soil of the mole hills makes splendid loam for potting composts.

4
Design and Maintenance

In Chapter 1 the importance of design in relation to maintenance has been discussed, and this relationship becomes particularly important when considering the rationalisation or simplification of an existing design with reduced maintenance as the main objective. For many with large gardens whose styles have basically remained unchanged for half a century or more, there may be a natural reluctance to change the established order, particularly where a family and the gardener have had a long association of traditional and successful management of a garden together.

This chapter examines various methods of bringing about changes in design without excessively altering the general character of the garden.

Design rationalisation

Two stages are suggested in the process of design rationalisation:

(a) The simplification of the existing designs.
(b) The introduction of 'new' features with reduced maintenance input.

Simplification of the existing design

An obvious first step is to carry out the exercise discussed in Chapter 2 of analysing the existing maintenance systems of the garden, to see if savings or economies can be made without the need to change the design. This is an important preliminary and is preferable to impulsive alterations in the character or design of the garden that may be regretted later. Design rationalisation is a very important stage, and one that needs undertaking with an objective, analytical approach, casting aside, if possible, nostalgic associations and tendencies to timid tamperings with a problem that may need a bold approach to succeed.

A closer look at the overall design is necessary, but particularly those features or areas that are the most labour intensive and where savings in man hours could be made. Some examples are plant borders, rose gardens, grass areas, paths and hedges.

Plant borders. Depending, naturally on their shapes, sizes and the actual planting design these are the first areas to look at, since in many gardens they are the most labour-intensive features to maintain. Table 4.1 shows that over 40% of the man hours are spent on maintaining planted areas.

The possibilities of eliminating or simplifying unnecessary or small flower beds, or those of awkward shapes should be examined. Small triangular or rectangular beds in lawns are always difficult to negotiate with a mower, and there are also the edges to be cut.

Where possible and appropriate, such borders should be redesigned or

Table 4.1 Wye College Gardens Department labour analysis, 1st January to 30th July, 1978 man hours gardens work

Operation	Withersdane gardens	College surrounds	Total	%
Weeding, etc.	1139	148	1287	47.3
Spraying	18	—	18	0.6
Mowing	362	207	569	20.8
Planting	177	19	196	7.2
Pruning	68	4	72	2.7
Hedging	31	72	103	3.8
Fertilising	4	—	4	—
'Tidying up'	249	117	366	13.4

reshaped to suit the mowing, with a reduction of those awkward angles that need more time and care to cut (see fig. 4.1).

(a)   (b)

Fig 4.1. Mowing and edging will be simpler and faster in (b) than (a)

Where marginal rectangular beds are placed like a fragmented picture frame to an expanse of lawn, with often a hedge or wall behind, a simpler, stronger and more easily maintained design may be effected by joining up all these smaller beds and creating a bolder, more effective and unified design (see fig. 4.2).

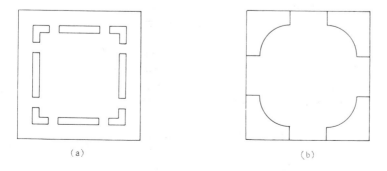

(a)   (b)

Fig. 4.2 Simplifying the same area by changing the angles to curves can reduce maintenance and often strengthen the design itself

In an intricate Edwardian-style rose garden or formal garden, for example, a proportion of the beds could be eliminated, and yet still have the same sense of the design, if carefully done. However, grassing down borders in such a symmetrical design needs doing with some care and thought for the design, which can easily be thrown out of balance by impulsive or haphazard rationalisation.

Mowing strips (see fig. 4.4), already referred to in Chapter 2 should be used where appropriate and if time and expense allow. The initial cost may be well worth the savings in maintenance later.

Rose gardens. In a fascinating article in the *Rose Annual* for 1980 Graham Stuart Thomas traces the origins of the rose garden in the mid-nineteenth century when the wealthy trend-setters intent upon re-establishing flower gardens returned to the geometric beds of the early-eighteenth century easily accessible by mown grass now that the mechanical lawn mower had been invented. However, the roses of this period were still of a short period of flowering, and rather flimsy growth, and for many months of the year were rather uninteresting, so they tended to be enclosed by protective evergeens like laurels, holly and laurustinus. Such rose gardens were for summer visiting only. The roses also needed rich cultivation. Also to quote Thomas:

'Some rose gardens (of this period) of those primarily interested in the show were at times boringly repetitive. To them the design of rose gardens was unimportant.'

However, tradition dies hard, and Gertrude Jekyll in her challenging *Roses for English Gardens* 1902 said:

'We are growing impatient of the usual rose gardens, generally a sort of target of concentric rings of beds placed upon turf, often with no special aim and connected design ... and filled with plants without a thought of their colour effect or any other worthy attention.'

The concept of the rose as a flowering shrub did not really emerge until the 1930s and even not until the 1950s for many people, with the revival of interest in the botanical roses and the older hybrids of the Elizabethan days. Today roses are increasingly used as shrubs in mixed plantings or for hedges, backgrounds, wild gardens and walls and coverings, having mercifully escaped from the confines of the labour-intensive and frequently dull rose garden.

In the rationalisation exercise of rose gardens therefore I would offer the following alternatives of design and plant selection.

Design. Simplification as far as possible of elaborate beds, and overall design and consideration of substitution of grass paths with paving or gravel.

Plant selection. Selection of roses that are as maintenance free as possible and that need little or no regular spraying against the usual problems, and use of ground cover, mulches and herbicides, to reduce the weed problems. A dense low ground cover of such plants as sedum, viola or *Stachys* can be used with some roses, to reduce the bare skeleton look in the winter, and edge species like pinks or chives are also an added attraction (plate 4.1).

There is also a widespread belief that chives planted near or among roses drive away pests, especially aphids or greenfly.

Alternatives. The rose garden could be dispensed with altogether and the roses used in their own right as shrubs in mixed borders or for enclosure and screenings, perhaps in place of a formal hedge.

Plate 4.1 Formal beds of standard roses look less stark and 'urbanesque' when generously underplanted with the silvery *Stachys lanata*. The winter effect is also far better

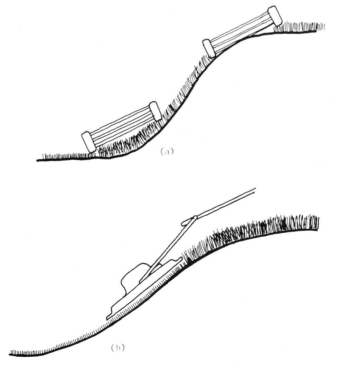

Fig. 4.3 Grass banks should be designed and shaped with more gentle curves and slopes to allow the use of a hover type 'Flymo' mower where gradients at the top or bottom of banks are too steep (b). Cylinder mowers are much less effective and can scalp or miss the grass (a)

Grass areas. Redesigning the shapes of borders and flower beds in mown grass has already been demonstrated in figs. 4.1 and 4.2 and further attention to other detailing in grass areas may also achieve saving in time and frustration. Figures 4.3 and 4.4 show some typical examples of this.

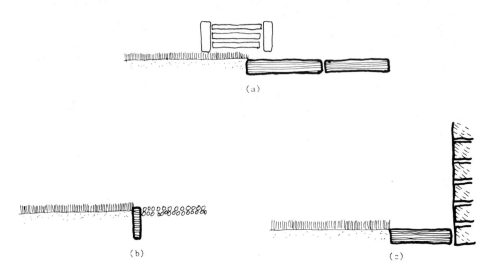

Fig. 4.4 Different design of mowing strips for grass/hard surface interfaces:
(a) Mowing strips against slabs. Successful if the grass level is 12-18 mm (½-¾ in) above the slabs
(b) Timber or concrete edging strips. Again the grass must be 12-18 mm (½-¾ in) higher than the strip
(c) Mowing strip against walls and buildings, statues, etc. The grass level is critical for maintenance

Paths. The use of mowing strips shown in fig. 4.4 makes a trim and effective finish to grass/path edges. Where large numbers of visitors are involved, paths should be wide enough or so designed and constructed to carry the traffic, and be safe and simple to maintain, and also in keeping with the design. Main access paths directly across gradients usually in conjunction with steps can lead to erosion and bypassing by the public (plate 4.2).

Hedges and backgrounds. Hedges, as already pointed out in Chapter 3, can be labour-intensive features, especially where the species are of the sort that need incessant clipping such as privet (*Ligustrum*) and *Lonicera*. The production of so much 'biomass' as the plant ecologists would say, or flushes of vegetative growth that are constantly being removed, invariably means that such vigorous hedges are nutrient and water-demanding and are less suitable as background features for planting, due to their competition and the need for access for clipping several times during the growing season.

An alternative, where the design is appropriate, is for background enclosure of massed, naturally green shrubs, which usually need little or no attention for years.

Heights of hedges can also be a critical factor in relation to maintenance (see table 3.5).

Plate 4.2 The design and construction of these steps across a fairly steep gradient needs re-assessing. Erosion, and excessive wear are a problem and maintenance is also difficult. Widths are critical where large numbers of visitors are involved

Introduction of new features

The wild garden. William Robinson defines the wild garden as:

'The naturalisation and natural grouping of hardy exotic plants including a garden of British wild flowers'.

In the foreword of the 1977 edition of Robinson's *The Wild Garden* there is an editorial comment by Robin Lane Fox:

'The arrival of Mr Budding's original lawn mower in the the scythed gardens of the mid-nineteenth century (Chapter 2) had done much to drive out the meadow style of wild gardens that Robinson wanted to revive. The shaven lawns that became the norm and the socially essential features of most gardens by the end of this century prompted Robinson to write in his book: 'Surely it is enough to have a portion of the lawn as smooth as a carpet at all times without shaving off the long and pleasant grass of the other points of the grounds. It would indeed be worthwhile to leave many points of the grass unmown for the sake of growing many beautiful plants. Mowing the grass once a fortnight as now practised is a costly mistake. We want shaven carpets of grass here and there, but what a nuisance it is to shave it as often as foolish men shave their faces. Who would not rather see the waving grass with countless flowers than a close surface without a blossom".'

The maintenance implications are also referred to in this prophetic and challenging attack on the mown lawn. (See also Chapter 3).

The floristic meadow or a meadow garden. The whole business of costs and labour involved in mowing turf is studied in Chapter 3, and now the ideas and challenges of William Robinson made a century ago are being eagerly sought by many garden owners and landscape managers as a possible alternative to at least some of the intensively managed turf under their care.

However, the 'countless flowers' referred to by Robinson and the romantic ideas of flowering meadows and the array of wild and perhaps suitable exotic flowers, is by no means as speedy to achieve as may be thought.

Soil nutrient status. One of the controlling characteristics of traditional flowering meadows including the alpine meadows of much upland and mountain country, is the comparatively low nutrient status of the soil. The usually thin soils of many of these meadows are further impoverished with continual removal of hay crops, but it is this characteristic that largely determines the diversity of species found. Where pastures are improved with the addition of fertilisers, the stronger growing grasses are encouraged to grow at the expense of many other herbaceous species and the swards become much more uniform in appearance with a decrease in the range of floristic species.

High N,P,K, levels favour the growth of the more vigorous coarser grasses such as rye (*Lolium perenne*), Yorkshire fog (*Holcus lanatus*) and cocksfoot (*Dactylis glomerata*), to the exclusion of the other grasses and herbs. The vigorous grasses and the presence of vigorous 'weed' species like nettles and docks are indicators of nutrient-rich soils. Reduction of the mineral levels can be a slow business and may be achieved by one or more of the following methods:

(a) (a) Existing coarse, vigorous turf. A regime of repeated close mowing with removal of all trimmings, and spot herbicide treatment of weed species for probably two to three years by which time significant reductions of vigorous species should have resulted. Begin the hay meadow treatment and add seed/plants of meadow grasses and herbs.

(b) Plough and cultivate the area proposed for the meadow. Fallow for one season to reduce weed populations and grow a nutrient-extractive crop such as potatoes and roots if feasible. Seed with a fescue/bent mixture plus small amounts of white clover and suitable herb species at a rate of 8-17 g/m² (¼-½ oz/sq. yd).

(c) Existing close mown turf. Avoid fertiliser treatments of any kind. Allow the sward to develop to hay length in designed zones appropriate for the site. If nutrients are at a reasonably low level as is often the case in lawns mown closely for many years, the potential for making a floristic meadow is good.

Introduction of species. Species enrichment of grassland areas may be achieved as follows:

(a) By natural colonisation with time and consistent management. This may be a slow process especially if few local seed sources for natural colonisation exist.

(b) By seeding. Introduction of species from seed. Grasses and herbs, if or when available, can be seeded into localised areas of the meadow to establish nuclei or colonies. Consistent hay meadow management should encourage the spread of these initial colonies. Small quantities of seed are usually all that are available and these should be mixed with seed compost and sown in autumn or early spring into shallow scrapes or divots in the existing turf. Legumes like vetches and clovers establish well this way.

(c) By planting. The common herb species like buttercups (*Ranunculus*) and ox-eye daisies (*Chrysanthemum*) can often be moved carefully from waste ground in early spring. Plants can be raised from seed in the garden or nursery and transplanted when large enough into the meadow. Cowslips (*Primula veris*), fritillaries (*Fritillaria meleagris*) and meadow cranesbill (*Geranium pratense*) can be treated in this way. If an old pasture, rich in meadow species is being destroyed by development or ploughing and there is a chance to rescue a few turves, these make an excellent nucleus for the future meadow flora.

Some species recommended for a floristic meadow. As a general rule native British species will be the most successful, but there are also exotic bulbs and herbs from the Continent, North America and elsewhere that may colonise grassland effectively.

Grasses.
Festuca rubra, creeping red fescue   - several strains available
Agrostis tenuis, brown top/brown bent
Agrostis canina, velvet bent (shaded areas)
Cynosurus cristatus, crested dog's-tail
Anthoxanthum odoratum, sweet vernal grass
Alopecurus pratensis, meadow foxtail

Herbs.

Legumes.
Trifolium repens, white clover
Trifolium pratense red clover and various strains
Lotus corniculatus, bird's-foot trefoil
Anthyllis vulneraria, kidney vetch
Lathyrus pratensis, yellow vetchling
Lathyrus nissolia, grass vetchling
Vicia cracca, tufted Vetch

Composites.
Chrysanthemum leucanthemum, ox-eye or moon daisies
Hieraceum spp., hawkweeds
Crepis spp., hawksbeard
Taraxacum officinale, dandelion

Other species.
Ranunculus, buttercup species
Cardamine pratensis, lady's smock
Geranium pratense, meadow Cranesbill
Primula spp., primroses, cowslip, etc.

Bulbs.
Narcissus spp. especially *N. pseudo-narcissus*
Narcissus spp. especially *N. poeticus*
Crocus sp. especially *C. tomasinianus*
Crocus sp. especially *C. chrysanthus*
Colchicum autumnale, autumn crocus
Fritillaria meleagris, fritillary
Tulipa sylvestris, native wild tulip

Camassia sp.
Endymion non-scripta, bluebell

Native orchids. On no account should these be dug up from the wild unless a rescue operation is justified where a habitat is being disturbed by development or ploughing. On the other hand, orchid seed is dust-like and wind blown and may colonise naturally in favourable meadow habitats in the course of time. (plate 4.3).

Plate 4.3 Native orchids and many herb species and fine grasses compose this meadow area that was once a close mown-lawn of a large house in the Kentish weald. Consistent management has induced a 'hungry' turf rich in wild flowers

Mowing. The ideal implements for the hay mowing operation in early to mid-July are either the hand scythe which is very effective with skill and practice, especially for banks and small areas or a forward-mounted cutter bar of an Allen-type Autoscythe. The latter are somewhat heavy but effective machines which can be hired for a few days for the job. Some small tractors also have side-mounted cutter bars. All hay mowings must be removed. The 'aftermath' cuts can be done with rotary mowers.

Woodland, copse and shrub gardens. Some of the maintenance aspects of these potentially attractive and rewarding habitats have already been considered and the case studies include one or two gardens that use this approach to gardening.

The wild garden approach is to use appropriate species of trees, or shrubs as groups or associations, usually with a ground base of the floristic meadow and naturalised bulbs, and such wild gardens may be made from new, or by converting an existing more formal or intensively managed design. Trees, and more especially shrubs, should be selected for their good visual appearance as specimens or as groups, and also for their ability to thrive with little or no maintenance in a grassland or ground-cover matrix. Native shrubs like *Viburnum* and *Cornus* can be blended with introduced species for woodland glade habitats or a more open scrub-like habitat. Grass paths can be mown through the longer grass zones in which the shrubs and trees will be growing depending on the habitat, the soil and the character of the garden. Such wild gardens once established are remarkably easy to maintain, provided one accepts the 'wild' character, and tolerates some 'weeds' as part of the scheme.

Wild water gardens or wetlands. There may be some parts of the garden or grounds that are naturally low lying, or poorly drained, and also areas of permanent open water as well as ponds and streams. Such damp areas or low-lying places are all too often dredged or 'tidied up' and here again is the opportunity of creating some dramatic wild effects by planting a range of moisture-loving plants in a natural or semi-wild association. There are some magnificent and spectacular herbaceous foliage plants like the *Ligularias*, ornamental rhubarbs (*Rheum*), *Rodgersias*, and all manner of ferns, as well as the more woody bamboos and willows.

Water areas as ponds or lakes are also themselves comparatively easy to maintain for long periods of time, and should also be considered as part of the design rationalisation exercise.

In conclusion, therefore, there are many other opportunities for the wild garden concept as an alternative or as a different style and for the most part the maintenance and upkeep is less in man hours, but nevertheless, does need an understanding of what one is trying to do. Where staff are employed therefore, they must be in sympathy with the idea or else misunderstandings and failures are bound to follow.

Gravel and dry gardens. Originating, perhaps from the materials used in Japanese gardens, and with contemporary influences from North America and Northern Europe, low maintenance compositions using blends of stone, gravel, paving and plants are appearing in more gardens and amenity areas. There is an interesting example being developed in the Savill Gardens at Windsor. Limestone chippings over good drainage encourage the growth of shrubs and mat-forming plants of which there is infinite variety.

Gravel gardens may be made in one of several ways:

(a) In weed-free well-drained and reasonably level sites, by consolidating with a light roller after levelling to suit the design and site, and then planting specimen trees or conifers, and placing any stones or rocks before applying a 50-75 mm (2-3 in) layer of chippings. Further planting of shrubs, or other plants can be done directly into the gravel.

(b) By converting an area of turf. The turf is killed off with a contact herbicide such as paraquat or 'Roundup', and after an interval of three to four weeks, key planting of trees and shrubs or other plants can take place in pits or cultivated areas in the killed sward. After any minor levelling, the area is covered with a layer of chippings or cobbles (see plate 2.3).

The subsequent maintenance of these gravel areas is with a residual herbicide carefully applied in the establishment period and depending on the species used, as an overall application each year. Some hand weeding may also be necessary. The gravel can be raked at intervals depending on the design and the time available.

Grass areas converted to gravel gardens can show a dramatic saving in man hours or maintenance.

There must be many more design aspects that could well have been tried, in this chapter, but these are left to the ingenuity of garden owners and their gardeners to explore.

Growth retardants

There are now a number of chemical growth-retarding sprays available for reducing the rates of growth of grasses, hedges and woody plants. Maleic hydrazide has been in use for some years for reducing the growth of vigorous grasses, particularly in inaccessible areas, on steep banks and around obstacles.

The timing and the rates of application are critical, but savings in man hours may be achieved for large areas. The use of these materials for curtailing the growth of hedges, etc., has not yet been shown to be a saving in man hours over mechanical methods of cutting. There may be a future for these, however.

5
The Restoration of Neglected or Abandoned Gardens

To quote Graham Stuart Thomas:

'Gardens are living entities constantly developing and decaying. The masonry trees and grass - whether formal or informal - last a long time. The richer embellishment of shrubs and plants has a shorter life. At no time in any of these planting schemes is the garden perfect, at no time can it be said that the art (coupled with the craft) which has brought all the ingredients together is in complete control. Nature governed by man's best abilities is in control.'

In other words, the time scale is of vital importance in any garden design, the only real art form that changes steadily, sometimes more rapidly with the years or perhaps the centuries. The whole complex assemblage, (of plants expecially) develops, matures and eventually decays at widely differing intervals of time, and one important aspect of maintenance and management is to hold as many of the planted elements in a healthy state for as long as possible, until restoration and renewal eventually become inevitable considerations.

Some principles of garden restoration

When a large garden or park is acquired by a new owner, or new management, there are two important preliminaries that should be undertaken before any actual physical work of restoration is started on the ground. These are both concerned with finding out as much as possible about the property and site and can be done in two stages: (a) research; (b) site survey.

Research
If the garden or park is of significant size and importance and perhaps asociated with a 'period' house and buildings then it is quite conceivable that it may be of some historic importance, and the gardens may also have some arboricultural or horticultural importance. This is where research is so important at the very outset, in order to find out as much as possible. Of course, the previous owners may have information, and in any case, the deeds and perhaps records will be passed on as a basis for this information gathering. There are a number of sources of information that can be consulted. For instance, if the garden seems to have historical importance, there may be regional (or in some British counties) county specialists usually in the County Council Planning Departments or the local District Council Planning Department who can advise, or better still, the Garden History Society has an increasing number of members across the country who will be pleased to advise or help, if consulted. Local libraries, and local historical societies should also be approached and there may be elderly individuals perhaps the retired gardeners or estate workers, still living nearby.

As regards the definition of an 'Historic Garden' (and this assessment may be a very useful one as a basis for a restoration programme), one can turn to the Garden

History society again for their definition, which is incidentally being used as a basis for a National Survey of historic gardens now gradually getting under way.

Historic garden definitions. Gardens, parks, designed landscapes, designed grounds and places of recreation are of historic interest:

(a) When they illustrate some aspects of the history of such places or of the history of gardening or horticulture. In this respect they may provide examples of the work of a particular designer, or have features of a particular period or of a particular style.
(b) When they have significant historic associations with perhaps a particular person or event.
(c) When they have a group value of buildings, and the group value is of historic interest or when they provide the setting for a building of historic interest.

The relative importance of a site is then assessed by reference to:

The general historical aspects revealed
The history of the particular site
The condition of the site and its remaining features
A comparison with other similar sites
The significance of the association
Other relevant factors.

So far this Research stage may seem to be very academic and perhaps unnecessary especially to an impatient owner or management group who are anxious to get on with the restoration work without delay. A timely reminder therefore to such people, should any read a book of this kind, and also as a matter of general interest, that there are values and possible benefits from any research exercise of the kind just described. Here are some of them:

If a designed garden of minor or major importance still survives in a neglected or abandoned state, the design was probably in keeping with the house, and therefore to restore as far as possible to the original design revealed by research, may be more satisfactory and more aesthetically pleasing than to establish a completely new style.

Grants may be available to help with a major and expensive piece of restoration, if the garden can be shown to be of historic and 'heritage' importance (see Chapter 7).

The garden buildings and other constructed features such as walls and terraces may already be 'listed' by the Historic Buildings Record Office in the same way that important buildings are listed in different categories. If research shows such listed artifacts it means that they do have legal protection, and demolition or drastic alterations cannot be undertaken without official approval or planning consent.

If the owners are considering any kind of commercial venture, visitors are more likely to be attracted to an authentically restored garden or part of a garden and if researches show a genuine connection with an important person or event such as the Churchill association with Chartwell in Kent.

Site surveys

However badly neglected or abandoned the garden or park may be, depending on the style, character, and condition of the 'patient', a reasonably thorough physical survey of the site is well worthwhile and should aim to cover the following:

Trees and significant woody vegetation. Trees are especially important and for extensive sites with many fine specimens or groups, probably in a neglected or dangerous condition, the aid of a reliable specialist should be considered not only to help in identifying the species of trees, but also in advising on their probable age, health and safety. Chapter 2 deals with Tree Management and the work of arboriculturalists who may be able to advise.

For those who wish to carry out their own tree surveys and have the time and adequate knowledge to do this, the *Tree Council's Tree Survey Guide* is recommended as a practical and helpful booklet which is very easy to follow. What will be more difficult is to assess the health and safety of the trees and if there are large trees about which one has any doubt, the local forester or tree officer of the local or county council may be able to help. In this respect, remember to check with the planning authority whether any of the trees are covered by a Tree Preservation Order and also ascertain one's legal responsibilities (summarised in Chapter 2) of trees overhanging roads or public thoroughfares or in gardens or parks open to the public.

Other woody vegetation, including scrub, but especially old hedges and shrubberies may be very neglected but may represent the remnants of a formal design, or may have some botanical interest. Therefore do not be in too much haste to renew all such features, having revealed them in the survey until it becomes obvious that they are no longer needed.

Lawns. Badly neglected lawns, even if uncut for years and resembling hay fields can be restored surprisingly well under certain conditions, and especially if the site is level and not too badly affected by ant hills or moles. The survey should note the condition of this 'lawn' and the potential for restoration.

Stonework, steps, terraces, walls, brickwork and garden buildings should, of course, be included in the survey. The help of a specialist architect is usually needed to advise on the condition of the stonework, buildings, etc. Hasty demolition may again be regretted, and, of course, some of these features may, in any case be officially 'listed'. There may also be a range of old glasshouses, potting sheds and other horticultural features to be noted.

Soil survey. It is quite important to carry out a soil survey if a wide range of plants is to be grown or the fertility is in question. Simple soil testing kits are available for pH and perhaps the main elements, but for a thorough analysis one will have to approach a testing laboratory, run, for example, by the local Agricultural Advisory Service, who regularly do soil testing for growers and farmers. Drainage and wet areas of the site should also be noted. The causes may be natural (i.e. springs or streams), or one may have to look for a blocked field drainage system.

Design objectives

This principle may not apply when a neglected garden still reveals most of the original design features which it is the intention to restore and maintain within the capacities of staff available and financial resources. It is more difficult when the garden has become virtually featureless through dereliction and perhaps pillaging by previous insensitive owners. In this case there are several options worth considering:

(a) To carry out the research and survey already discussed to see if anything from the past emerges that can be used as a basis for a layout. If enough can be found, then the original as far as possible or feasible can be re-instated.

(b) To establish a new style within what remains of any skeleton of the older or original layout and aiming for something in scale and sympathy with the house (see chapter 6). In the case of this option it is important to try and retain any features that may be worthy of inclusion in the new design. In the case of overmature trees, however, one may have to be rather ruthless, since if there is any risk of subsequent collapse or decay soon after the new scheme is established the upheaval or damage that could be involved can be very expensive and disrupting. All major tree work is expensive if contractors are called in. it is therefore far better to plant new trees, of appropriate or similar species to those removed. One should look many years ahead with an exercise of this kind.

(c) Possibly similar to the above to evolve a design which broadly reflects the image of a possible known original. This would be a fascinating exercise calling for some imagination and sensitivity.

(d) The case may also arise where a new house is 'inserted' into an old mature landscape or garden, and the house may be of a contemporary design that really has little to relate it to its setting. This, of course, can become a subjective matter and one can meet persuasive architects who are convinced that even the most *avant garde* design will look appropriate in any 'green' setting. Nevertheless some attempt should be made to relate new with old at the design stage.

Restoration procedures

This section summarises the broad guidelines to follow in the restoration process of the garden elements and vegation features only. The constructed elements must be left to other experts to deal with. As the emphasis throughout is on subsequent maintenance, there is this underlying motif in the guidelines that follow.

Protection of agreed features to be retained

This should follow the survey stage, and where contractors are involved, as is the most likely case, it is essential to indicate clearly on the plan and on site all these features such as trees, shrubs, old ponds or constructed elements that are to be left intact. Protective fencing barriers or temporary enclosures may be necessary on a large site, but one has to remember that contractors do need room to manoeuvre and work, so the protection will have to be realistic. Old lawns or areas of shrubbery may have to be sacrificed if access is essential by machinery for restoration activities. The place is inevitably going to look a dreadful mess while restoration work is in progress.

Clearance of excessive and unwanted vegetation
For those doing their own restoration work, neglected gardens are bound to be jungles in places where seedling trees, scrub and vigorous herbs like nettles have taken over. Total clearance of all scrub may not be necessary or desirable in woodland areas or the more natural garden where the occasional clump or specimen of hazel, elder, or similar shrub may help to give some character and shelter while the new planting is establishing.

Treatment of overgrown hedges and topiary
This has already been outlined in Chapter 3 but a reminder here that the species or kind of hedge is very critical if any drastic cutting back or rejuvenation is necessary.
   The following can normally be cut back very hard to make a new hedge:

Yew	*Taxus baccata*
Holly	*Ilex aquifolium*
Laurel	*Prunus laurocerasus*
Privet	*Ligustrum ovalifolium*
Box	*Buxux sempervirens* (not too drastic)

The following cannot be:

Lawsons cypress	*Chamaecyparis lawsoniana*
Leyland cypress	*Cupressocyparis leylandii*
Wester red cedar	*Thuya plicata*
Pines of any species	

   After cutting back the appropriate species follow with a slow-acting fertiliser and mulch dressing.

Treatment of overgrown shrubberies and shrubs including roses and climbers
There may be some valuable and unusual shrubs growing in the jungle such as magnolia, camellia, hammamelis and others that would not take kindly to clear felling tactics. These, if identified, may need a little regulation pruning (see Chapter 3) and then may live on to a venerable age. The shorter-lived shrubs like weigela, buddleia, broom (*Cytisus*) if very old and misshapen, should be cut down and grubbed out. This may also apply to old hybrid roses. Many of the longer-lived evergreen shrubs and some climbers, and the species roses or the older shrub types can be rejuvenated by hard pruning and mulching. As a general point of advice, it is often a good thing to delay cutting back anything until one growing season has passed, to enable one to identify the varieties or species in flower. This is especially so with roses, and also lilacs and rhododendrons.
   Finally, do not forget that overgrown shrubberies may be doing an excellent job of screening and sheltering the garden, so some thoughts on the effect of cutting back or removal are worthwhile before going into action.

Rock gardens and rockeries
As already referred to in Chapter 3 the era of rock garden building on an ambitious scale in the period 1900-39 has left a legacy of such features in some of the larger gardens which may have been neglected for many years. What can one do with these

today with limited labour resources and the sheer problem of dealing with perhaps, years of abandonment?

Restoration. This can be a problem indeed, especially if the period of neglect has been long enough to allow scrub and seedling trees to invade. In most cases all the real alpines and rock plants will have gone long ago as the buttercups, ground elder, grasses and bindweed moved in but there may be some surviving shrubs or conifers, perhaps outgrown dwarf types, worthy of retention. Chemical herbicides can be a real means of reclaiming a rock garden. Protect or mark any plants to be kept, and then cut back all scrub and weed growth in the autumn or winter with hand tools or a brush cutter. Spray the whole rock garden with a translocated herbicide, like 'Roundup' in the spring when weed and scrub growth is beginning, and repeat again later if necessary. This will create a temporary bareness, but at least the rocks will be revealed and most of the persistent weeds will be killed. If not, repeat again, leaving fallow for one season at least until all perennial weeds have been killed. This is important if the feature is to be used for alpine and rock plants since partially killed weeds, whose roots are well established among or beneath the rocks will only take over again, if not really dead. The next stage is to fork over all the pockets and areas between stones for planting, removing dead roots and debris, and add a 75 mm (3 in) layer of a gritty compost in which the new plants will grow also between the rocks. After planting, a really good effect is achieved by top dressing with a 25 mm (1 in) layer of gravel or chippings. The alternative to restoration is to dismantle the whole affair and use the stones for some other purpose, perhaps a more manageable rock terrace or for raised beds or dry stone walls.

A rockery/fernery feature. If the site is partially shaded (and this may not have been the case, of course, when the rock feature was originally built) overhanging branches and encroaching dense growth, should be cut back as far as is possible and instead of attempting to grow alpines and rock plants (which generally dislike shade any way) to exploit the habitat for a natural-style planting of ferns and other shade- and rock-loving plant associations. The weed control stage will still have to be done, of course, before planting, and instead of gritty compost before planting use a more leafy peaty mixture. Ferns are becoming very popular again and there are more nurseries now beginning to offer them. A blend of spring bulbs, ferns, welsh poppies (*Meconopsis*), columbines (*Aquilegia*), *Epimediums* and many others will be effective and reasonably low maintenance, provided the weeding was done effectively before planting.

Lawns

Lawns neglected or abandoned for long periods of years, have been referred to briefly in this chapter at the survey stage. No cutting and a period of accumulated organic matter from unmown grass and herbs, tend to make the once level surface uneven, with mole hills and ant hills in lighter soils, coarse tussocky grasses and even scrub and seedling tree growth, as the natural ecological succession from grassland to scrub gradually takes place. it is nevertheless quite surprising how comparatively quickly and successfully an area of turf can be reclaimed for general purposes. Naturally, if it is to be used for special purposes such as tennis or bowling, then a more drastic renovation is needed, but the following summarises a restoration programme for most general-purpose lawns:

Remove scrub and woody growth by grubbing out, and chopping off below ground level. Level off tussocks, ant hills, and fill hollows or pockets. A scraper blade attached to a tractor may be used for large areas. Cut over the whole area with a strong rotary mower set at about 50 mm (2 in) cutting height and if possible rake off debris and mowings. Repeat if necessary, and if a light roller is available, roll once or twice to consolidate the surface.

The area should be looking more like lawn now, but much of course depends on the proportion of grass species present in relation to other herb species (or weeds). If extensive bare patches are revealed, overseeding can be done with a suitable grass mixture in spring or autumn by simply scarifying or raking the surface and seeding at a rate of 34 g/m² (1 oz/sq. yd). If only coarse grasses and weeds are present, or little grass at all, another treatment worth considering is to adopt the farmers' method of direct drilling to convert the undesirable herb layer into something more suitable and potentially less maintenance intensive. This involves killing off the whole surface population of grasses and weed species with a contact/selective herbicide mixture preferably in early spring or late summer. After three or four weeks most of the vegetation will be dead or dying, and this layer should be scarified mechanically over large areas, or with a strong rake for small areas, and then a new grass seed mixture sown at the rate of 34 g/m² (1 oz/sq. yd). If finer, slow-growing grasses predominate in the new mixture, this will mean less frequent mowing of the restored lawn.

The final stages of renovation can be the closer mowing with a cylinder mower (once all stems have been removed) to about 25-35 mm (1-1½ in) or with a rotary mower set to about this height.

This restoration programme is generally preferable to the process of ploughing, cultivating and relevelling for turfing and seeding.

Drives and paths

Long-neglected gravel drives and paths may have become so invaded by grasses and weeds as to be almost indistinguishable from the surrounding grass areas. Indeed in extreme cases it may only be the change in level that marks the site of the path. Depending on the objectives of restoration and the attitude of the restorers there are again several alternatives here:

(a) To leave well alone and accept that the path, if only casually used can remain covered with grass and vegetation provided it can be mown and the levels are appropriate for this. Access drives are usually a different matter.

(b) To restore to the gravel surface. Here chemicals are invaluable and one of the most successful is the granular 'Casoron G'. Applied carefully in the late winter or early spring it should kill most growth in one application with a second one if necessary in the autumn. It is far far easier and less tedious to use herbicides than hoeing drives and paths, and much more successful. Follow with a top dressing of fresh gravel or chippings in 25-50 mm (1-2 in) layers and apply annually a residual herbicide like simazine or 'Casoron' as a routine.

(c) A modified gravel garden can be developed where extensive drives and gravelled terraced walks are on light soils, and where one can accept the colonisation of the gravel areas with a selection of spreading mat-forming species such as thymes, *Dianthus, Helianthemum* and many more. The pristine effect of a gravel drive or path admittedly will be missing but this may not matter and there are some good examples of gravelled areas like these that have become almost alpine lawns. In one, *Dryas octopetala* has formed large mats of its small 'oak' leaves studded with single white flowers in early summer. (See also Chapter 4 Gravel Gardens.)

6

The Maintenance and Management of Historic Gardens

Much of the nucleus of this chapter has already been covered in various sections of other chapters, and Chapter 5 in particular. Logically, maintenance and management of historic gardens follows on from a continuous process of renewal or restoration that will, of course, have been in progress at various intervals over the centuries since the gardens were first started. Historic gardens by their very character may need rather specialist and sometimes more intensive maintenance programmes than their more modern counterparts and also longer-term management plans to allow for phased renewal and replacement as these become necessary.

The design aspects

The question of alteration or modification of the original design for future management is one that invariably may have to be faced. Geoffrey Jellicoe, that great contemporary architect and landscape architect, who has specialised in much landscape and garden design schemes within classical or historic settings observed in an excellent paper to the Royal Society of Arts in 1980.

'In historic English gardens there may be more than *six layers* of time - medieval, renaissance, French formal, The English School, the gardenesque, and the Victorian/Edwardian ... and there is the added problem of a twentieth century owner who sees no reason why his own age and thought ... should not be included in the historic saga'.

In other words, Jellicoe considers the ethics and the possibilities of adding a contemporary 'layer' from the designer's point of view, and in this interesting context we could also consider the implications of this from the management view point. He also goes on in this paper to consider the problems and the potentialities of inserting a new garden, or parts of a new garden into an old setting: and uses the term 'creative conservation' which adds continuity to the arts and the function of the garden, while taking into account modern usage and also the maintenance and management factors. His sympathetic and functional designs for Horsted Place, Sussex and Ditchley Park, Oxford show what can be done. However, great dangers can lie in the paths of those setting out on such policies, since excessive or insensitive alterations can badly affect or even destroy the character and the quality of a garden. Marcus Binney, that great present-day exponent of Britain's and Europe's heritage of great houses and gardens, shows dramatically in his publication *Elysian Gardens* how the sheer pressure of economics (and usually this means a drastic reduction in the numbers of gardeners) is eroding away the original character of many fine gardens as one feature after another is eliminated or much modified. On the other hand, mechanical and other modern aids, as has already been shown, do enable often quite formal and intricate designs to be maintained with surprising economy and all such aids should be considered before there is any over-hasty removal of earlier labour-intensive 'layers' of the designs. In this respect, there must be a considerable number of owners or managers of large historic gardens throughout Europe today, who are succeeding or not succeeding as the case may be, in maintaining a legacy of these 'layers' from the past and who will be asking themselves how much design modification will become essential in order to cope with future upkeep.

Design modifications for maintenance

Are modifications necessary?
The research and survey stage outlined in Chapter 5 should be extended to include a thorough analysis of the existing maintenance organisation and staff involved. Admittedly this may only be the owner and a few family or paid part-time helpers but economies and greater efficiency can often be achieved by a few hours of concentrated reflection on what is being done, and how it is being done. There may thus be no need at this stage to consider altering any existing design if changes in organisation methods can bring about the economies for at least the immediate future. However, the longer-term management implications should not be overlooked, and such major restoration projects as lake dredging, woodland or avenue renewal and scrub clearance are not out of the question these days with the Job Creation and Man Power Services Schemes available in some regions, and also grant aid for some projects.

Design simplification
A careful and deliberate study of the design and style of the gardens depending on its heritage importance and rating is necessary, looking especially for such features as labour-intensive areas that could be discreetly removed or simplified without altering the overall design too seriously. It could be that a later Victorian/Edwardian 'layer' to use Jellicoe's expression again, could be simplified or adapted or even removed. In this respect one is reminded of the successful design solution that was adopted at Blickling Hall, Norfolk as long ago as 1930 by the famous garden designer of that period, Norah Lindsay to replace an elaborate Edwardian *parterre*. It is the detailed complex flower beds with too many labour-intensive annuals that can so often take up the man hours.

   A much more drastic example of an enforced solution is quoted by Marcus Binney in *Elysian Gardens*, of the once famous Victorian show place Shrublands, in Suffolk designed by Sir Charles Barry and laid out in 1848-52. In 1900 there were twenty-five to thirty gardeners falling to twenty to twenty-five in 1925 but dramatically to three in 1960. In 1979 there was one fulltime gardener plus two boys and three pensioners. The resulting changes in layout and planting were:

'The elimination of 400 yards of herbaceous borders, of twenty other beds, and a number of grass courts, turning over two thirds of the lawns which remain to hayter or rough cut grass, and the elimination of box and yew hedges'.

Marcus Binney's final comment is particularly relevant however,

'Even today, however, it is remarkable how much survives at Shrublands, and how well maintained the gardens are, but evidently any further cut back could severely affect the character of the garden particularly as such major items as the maintenance of loggias, terraces and stone work (including statuary and vases) now runs into £3-4000 a year.' (1979)

Creative conservation

Another alternative is the concept of creative conservation as put forward by Geoffrey Jellicoe by rethinking the whole design from its earliest records or beginnings and perhaps evolving a new, simple or appropriate late-twentieth century layer, provided one does not destroy or alter too much the character of the 'listed' features (if any) in the process!

Reinstatement and maintenance

The National Trust with its positive decision-making policies and expert staff and resources usually aim for the reinstatement of a particular historic garden they acquire which is in a state of prolonged dereliction or serious neglect. To quote John Sales, the National Trust's Garden Advisor:

'Here the approach demanded should be of *informed objectivity* with a clear statement of policy arrived at by the combined efforts of historians, aesthetes and horticulturalists, together with those who have a special knowledge of the area, the property and its associations; and the former owner or creator of the gardens.'

The Trust has now to its credit several very successful examples of historic gardens restored during the last decade or less, notably Westbury Court (Gloucestershire), Claremont (Surrey), Ham House (Richmond near London) and Erddig (Clwyd). It should be added that the reinstatement has not always been back to the detailed authenticity of the layer or the period of its design since maintenance costs alone would be prohibitive, but the overall schemes have been recreated in all cases with faithful and painstaking thoroughness. The decision also has to be made as to which historic layer is to be agreed upon for the reinstatement, and certainly at Claremont later plantings of cedars and other trees, as well as the invasion of rhododendrons and scrub all had to be cleared to return to the early-eighteenth century design. Owners and managers of historic gardens who are faced with restoration or reinstatement will clearly have in mind the degree of authenticity to be adopted, including the use of plants from the period, which of course the public always like to see. One of the greatest considerations, however, will be the future manning levels available for maintenance and management. The examples quoted by Marcus Binney are mostly of enforced staff reductions and the impact on the garden style or character, but perhaps there should be more positive planning ahead with the staff and resources likely to be available clearly built into the restoration and management programme. This might even include the restoration of a kitchen or walled garden of the nineteenth or early-twentieth century, with its fascinating range of vegetable and fruit crops, glasshouses and frames. This is being considered by some owners as a public visiting venture and one example is at Croxteth Hall, Cheshire where the local authority as owners have successfully restored one of these features.

Management plans for historic gardens

A management plan for an historic garden should be based on the following information:

(a) A statement or review of the general aims or objectives of the Plan in the short, middle- or long-term periods. The title 'historic garden' implies a long-term existence, thus a management plan should look well ahead.

(b) An analysis of the main components of the garden or park in terms of areas of grass, length of hedges, specimen trees, etc. and all the other features that are to be maintained and their general condition (see Chapter 2).

(c) An analysis of the existing maintenance methods or techniques being used, including equipment, machinery, staff and perhaps outside contractors.

(d) The future phased renewal of major features such as specimen trees, avenues or important groups of trees, and the timing of carrying out expensive work like lake dredging or the repairs to garden buildings and other constructed features.

(e) The present and future impact of public access and commercial undertakings.

When existing resources are inadequate to cope effectively with the total requirements of the plan and are unlikely to be increased then the plan should be flexible enough to allow for a phased or priority series of work programmes to be undertaken over a period of years. If these are built into the management plan and dealt with on this basis, there is less likely to be 'management by crisis' situations that can so often happen where management is only concerned with the present *status quo* and has not anticipated the needs of the future. It is, of course, so easy to write all this down on paper in the calm of an arm chair, since even with the best laid plans, crises and emergencies are bound to arise. In any event all management plans and schedules are just so many pieces of papers, as written guidelines, and will only be effective if successfully transmitted to the staff on the ground who always hold the keys to success or failure of any schemes.

One particular value of written Management Plans is that they should help to ensure the continuity of the management programme when senior staff changes take place. The plan is an important reference document for succeeding generations of staff, owners and agents.

Techniques of management

Many of the techniques of maintaining the features usually found in historic gardens have been already included in previous chapters of the book, and this section therefore concentrates briefly on some special problems and techniques that are more likely to arise in historic gardens.

Trees

The situation of removing and renewing overmature or decaying trees frequently has to be faced. When these are in key positions or where access is difficult such work is possibly best done by a specialist contractor (see Chapter 3). The incidence of replacement following removal is obviously more likely to increase with the age of the garden or park. It is often possible to detect at least five main tree planting eras or 'renewal layers' in many of our heritage gardens and parks. These are broadly as follows:

(a) *Ancient woodland or forest* which has been developed for a garden or park. The case study of High Beeches, Sussex is one where ancient oaks from even more ancient forest remnants still survive and regenerate. The problem of removing very old trees can be a major one when the time comes for them to go.

(b) *The avenue planting period* of the seventeenth and early-eighteenth centuries. Some ancient or partially renewed avenues still survive in a state of magnificent decadence particularly of London plane (*Platanus*), sweet chestnut (*Castanea*), limes (*Tilia*) and beech (*Fagus*). There may also be parkland or garden trees dating from this period and the question of their removal or treatment has to be faced in the not too distant future. Discreet tree surgery and remedial work as described in Chapter 3 may help to keep the tree going for a few more years.

(c) *The great eighteenth century era of parkland tree planting*, especially in the many great landscape parks created by Brown and Repton and their disciples. The majority of the trees planted in these parks are native or introduced broad-leaf deciduous species in belts, clumps, copses and as specimens. Many of these if not already replaced, are nearing the end of their lives and a phased programme of replacement is advised as discussed in Chapter 3. Cedar of Lebanon (*Cedrus libani*) and some pines and firs were also used, their form being particularly associated with gothic and classical buildings. Now two centuries old or more, they are gradually disintegrating, the process being hastened by snow or severe winter gales.

(d) *The nineteenth century era of exotic trees and conifers* especially the American conifers used widely in arboreta, woodland gardens and botanic gardens. Many of these at 100-150 years old are still in moderate shape, except the firs (*Abies*) which tend to lose their tops or die in the upper parts. The earliest Californian redwood (*Sequoia sempervirens*) and Wellingtonias (*Sequoiadendron gigantea*) dating form the late 1850s are still growing well, especially in their favourite habitats in the west and north-west of Britain and their heights are recorded at intervals. As many conifers of this era are found in mixed collections in pineta or arboreta often planted in a more random manner their specific removal and renewal is less critical from a design point of view.

(e) *Twentieth century flowering trees*. In the first three decades of this century there was profuse planting of many exotic species and trees of garden origin, especially flowering trees such as ornamental cherries *Prunus*, crabs (*Malus*), laburnum and thorn (*Crataegus*). These have often been branded as 'suburban trees' since so many were used to enliven the new gardens and roads in this period of rapid metropolitan growth.

Some garden designers did use them in the larger, contemporary or historic gardens and the late Percy Cane introduced Japanese cherries to such gardens as Dartington Hall (Devon) and Hascombe Court (Surrey). Most of these flowering trees, and especially cherries, do have a comparatively short life span (forty to fifty years) and as they can look out of place in historic gardens their replacement is **justified unless considered really appropriate for a particular scheme or period.**

Malus are usually longer lived and species like *M. floribunda* or *M. hupehensis* can still be spectacular and flourishing at fifty years of age.

Woodland

Historic or planted woodland when all the trees tend to be of the same age, should also be the subject of a long-term renewal management plan. The advice of a forester or woodland estates advisor should really be sought, but this will depend **on whether the woodland is primarily for timber production, or as an amenity** feature, or as a setting to the house and garden. As few people these days can afford the luxury of purely amenity woodlands on any extensive scale, except possibly for sporting purposes, a felling and renewal programme should be broadly based on the following guidelines by John Workman, the National Trust's Woodland Adviser for many years:

'An approximate formula is to replace 1/20 or 5% of the area every decade so that with a crop of broad leaf tree maturing in 200 years, the total area will have been replaced by the end of that period. This is long-term management planning indeed but part of the normal forester's way of thinking! However, to begin such a policy with a woodland already 150 years old would mean a failure even to catch up with the programme so therefore a faster rate of renewal will be needed, such as 1/5 or 20% of the area each decade for the first three decades and then perhaps a slower rate depending on how the woodland appears. A woodland therefore of even age of about 100 years would mean a replacement rate of about 1/10 or 10% of the area per decade for 40 years followed by 1/20 or the norm per decade. Much also depends on the species, growth rates and the trees themselves.

Shelter belts
Shelter belts, to live up to their functional name, should be sufficiently dense and sufficiently wide, and they may be composed of a range of species including conifers and scrub margins. When the majority of trees in the belt are broad-leaf species like beech or sycamore, it is conceivable that they were all planted at about the same time and may therefore have the same even age structure as the woodlands already described. A definite phased renewal programme is then called for by complete replacement of the belt by clear felling in sections perhaps 100 m (328 ft) at a time and replanting with 1-1.25 m (3-4 ft) feathered whips as an optimum size. Protection of the new belt from animals and grazing stock is essential in the establishment period and even when mature, excessive cattle trampling beneath trees may cause root compaction and damage. Interplanting new trees in an ageing belt is seldom successful.

Clumps
These first appeared as designed features in eighteenth century landscape parkland as circular features (also called 'roundels') dispersed across the parkland according to the character and the design of the latter. Brown and Repton both used these, and laid down planting details for them. They were usually composed of native deciduous species, such as beech, elm, oak or sweet chestnut, and were fenced against cattle and grazing animals. At the planting stage coniferous nurse or 'filler' species of pine or fir (*Abies*) were included in a ratio of about one long-term tree to five or ten 'fillers', the latter being removed in stages as the clump developed. This was Humphry Repton's formula based on forestry practice. Whereas shelter belts have a functional role to play, and may have some timber production value also, clumps are almost entirely visual, and as such have suffered more with the development of parkland for agriculture and have simply become a low priority for renewal. Two particular problems are often encountered with clumps of this sort: the overmaturity and senescence of the main trees and the question of replacement, especially if the clumps are original key points in a Brown landscape. Interplanting new with old, as we have seen, is seldom successful so some alternatives are:

(a) To clear fell selected clumps on a phased basis and replant with similar species, using the Repton planting formula or something similar. Feathered whips at about 1-1.5m (39-59 in) high and about 1 m (39 in) apart are an ideal size planted with Austrian pine (*Pinus nigra*), or Scots pine (*Pinus sylvestris*) as nurse species at a ratio of one broad-leaf to five nurse trees and well fenced against stock. Rabbits may also be a problem. The conifers should then be thinned gradually over a period of ten to twenty years or more depending on how rapidly the main clump trees grow. Clumps in the nineteenth century were sometimes composed entirely of conifers, and one also sees cases where the firs were never properly thinned or removed, causing a dense overcrowded mixed clump (plate 6.1).

Plate 6.1 A clump of Scots pine (*Pinus sylvestris*), in parkland in Kent. These are all of an even age and should really have been thinned many years before

(b) Another alternative is to resite a new clump or clumps as close as possible to the original, where this is practicable. This does, of course, mean taking more land out of agriculture or other uses if the new clumps are allowed to establish before the old ones are removed. To make any impact in a panoramic landscape, a clump needs to be at least 50 m (55 yd) across.

For landowners who really need the parkland and who are unable to face the costs of replanting many clumps, aged features should be clear felled leaving if possible a few strategically sited features based on the original design. The survey stage may be important here.

(c) Tree clumps, where original stately broad-leaved species have been lost so that only an insignificant or scrubby population of conifers or seedling trees survive, leave no option other than removal or thinning or replanting (plate 6.2).

Specimen trees
These were once an important characteristic of designed historic parkland as

Plate 6.2 A rather scattered and very mixed 'clump' of mostly deciduous species, some of which are in a state of decay. Felling of these and replanting with transplants of appropriate species is recommended for such a dominant feature

scattered individuals carefully sited into a panoramic landscape. Original plans by Brown or Repton show these features, of which many still survive today in protected or conserved historic gardens and parkland as gnarled veterans of beech, oak, sweet chestnut, plane and cedar of Lebanon. However, very many have been lost due to old age, or the need to develop such parkland for arable production and single trees are particularly vulnerable to damage and removal.

Another real problem with all ancient trees is their potential danger if in areas of public access due to falling branches and collapse. The answer is all too often to remove the tree altogether. However, I have already referred to the role of the arboriculturalist or tree surgeon, and even with overmature trees, it is possible to do remedial work on veteran trees. As John Workman comments:

'Pruning may in itself not actually prolong the life of a tree but by making the tree safer one can obviously retain it longer in sensitive areas.'

Specimen or groups of trees should be replaced wherever possible, even if only a fraction of those once featuring in the original park, and these new trees will need strong, durable guards against cattle in particular (see Chapter 3).

Avenues
These are undoubtedly one of the greatest problems facing landowners and managers today who have such features to manage. Mature intact avenues, often

planted two centuries or more ago are unique features, whose very character and drama depend on the long cathedral-like perspective of even columns and arching tops. Once they become uneven, and 'gap-toothed' due to death or decay, they are really a poor substitute for the real thing.

Again, turning to John Workman who has a special interest in, and concern for ancient avenues, since the National Trust and many other owners of such historic features are seeking solutions to the renewal problems facing them in the immediate or very near future, one finds the following series of alternatives for the treatment of avenues:

(a) Clear fell and replant the entire feature. A bold, drastic decision but the visual shock is bound to be sensational. The big problem is usually of timing the felling of the avenue.

(b) Clear fell sections of a long avenue, preferably of significant lengths, of about 30 m (33 yd) at a time, and adjacent sides and replace with even-age, well-grown nursery stock, at ten year intervals. Stump removal and ground preparation will have to be as thorough as possible (see Chapter 3).

(c) Cut out every other tree and replant. This is generally never too successful, since the new trees will face competition for light, and water and nutrients and may be slow to establish and become poor distorted specimens. Shade-loving species like beech or oak may stand this treatment but the long-term results will never be as dramatic as the even-aged trees.

(d) Double avenues, remove the inner or outer row and replace on a phased basis. However, if the rows are too close, the row of younger trees will still be overshadowed by the mature row alongside and will tend to grow out at an angle towards the light, and retain this shape in the future.

(e) Plant a new avenue on the inside or the outside of the existing line, if space allows. This can be very effective if the design is acceptable, but can be very demanding of land space.

(f) Enjoy the old avenue as long as possible, and plant an equivalent new one somewhere else in the park.

(g) Replace trees individually as they fall. The most common remedy and in the long term the least rewarding one. The avenue will always look uneven, without the fine colonnade effect.

(h) Accept an heterogenous or mixed avenue, with flowering trees or evergreens. This is fine in its way, but it is not really an avenue. To quote John Workman: 'Avenues ought to be superlative!'

(i) If more than one avenue occurs on the same property, consider eventually having each one of a different species to ensure against disease or other casualities.

Planting grants. It may be possible to have grant aid for the renewal of historic trees as just reviewed, and more information on this is summarised in Chapter 7.

Knot gardens and parterres
The advent of herbicides and mechanical trimmers has simplified the lengthy

hand-work operations of weeding and clipping, and if both these aids are used with care and understanding, maintenance standards for extensive areas of such features can be held with fewer staff. Gravel areas between box hedges for example should be treated with precise rates of a contact or residual herbicide. Any excess doses of the latter or careless application will damage the box.

Planting designs can be adjusted to match the maintenance resources and the setting and there are many low, compact growing and reasonably persistent species such as *Santolina*, dwarf lavenders, thymes, hyssop, pinks, burnet roses and many others suitable for knot gardens.

7

Economic Aspects of Garden Maintenance and Management

The previous chapters have concentrated on the principles and practices and the arts, science and craft of garden maintenance, yet the most critical factor of all for so many today is the economic one, largely accounting for the difficulties facing garden owners and the decline or loss of many larger gardens referred to in Chapter 1 and elsewhere.

It is proposed to look a little more closely at the following aspects that largely apply to situations where staff are employed:

(a) The costs of running a garden
(b) Tax concessions and maintenance funds.
(c) Grants for gardens
(d) Revenue-raising ventures.

Table 7.1 A garden in Scotland: expenses in 1977-78 (Adapted from figures produced in the Bellchamber Report on Scottish gardens.)

Items	Percentage of total expenditure	Expenditure (£)
Total wages (two full-time, two part-time gardeners)		7670.00
Rates on three cottages	75	270.00
Electricity		330.00
Fuel etc.		150.00
Total expenses staff items		8420.00
Heating glasshouse	7	600.00
General expenses		180.00
Machinery repairs overhaul		350.00
Depreciation		200.00
Fuel	10	120.00
Replacement		360.00
Weed killer and fertiliser		200.00
Plant bulbs and seeds		450.00
Tools etc.	8	100.00
Fencing, tree guards		70.00
Protective clothing etc.		150.00
Total		11 200.00

In this particular privately owned garden both owners also work ten hours per week which does not, of course, show in the above figures, but is a significant input to take into account.

The costs of running a garden

Analysis of some garden expenses carried out in recent studies shows more or less the same result, namely that labour costs can account for over 70% of total expenditure and this proportion also applies to landscape contracting and maintenance work generally. In a little more detail, two sets of expenses of large gardens in different parts of the country are reproduced taking examples where several gardeners are employed in each case (see tables 7.1 and 7.2).

Table 7.2 A garden in the south of England: A comparison of costs over three years

	1978 £	1978 %	1979 £	1979 %	1980 £	1980 %
Labour (4 staff)	16375	78.8	17012	69.2	18001	66.4
Plants and seeds	405	1.9	771	3.1	716	2.6
Fertilisers	458	2.2	498	2.0	854	3.1
Sprays and dusts	318	1.5	482	2.0	988	3.6
Hortic. sundries	15	0.07	99	0.4	323	1.2
Glasshouse fuel	505	2.4	516	2.1	685	2.5
Other fuel and oil	172	0.8	460	1.9	626	2.3
Repairs and maintenance- machinery	1062	5.1	1869	7.6	1165	4.3
Vehicle tax and insurance	109	0.5	136	0.6	130	0.5
Maintenance charges	111	0.5	142	0.6	761	2.8
Small tools	534	2.6	1233	5.0	1038	3.8
Contract			29	0.1	16	0.06
Miscellaneous	55	0.3	99	0.4	116	0.4
Depreciation Machinery and equipment	685	3.3	1237	5.0	1699	6.3
Total gardens operating costs	20804		24583		27118	

(1) The general increase in expenditure costs on most items and especially sprays (more herbicides used), small tools (includes brush cutters etc.) and machinery.

(2) Most of the main items of machinery such as tractor, triple mower and other mowers are over five years old and the depreciation figure starts to look alarming.

(3) Glasshouse heating oil for one propagating and growing-on house of 142 m³ (5000 cu. ft) is also becoming an expensive item.

In both these examples therefore labour emerges as by far the greatest item of expenditure with machinery next, and of particular note, the high costs today of running heated glasshouses, due largely to the increasing costs of fuel, and if labour is added, the detailed and often time-consuming hand work involved in glasshouse management and the crops therein.

Estimating costs

There are, of course, very many smaller gardens perhaps employing one full-time, or a part-time gardener. These are referred to in the Bellchamber Report, as those where the labour input is usually less than eighty hours per week. In the Scottish Gardens Survey it was found that many owners in this category had imprecise information on their running costs (either by intention or lack of need) and for these owners a quick method of estimating the total annual costs is suggested:

(a) Calculate total wages (70 % of total costs).
(b) Add 10 % for overheads, perks, etc. This figure then gives a total of about 80 % of the costs of running the garden.
(c) Divide this total by eight.
(d) Multiply then by ten to give estimated total annual costs. An example is quoted thus:

$$
\begin{array}{llr}
\text{Total wages} & = \pounds1232 \\
\text{Add 10\% overheads} & = \pounds\ 123 \\
\hline
& \pounds1355 \\
\text{Divide by eight} & = \pounds\ 169.37 \\
\text{Multiply by ten} & = \pounds1693.70
\end{array}
$$

Thus £1693.70 is the estimated total annual cost.

Chapter 2 examined measures that could be taken to reduce costs, especially of man power, and clearly in all these figures the input of the owner and his family has to be taken into account. One rather sad but inevitable fact that also emerges from most garden accounts is the rather low figure being spent on new planting and development. An exception, described in Chapter 8, is Castle Howard where considerable resources have been devoted recently to a new rose garden and arboreta. For the majority, however, most expenditure has to go on short-term maintenance and money-raising ventures.

Taxation and gardens

H.M. Treasury Memorandum *Capital Taxation and the National Heritage,* published in December 1980 quotes as follows in its introduction:

'Historic properties and land of scenic and scientific interest, individual objects of artistic, botanic or scientific interest ... form an integral and major part of the cultural life of this country. It has been the policy of successive governments that this national heritage should be conserved and protected for the benefit of the community. They have taken the view that where such property remains in private hands, the owners should be encouraged, wherever possible, to retain and care for it and display it to the public; and that where this is no longer possible they should dispose of it to those bodies in the country which have been set up specifically to hold such property in trust for the community.'

These are altruistic and encouraging words from the treasury and government but as will be seen there is still considerable cause for concern when it comes to the 'encouragement' actually available to garden owners.

Tax treatment of historic houses and gardens open to the public
The situation is always under review in this respect, but summarised here is the position as it stood in November 1980 based on information kindly supplied by Norman Hudson, Technical Adviser to the Historic Houses Association in a memorandum providing guidance for owners of houses and gardens opening to the public. Liability to tax is based not on the full amount of the admission fees but on the balance of profit remaining after deducting from the receipts any allowable expenses. Those expenses allowable, and the ways in which relief is allowed for a

loss, (if one occurs and it usually does) differ according to the treatment of the opening of the property for tax purposes. There are two main categories.

A house and garden maintained solely or mainly as a show place. Here if an occupier is carrying on a trade of showing the house and/or garden to the public 'managed on a commercial basis with a view to the realisation of profit' the profits will fall within Section 110 (3) ICTA 1970 and will be taxed under Case I of Schedule D. The occupier will be entitled to claim as a deduction in calculating the profit, so much of any expenditure which is incurred in the upkeep of the house, its contents and gardens as is preferable to the trading activity. Capital expenditure incurred on the provision of machinery etc., for maintenance may qualify for capital allowance. Any grant under Section 4 of the Historic Buildings and Ancient Monument Act 1953 which is used wholly or partly to meet expenses attributable to the opening of the property to the public will be taken into account in computing profit.

If there is a trading loss in any year relief from tax on the amount of the loss is allowed either by setting it against other income for the year or against increase from all sources for the following year.

'Going commercial' with a house or garden does need to satisfy the Inspectors of Taxes and they do look at the following points in making their assessments:

(a) The extent to which the property is likely to attract visitors having regard to its historic, architectural and in the case of gardens, horticultural interest.

(b) How much of the property is set aside as a show place. Usually a substantial part should be open to visitors, with due allowance made for utility and privacy of the occupier and the family.

(c) The number of days on which the property is open to the public usually compatible with the aim of making a profit from opening. A substantial number of open days are normally expected including those days on which the house is open by appointment to groups or parties.

(d) The amount of organisation for the attraction and reception of visitors by adequate advertising and publicity, provision of ticket offices, car parks, refreshments, guides, sales of guide books, etc. In other words, it must be demonstrated that a definite organisation has been set up for attracting and dealing with visitors.

Realisation of profits. It must be shown that the whole activity is undertaken with the intention of making a profit and not for purely altruistic motives or with a view to getting relief from tax.

New ventures. Where a property is opened to the public for the first time, the **realisation of profit test will be regarded as provisionally satisfied** if a sufficient number of visitors is attracted to suggest that there is a reasonable prospect of profits being made in the foreseeable future. Thus for example, receiving 15 000 visitors a year with regular opening will be regarded as satisfying the test in the early years from first opening. The actual number of visitors a place receives to satisfy the profit test is related to the actual profitability and the level of visitors the property can receive without excess wear and tear.

Continuing losses. When prolonged losses occur, the Inspector will need to be satisfied that the property really is being managed on a commercial basis or if after periodic reviews the situation does not improve the Inspector may consider that the venture is not viable.

Other receipts. In practice, the net proceeds for special attractions, events, tea rooms, etc., which can be associated with the showing of the property to the public will be taken into account in determining whether the realisation of profits test is satisfied and will not be separately assessed for tax.

Houses and gardens not maintained solely or mainly as show places. If the house or garden is not maintained wholly or mainly for making a profit from the admission of the public, i.e. if there is no commercial organisation, or simply the receipt of fees from casual visitors, profits will normally fall under Case VI of Schedule D. In computing profits for assessment under Case VI, deductions are normally only allowable for the additional expenses incurred as a result of opening, i.e. wages for a person to collect gate money, or for cleaning, etc. Relief for any loss so computed, is allowed, not against income generally, but only against profits from any other transaction taxed under Case VI of Schedule D either for the same or future years.

Capital taxation

This can be divided into two headings for the purpose of this section: (a) Capital Transfer Tax (C.T.T.); (b) Capital Gains Tax (C.G.T.).

Capital Transfer Tax (C.T.T.). This was introduced in the 1975 Finance Act. It applies to lifetime transfers made on or after 27th March 1974 and to all deaths occurring on or after 13th March 1975. There is a lower scale of rates for lifetime transfers (up to £310000) and C.T.T. is not charged on the first £3000 of a person's lifetime transfers in any one tax year. Transfers between a husband and wife living in the United Kingdom can also be exempt. There are numerous exemptions from C.T.T. as detailed in the Treasury Memorandum, but the Clause in respect of gardens is summarised here. It comes under the heading 'Outstanding Land'.

Exemption may be given for land which in the opinion of the Treasury is of outstanding, scenic, historic or scientific interest. These three categories cover botanical, horticultural, silvicultural, arboricultural and agricultural interest and include created landscapes. Buildings erected on outstanding land may also qualify, either on their own merits or because of their contribution to the interest of the land. The views of relevant advisory bodies will be sought before a decision on exemption, is taken.

Conditions of exemption. The usual undertakings are that reasonable steps will be taken to maintain the land or garden and the preservation of its character, and for securing reasonable public access.

Woodlands. Beyond the scope of this book but full information can be found in the Treasury Memorandum or in the Forestry Commission's leaflet No. 12 *Taxation of Woodlands* (see References).

Capital Gains Tax (C.G.T.). This tax was introduced by the Finance Act 1965 and is chargeable on gains which arise on the disposal of assets subject to certain exemption. In broad terms the amount of the chargeable gain is the differences between the cost of the asset and the sale proceeds. Exemptions are given for a variety of conditions but usually when a national heritage property is transferred by way of a gift from one individual to another or to one of the charities or national heritage bodies approved by the Treasury for this purpose. These are usually museums, libraries, universities or local or county councils. The criteria are similar to the C.T.T. and a direction will only be made if the body receiving the gift is considered suitable to assume responsibility for its preservation.

Other conditions also are:

(a) The receiving body must have financial capacity to maintain the property. Full details are therefore required of the body's assets and expected income and the terms of application.
(b) Undertakings will be required in respect of public access, restriction of use and preservation of this property and its dispersal.
(c) The donor cannot reserve any interest in the property for him or herself.

Transfer of any property to a maintenance fund is charged to C.G.T. on the transfer.

Maintenance funds

The Finance Act of 1975 which introduced Capital Transfer Tax also introduced the concept of conditional exemption to protect heritage property. The Historic Houses Association in particular while welcoming this concept felt that it was not sufficient to protect the heritage property itself from capital taxes without also protecting the capital needed to support it. Fairly close and protracted negotiations between these Associations, the Joint Committee of the Amenity Societies, and various Treasury Tax Committees eventually led to the Finance Act of 1980, which included among other proposals the setting up of maintenance funds provisions for historic houses and gardens.

Maintenance funds are designed to encourage owners of heritage property to set aside capital to keep their property in good repair and to make provision for reasonable public access to it. While there is a measure of income tax relief available which may be advantageous in certain circumstances, the maintenance fund is essentially a means of protecting capital from (C.T.T.) Capital Transfer Tax.

A maintenance fund is a trust fund which may be set up by an individual, or by trustees through an individual, and this fund may continue in existence without payment of C.T.T. regardless of who owns the property. The income or capital of the fund may only be used for approved heritage purposes during the first six years of its life. Other conditions apply after that.

The property in the maintenance fund to qualify can either be an outstanding building and its adjoining amenity land, or it may be land of outstanding scenic, scientific or historic interest. The latter category would normally include the outstanding garden in its own right. The heritage property does not have to have been granted conditional exemption from C.T.T. but it has to meet the test of designation for that purpose and the relevant undertakings must be agreed and observed. Such a fund is still in its early stages but with favourable government interpretation and numbers of property owners taking part this could be one answer to the long-term future and upkeep of some private gardens at least. More details of this fund are available from the Historic Houses Association.

Other alternatives to maintenance funds

Charitable Trusts. A number of gardens have become a Charitable Trust which constitutes a gift or donation of the property and its land to the nation. Usually a sufficient sum of money is given with the property to safeguard its maintenance and any income from this fund is exempt from taxation. There are some disadvantages, such as the ownership of the property and garden passing to the Trust. A fairly large sum of money is now needed to transfer to the Charitable Trust fund in order to yield enough income to cover the running costs of the garden especially with inflation. This may well be a deterrent. Also the designation of the garden as a Charitable Trust has to be critically assessed by the Charity Commissioners. A management committee is appointed to administer the Trust and run the garden and this usually includes the owner and perhaps members of the family and the agent or head gardener.

The National Trust. A property and its land and garden can be bequeathed to the National Trust normally with a substantial endowment to cover running costs for a number of years. A direct approach to the Trust is advised by an owner considering this cause of action. Again the Trust have to be selective and discerning as to the type of property they will take on.

Revenue from grants

Although available grants are limited, according to the Bellchambers Report little advantage seems to have been taken of such grants presently available, and the view seems to be that the tax concession method, so far, is the better method of helping garden owners. Three main reasons are put forward for this in the Report:

(a) The grants available cover capital investment only, not maintenance. From the Scottish gardens survey, the average garden is spending only 5% of its total expenditure on new plants, paths, etc. 95% of its expenditure goes on maintenance which is where most urgent financial help is needed.
(b) There is general fear or suspicion of government interference, and of the conditions that might be attracted to any grants.
(c) The general lack of knowledge among private gardens certainly of the sort of grants that are available.

Grants generally come from these sources:

(a) Historic Buildings Council grant for garden repairs.
(b) Countryside Commission grants for amenity tree planting.
(c) Local authority grants and loans for repair and maintenance.

The availability of the grants is generally linked to the importance of the historic property and this is where the listing of gardens already referred to on a national basis will help to produce criteria for deciding on the deserving cases. Conditions are imposed, but with the growing evidence of the need to conserve heritage, approaches to the above bodies and to the local councils also are suggested. Occasionally grants may come from the Tourist Boards, and, of course, where woodlands are involved there are various Forestry Commission schemes that should be considered.

Income-raising ventures

The preceding sections on taxation and related matters do emphasise one point
that needs making with any ventures into the money-raising business in gardens
and parks. This is the importance of the 'realisation of profits' objectives of any
enterprises projected, whether it be from visitors only, or visitors and plant and
other sales, or commercial horticultural production or anything else.

Horticultural production and plant sales
Many of the larger historic and landscaped gardens and parks have a considerable
area once used for food production as walled or kitchen gardens, glasshouses and
frames and the various ancillary buildings to go with them. Careful siting on
south-or west-facing slopes maximises the production and soils have been built up
in fertility over the centuries of garden craft and management.

  Many of these facilities still survive, and unless converted into car parks or
pleasure gardens some, or all, of the areas can be considered for intensive
production of suitable crops. Other places may have spare land available for crop
production but whatever land is available there are some very important questions
that must be answered before undertaking any enterprise with a view to raising
significant income:

(a) *What are the existing or potential markets or outlets?* It is advisable to explore
these in local shops, hotels, wholesale markets, and the demand from visitors at the
gate or other nurseries. These need investigating fairly thoroughly. There are too
many gardeners and horticulturalists who are good growers of good produce, but
poor on the sales and marketing side. Glasshouses full of pot plants, or a kitchen
garden with prime vegetables can be most satisfying to look upon but an expensive
luxury if only a proportion are sold at a market price or made available on a casual
basis to staff or local callers. Losses are often covered up or ignored, or simply not
calulated.

(b) *What is the scale or scope of the enterprise?* Think carefully about this. It is
generally preferable, having decided on one's markets, to aim to produce good
quality stock in a limited range directed at these markets, than to indulge in too
many enterprises or a wide range of crops that may be more expensive to produce
and more difficult to sell. For example if a hardy plant sales venture attached to a
garden open to the public is planned, it might be better to produce agreed
quantities of certain notable plants visitors have seen growing in the garden itself,
such as old roses, the more unusual cultivars of herbaceous plants or indeed of
plants that help to determine the character of the garden, and that cannot easily be
obtained at a local nursery. It seems rather pointless for a perhaps unique garden
containing many unusual plants having a plant sales centre that sells mainly the
everyday plants and shrubs one can buy 'down the road'. Go for quality and
uniqueness. Another example might be supplies of fruit or vegetables, and
especially salad crops to local hotels or specialist shops that want to get a name for
locally grown fresh produce that customers can rely on. Negotiated contracts need
'looking after' and quantities must usually be regular and adequate to meet the
fluctuating demands especially in tourist areas.

(c) *Are manpower and resources available?* These can also be critical questions
since with most garden staff working flat out in the spring and summer months, it

may be that the last thing they want to do is to stop and pick vegetables or fruit in the height of the 'hump'! Hence the advantage of hardy plant production since much of the propagation and growing on can be done in the autumn, winter and spring, with sales of container-grown plants being more easily handled by assistants perhaps attached to the local shop or visitor centre and without affecting the garden staff too closely. Old glasshouses and frames can be cheaply converted to propagation and production using polythene lining and insulation and introducing simple propagation methods. Walk-in polythene tunnels are also reasonably inexpensive to erect and manage and are useful for production of many crops. Look for essentially simple, economic and efficient systems of production avoiding too many mist units or too much heated glass that can run away with the profit. For anyone considering beginning a plant-raising or nursery stock venture the excellent Grower Book *A Nursery Stock Manual* is recommended reading, being extremely useful up-to-date and very practical handbook on the subject, and especially good on the various alternative propagation systems available today. Cold glass or polythene tunnel flower crops maturing in early spring before the peak begins are also worth considering, such as pinks (*Dianthus*), Peruvian lilies (*Alstroemeria*) and perhaps bulb flowers. Herbs as young container-raised plants are easily and quickly produced from seed or cuttings and are usually sought after by visitors to historic properties especially if there is a herb garden feature. A small area of heated glass for plant raising is sufficient to produce growing-on plants under plastic tunnels or houses.

Cold lettuce crops are also a possibility for late winter or spring production. Summer-maturing vegetables, cut flowers and fruit crops are the 'problem areas' competing with the limited labour available and to be successful the production of these crops needs to be on a sufficient scale to carry the costs of one full-time or part-time person, especially during the periods of production, harvesting and marketing. It is usually not sufficient to divert existing garden staff away from summer maintenance work, as has been mentioned. Also prices of produce can fluctuate wildly in the 'glut' period and high marketing costs are usually not justified.

Other alternatives

Pick your own. The self picking or pick your own enterprise when the visitors and public are invited to pick from selected areas of the crops to be harvested is certainly worth considering, but competition is strong in areas of soft fruit and market garden production. However, attached to an historic house and walled garden, this could be an additional attraction, provided some sort of control can be exercised over the public once they get 'behind the scenes'. Experience in Kent has shown that in general the public do less damage to crops they harvest, than groups of casual workers called in on a piece-work basis, which is another alternative of course. The following crops have been found to be suitable for pick your own enterprises: strawberries, raspberries, brussel sprouts, rhubarb and even potatoes.

A tenant. Another possibility is to let the walled garden or production areas to a suitable tenant for a market garden venture. This solution has been adopted by many owners where they can be sure of reasonable maintenance and care of the holding by the tenant and there will be a small rent coming in!

Garden shops or plant sales. Such ventures may also be stocked with bought-in produce, provided a really reliable local supplier can be found to keep regular supplies of good quality plants of the sort of range and character that fits the property and its character.

Other ventures are really beyond the scope of this book in so far as they affect the gardens and their management. Certainly guides and books are popular, and there is probably far more scope for garden trails or self-guided leaflets. So often the house of a heritage property has plenty of interpretation literature and guides in person to show visitors round, whereas the gardens are often overlooked or rather scantily covered in the literature available. Peter Blake, the Horticultural Officer of Cornwall County Council created a most original and educational demonstration garden at Probus in Cornwall some years ago since he felt very strongly that there is a largely unexploited potential in gardens and parks for the education and enlightenment of the visiting public.

The far more ambitious and larger-scale ventures like safari parks and public entertainment affairs can certainly be profitable but they need careful planning at the outset, and managing with skill and ingenuity. Restaurants on the other hand are invariably well supported, whatever the scale of the operation and in a picturesque and comfortable setting may certainly add to the visitor numbers.

Visitor pressures on gardens. Although large numbers of visitors can add to the problems of garden management, an initial survey seems to show that where maintenance is good anyway, the damage and wear and tear are not a serious matter. The removal of litter containers as practised for sometime now by the National Trust, has greatly reduced the litter problem (never really serious in gardens) and reduced opening times for the pressurised gardens have enabled the garden staff to get through their work with less inconvenience. Plant pilfering does however, seem to be on the increase.

The important subject of visitor handling and management in gardens really deserves a book in itself, and regrettably space has not allowed this rather specialised subject to be covered adequately in this work.

8
Case Studies

Historic and horticulturally important gardens need very special and careful techniques to maintain their character and quality. Many in the past were able to do this with a large staff of skilled gardeners that are out of the question in 1981.

To demonstrate the different management systems that have been devised to run such large gardens, seven different gardens are discussed in this chapter and the maintenance and management systems examined in each case. The gardens have been selected from French and British examples representing contrasting styles of historic or horticultural importance with quite different intensitities of manpower input needed to run them. All the studies were carried out in co-operation with the owners or the head gardeners in 1981.

Vaux-Le-Vicomte, France

Location: 77950 Maincy, 5 km E. of Melun, 40 km (25 miles) S. of Paris.

Owner: Comte Patrice de Voguë

Opening: March 1st-October 31st most days from 10.00 a.m. to 6.00 p.m.

Background
The chateau and gardens are among the finest surviving seventeenth century masterpieces in the whole of France.
   They were created in the late 1650s by the Superintendent of Finances to Louis XIV, Nicolas Fouquet, helped by three talented artists - the architect, Le Vau (1612-70), the interior decorator, Charles Le Brun (1619-90) (ceilings, tapestries, furniture, etc.) and the landscape gardener, Andre Le Notre. In one single uninterrupted five year period 1656-61 the superb house and gardens took shape.
   In 1875 Alfred Sommier purchased the property and its estate and proceeded on a lengthy programme of restoration, including the very neglected gardens which took fifty years to restore to the condition in which they are seen today. It is a descendant of the Sommiers who owns the property now.

The gardens
The bird's eye view conveys (plate 8.1) the scale and magnificence of Vaux. The total area of maintained gardens is 70 ha (173 acres) of which 20 ha (49 acres) are mown grass, 20 ha (49 acres) parterres and *allées*, and the remainder water features (*pieces d'eaux*), gravel paths, bosquets, etc. The length of the grand axis is 1300 m (1422 yd).

Maintenance staff
There are eight full-time gardeners under the head gardener, Louis Bastard, who are all responsible to the owner Comte Patrice de Voguë. In the pre Second World

Plate 8.1 Vaux le Vicomte from the air looking down the main east-west axis of Le Notre's dramatic design. note the enclosing woodlands and the proportions of hard areas to grass and parterres.

War days a staff of fifteen were employed including those involved in intensive cultivation of a large kitchen garden or potager (at present uncultivated). All staff share the work of the gardens, with no specialists for certain jobs.

Plate 8.2 The 'afternoon' rotary mowing in progress. Level, unbroken expanses of grass are cut very quickly with these two machines, and the finish is good

Management systems

Grass areas. The majority of the 20 ha (49 acres) of 'pelouses' or main lawns are cut speedily and effectively with two modern rotary mowers: a Japanese Kubota L175 tractor with a 1.5 m (5 ft) cutting width and a Trojan Toro 1.2 m (4 ft) cutting width. These two mowers can cut all the main areas on two afternoons per week cutting at rates of 6000-10 000 m² (1.5-2.0 acres) per hour. The height is about 35-50 mm (1¼-2 in) and in March, April and May, usually all three areas are cut twice weekly. In the drier summer months the rate usually falls to once per week or less frequently (plate 8.2).

The smaller more detailed parterres and enclosed areas of grass are cut with three hand propelled Wolf 55 cm (22 in) rotary mowers, sturdy, reliable and very effective machines. As in most French gardens, no grass clippings are collected. an annual fertiliser application is given to all the grass which obviously encourages growth, and possibly necessitates rather more frequent cutting than one would think necessary for grass of this length and character.

Hedges. There are two types of hedges at Vaux:

The taller hornbeam (Carpinus betulus) hedges or '*Charmilles*' that frame most of the *allees* and bosquets. There are some 12 km (7.5 miles) and these are done annually by hand in late summer with the very traditional bill hook or *Croissant Pour les Charmilles* that the present gardeners are accustomed to using. Four men can cut the 12 km (7.5 miles) of hedges in fifteen days.

The small parterre box hedges in the intricate design of the period are cut once or twice in the growing season using two electric cutter bars driven by a mobile generator.

Topiary features. There are some 300 of these features mostly in box or yew also cut with the electric trimmers. Where any are looking impoverished or dying back, fertilisers are injected into the soil or gravel paths in the late winter. Renewal is a problem with some of these features.

Weed control. This is one of the biggest problems in a large formal garden. Paths, drives and gravel areas are treated with a residual herbicide but the most serious and tedious problem at present is the hand weeding of the box hedges in the parterres. These have become invaded with such perennial weeds as lesser bindweed (*Convolvulus arvensis*), couch grass (*Agropyron*) and others. Herbicides have not been considered safe on these so far, so many hours of repetitive hand weeding are necessary to keep these weeds at bay.

Other areas and operations. There are few flowers at Vaux. A number of large urns and vases are planted with pink pelargoniums throughout, these being supplied by a contractor. Only a small area of 'domestic glass' is maintained.

Woodlands and bosquets. The blocks and compartments of fine trees and woodland that define the great spaces of Vaux are composed of mixed broad-leaf species especially oak (*Quercus robur*), beech (*Fagus sylvatica*), hornbeam (*Carpinus betulus*) and sycamore (*Acer pseudoplatanus*). The margins of the main axis are framed by tall horse chestnuts (*Aesculus hippocastanum*) and along the great canal by lofty planes (*Platanus*). The trees and woods are of moderate age with dense regeneration in most blocks. Some periodic thinning is carried out by estate staff. Extensive forests and woodland to the south and west of the Vaux gardens are dominated by oak and hornbeam.

Irrigation is occasionally used for the parterres.

Autumn leaves are a problem and over two months are spent collecting these by a combination of machine raking and hand sweeping and carting.

Water features. Some of the fountains are operational, others are out of action and in need of repair. There are two main problems here: firstly the supply of water needed to operate all the many cascades, jets and fountains is probably inadequate due to increased local use. Secondly the repair and renewal of pipes, stonework and basins is a formidable undertaking and with the present level of visitors and the political climate, the owners could not contemplate a major programme of this sort.

Visitors
Some 250 000 visitors came to Vaux in 1979 and usually presented no problems to the staff.

Summary
The maintenance systems used for Vaux, one of the greatest formal gardens in Europe, are traditional and effective with the emphasis being on the upkeep of the main vegetation features. There is potential for restoration of more contemporary features in the future and as with most houses and gardens of this period, there is a continuous programme of repair and restoration of the stonework and statuary that is quite a formidable task in the present economic and social climate of Europe. Long-term management policies are not a priority at present.

Chateau de Courances, France

Location: Courances 91490, Milly-La-Foret, 48 km (30 miles) S. of Paris, near Fountainbleau.

Owner: Marquis de Ganay

Opening: By arrangement with the owner.

Background
The chateau was built in 1622 for Claud Gallard, son of one of Louis XIII's officials. He was also largely responsible for the original gardens. It is possible that a pupil of Le Notre, or Le Notre himself may have been involved with the garden design, but there is no record of this. The great grandfather of the present Marquis de Ganay bought the property in 1872 and carried out a complete restoration programme including the surrounding parklands. The years 1880-1914 were the halcyon days of Courances with ten full time gardeners and many estate staff. In 1930 a romantic Anglo-Japanese garden was laid out by the present owner's grandmother, the then Marquise de Ganay. The chateau and gardens suffered a further period of neglect in the 1939-45 war but the present Marquis de Ganay has since been carrying out an energetic programme of restoration.

The gardens and their management

The garden and park total 75 ha (185 acres) plus a farm and wooded estate. This figure comprises 15 ha (37 acres) of maintained garden and 60 ha (148 acres) of woodlands, bosquets and rough grass (plate 8.3).

Plate 8.3 The Chateau de Courances from the east. The planes are nearly 200 years of age, and typical of many others like these at Courances

Courances is a remarkable example of the achievements of a dedicated and much involved husband and wife partnership who, on inheriting the property, after years of war time neglect are facing the tasks of restoration and maintenance with energy and enterprise.

In place of the ten gardeners of pre-war days, there are now three full-time men working a total of about 6000 hours per annum (this compares with a total of very approximately 50 000 man hours early in this century). The Marquis is closely involved with the maintenance programme and has compensated for the lack of gardening staff, by the ingenious and enterprising use of mechanisation and equipment, without which he is firmly convinced the gardens could not survive.

He is in effect the owner/manager and personally directs the running of the gardens and parks. His wife the Marquise also assists with the more detailed designs around the house, and both manage the Japanese Garden with great sensitivity and success. The management methods for the various components at Courances can be summarised as follows:

Woods and bosquets. These are composed of broad-leaf hardwood species such as planes (*Platanus*), limes (*Tilia*), horse chestnut (*Aesculus*), oak (*Quercus*), hornbeam (*Carpinus*) and others. The planting is dense, and regeneration has encouragd this thicket effect. For the mature avenue trees and other large specimens tree surgeons are called in for the technical work. These are expensive in France. The main woodland areas that flank the gardens are renewed in compartments of 6 ha (13.5 acres) per felling, on a ten year cycle of felling and planting.

Hedges. These are structural frames to the bosquets and margins to the *allées* and are mainly of box (*Buxus*), and they also compose the designs of the parterre. All hedges are given an annual cut, but two levels of maintenance are adopted:

(a) Prestige hedges of the parterre and around the chateau, demand crisp, architectural, lines and are cut between July and September with machine-powered shears or hand shears. One man is responsible for all these hedges and when they exceed 1.5-2.0 m (4-6 ft) in height a tractor trailer unit is used as a platform from which to work. Occasionally two cuts are needed for the dwarf box hedges of the parterre.

(b) The 3 km (1.86 miles) of box hedges ranging from 1 m to 2 m (3-6 ft) in height that line the bosquets and the glades are very important frames to the *allées* and these are cut with a tractor-mounted McConnell 120 cm (48 in) reciprocating cutter bar operated usually by an experienced member of the farm estate staff. This can deal with all these hedges very quickly. The flexible arm also allows the pleaching of the bosquets (see plate 8.4). One cut in the summer is usually given, the normal cutting rate being one mile of hedge per hour. The main drawback is the unevenness of the terrain that makes precise level cuts of the hedges, especially the tops, sometimes difficult.

Plate 8.4 Hedge management at Courances. These box hedges are cut with a tractor-mounted cutter bar which also cuts the 'curtain' of woods behind the statue (pleaching)

The grass. Seventy per cent of the park is grass covered, the management varying with the different areas and character of the garden.

The swards around the chateau must be of smooth velvety turf as a foil to the fine building and the formal hedges and parterre, and where space allows this is achieved with an Atco triple gang mower drawn by a farm-size massey Ferguson tractor set to cut at 25 mm (1 in). This achieves a quick effective cut, the only problem being, that in wet conditions, the tractor may leave tyre marks. The best lawns, however, are cut with a hand-propelled cylinder mower.

The longer grass areas are cut with a four wheel rotary Hayter-type mower with a Flymo hover mower for banks and slopes.

Mowing strips have been incorporated along the main drives to reduce costs of edging and give a trim effect.

Water areas. The extensive formal water features (*pieces d'eaux*) present little immediate maintenance problems and the springs that feed them provide a constant flow of crystal-clear water. The two main problems are the prolific weed growth now appearing in some water areas due to nutrient run off from adjacent farm land, and the longer term need of eventual repairs to the stonework of the basins and canals and statuary.

Herbicides are considered absolutely essential for the extensive hard areas such as the drives, paths and cobbles or setts. Sodium chlorate was used but there were the usual run-off problems and even simazine caused some damage. Now a paraquat/diquat mixture is used applied from an 800 litre (176 gallon) tractor-mounted tank (plate 8.5) and from two lance sprayers with the use of a hand-held

Plate 8.5 Courances. Herbicide spraying in progress. This two-man unit can deal with extensive areas of drives and gravel walks speedily and effectively.

plastic shield to prevent damage to the grass (plate 8.6). One or two applications are made per year. The result if very fast and effective.

Plate 8.6 Courances. The hand-held plastic roof panel provides an effective guard against spray drift and allows precise and safe weed control

Leaves. Fallen leaves are a major job in the autumn with so many deciduous trees, especially planes. In general various blowing systems are used to deal with these:

(a) Leaves are blown into windrows in the *allées* and paths and then burnt in localised heaps where it is safe to do so. A Winro blower is used.
(b) Near hedges and the main grass rides, leaves are blown into windrows close to the hedges and these are then sucked up by a 'Giant Vac' type machine that blows them behind the hedges or into the wooded bosquets.
(c) The same machine can blow the leaves into trailers for removal to composting for mulches, or burying in pits, usually done in frosty weather when the ground is hard enough to take the tractors, trailers and vacuum blowers.

Visitors
In 1980 there were 15 000 visitors as organised groups in the spring and summer, in contrast to Vaux le Vicomte, and there are thus few problems with visitors in these small numbers.

General comment
The owner considers that it would be very difficult to manage the Chateau gardens without the associated farm unit giving support in terms of occasional extra staff, tractors and equipment. Despite fears for the future he and the Marquise still have plans for the restoration of various original features in the park. The emphasis at present is on shorter-term maintenance rather than long-term management.

Castle Howard, Britain

Location: North Yorkshire, 24 km (15 miles) N.E. of York 10 km (6 miles) W. of
Malton off the A64 highway.

Owner: George Howard

Opening: Usually Good Friday to October 31st daily.

Comment
One of the most magnificent examples of the eighteenth century English landscape
style with a palatial mansion matched by gardens and parks of a similar scale and
quality. Horace Walpole described the designs of Castle Howard in 1722 as 'the
grandest scenes of rural magnificence'.

Background
In 1699 Charles Howard, 3rd Earl of Carlisle, commissioned John Vanbrugh to
build Castle Howard on the site of Henderskelfe Castle, a much older building
partially destroyed by fire in 1693. He was assisted in this great task by Nicholas
Hawksmoor, and the work of creation continued for more than thirty years.

From more formal beginnings (like Blenheim Palace in Oxfordshire) the concept
gradually softened and broadened into the composition of the English landscape
school. Woodlands were planted, classical buildings added and not until 1795 was
the great 28 ha (70 acre) lake created by damning a shallow valley to the north of the
house. The walled garden was also doubled in size, so that by 1750 it extended to
about 4½ ha (11 acres). The main features of Castle Howard park and garden as they
exist today are shown in plate 8.7.

The Howard family have continued to live at Castle Howard up to the present
day.

The gardens and their management

Approximate components. The maintained garden and grounds comprise about
62 ha (155 acres) made up as follows:

grass areas	1.2 ha (30 acres)	
lakes	2.2 ha (5.5 acres)	much reduced since the late eighteenth century)
plant borders	1.4 ha (3.5 acres)	excluding the rose garden)
gravel paths	0.4 ha (1 acre)	
hedges	over 1.3 km (1400 yd)	(mostly yew and box)
walled garden	4.4 ha (11 acres)	made up as follows:
new rose garden	1 ha (2.5 acres)	
market garden area	3.4 ha (8.5 acres)	
ornamental woodland	7.2 ha (18 acres)	
new arboretum	30 ha (75 acres)	

Staff. The present staff comprise nine full-time and six part-time persons,

Plate 8.7 Castle Howard. A dramatic aerial view showing the contrasts between extensive, informal parkland and intensive more formal gardens that both require very different levels of maintenance. Note part of the lake as a middle-distance feature to the north of the house

representing an increase in the last five years from seven full time and one part time. This is due to the expansion of successful activities.

Maintenance and management policy
The successful expansion of many activities has created additional maintenance responsibilities which have been met by some increase in staff, but mainly by the following policies:

(a) A much greater emphasis on the use of machinery and equipment, and of chemicals to maintain a better standard at lower cost, and to create more time for development work.
(b) Carefully planned organisation of staff and work schedules. The present head gardener Brian Hutchinson firmly believes in promoting greater incentives and interest by giving individual staff specific areas of responsibility.
(c) Close liaison with the owner, and also meetings with other garden managers and staff through the Professional Gardeners Guild.

Some maintenance techniques

Grass areas. The 2.4 ha (6 acres) of close-mown lawns are cut with three machines a 90 cm (36 in) Ransome Mastiff, a 70 cm (28 in) Atco and a 60 cm (24 in) Matador cylinder mower.

The 4.4 ha (10 acres) of gang-mown grass are cut with a Ransome 5/7 unit cylinder gang mower and the remaining rough grass with tractor-mounted 2 m (6 ft) Votex rotary cutter and a 105 cm (42 in) rotary on a 12 h.p. Kubota mini-tractor. Other smaller machines like the Hayterette and Flymo rotary mowers are used for limited areas, banks and the lake, etc. Brushwood cutters are also used.

Hedges. There are some 1.2 km (1300 yd) of yew hedges and 110 m (120 yd) of box hedges all cut by two electric Marples hedge trimmers powered from a compressor on the tractor.

Weed control. The gravel paths and drives are treated with simazine and a paraquat/simazine mix. Simazine is also used on some planted areas and borders.

'Kerb' and 'Roundup' are also used widely. An annual application of herbicide is also given round the base of newly planted trees, and along the rides and vistas.

Woodlands and trees. Tree surgery is carried out by the garden staff on most specimen trees when necessary.

The market garden, walled garden area is intensively cultivated producing a range of vegetables, soft fruit and flower crops for local markets and for sale to visitors. For the latter a recent development has been a plant centre and a pick-your-own enterprise of strawberries and raspberries as an important part of the market garden enterprise. This is very successful.

Recent developments include the rose garden developed in a section of the walled garden, and representing one of the largest collections of roses of the older varieties; the Ray Wood woodland garden, planted since 1975 with a large collection of ornamental trees including over 700 species of rhododendrons, acers, nothofagus, styrax, magnolias and conifers; and the arboretum begun in 1979 in a run-down area of parkland, as a project for posterity being still very much in its early stages. As with the rose garden it has been developed with the expert advice of James Russell the former Surrey nurseryman who is assisting with developments at Castle Howard.

Visitors
Castle Howard receives many visitors per year who from the garden maintenance point of view present very little wear and tear problems and leave very little litter.

Summary
This is an exception to most studies of large privately owned establishments increasing its staff and activities as a result of good staff organisation and management, and the use of modern aids wherever possible. Short-term maintenance and long-term management are both characteristics of Castle Howard where the present owner has an eye for posterity.

Hall Place Gardens, Britain

Location: Mid-Kent, 6.4 km (4 miles) W. of Tonbridge on the B2027 Tonbridge -
          Penshurst Road, Leigh.

Owner: Lord Hollenden

Opening: Some Sundays and other Charity Days for the Gardener Sundays,
         National Garden Scheme, The Army Benevolent Fund and others.

Background
A high-Victorian mansion (now reduced in size) and associated spacious gardens
and grounds including an 4.8 ha (11 acre) lake. The mansion was built in 1871-2 on
the site of an earlier house in the neo-Elizabethan Victorian manner by George
Devey the revivalist architect for Samuel Morley M.P. and it had extensive gardens
laid out at the same time. There were formal terraced gardens near the house, and an
elaborate Dutch garden and rose garden with 60 m (200 ft) pergola that still survives
today; and a gradual transition to a more natural shrub and wild garden area near
and around the lake. There were also extensive kitchen gardens and ranges of
outbuildings, glasshouses as befitted a large mansion of the time. Lord Hollenden
the present owner is a direct descendent of the original Morley family.

The gardens and their maintenance
The gardens at Hall Place extend to about 10.5 ha (26 acres) which includes the lake
of 4.4 ha (11 acres). Soils are heavy acidic clay loams which support excellent
growth of trees and shrubs.

   The original estate of farm, park, pleasure gardens and kitchen garden were
staffed by at least eighteen gardeners and estates staff, but in 1973 the garden staff
were reduced to three and a policy was implemented to meet this drastic staff
reduction. One wing of the great house was demolished and its basal walls and
doorways cleverly converted into gravelled planted courts, and there were
considerable modifications to the more elaborate features of the formal gardens.
The implementation of this policy has involved the following:

(a) Grass verges in front of the formal beds along the drives have been removed and
    planted to suit the situation (see plate 8.8.)
(b) Difficult areas of mowing have been removed and plant beds have been joined
    together to make larger beds of predominately shrubs.
(c) The widespread use of leaf mould as a mulch has been introduced to make beds
    easier to maintain, and ground cover planted wherever possible.
(d) Approximately 1.2 ha (3 acres) of the rough grass is either cut for hay by a local
    farmer or grazed by his sheep. Areas not grazed or cut for hay, are cut with rotary
    mowers.
(e) Some yew hedges were removed altogether, where the design did not suffer too
    much and others that were overgrown or too large have been drastically reduced
    in size.
(f) All annuals, and bedding displays, once a great feature of the Victorian and
    Edwardian layout were virtually eliminated. These were mainly on the terraces
    and in the Dutch garden. In their place in 1970 were planted suitable massed
    shrubs and ground cover, including perennial herbaceous plants on the

Plate 8.8 Hall Place. Massed foliage and colour plantings of shrubs and herbaceous species replaces the bedding displays beside the gravel walks

recommendations of Lanning Roper. Most plants used in the gardens now are home grown (see plate 8.8).

(g) Overmature trees or dead trees in the park areas known as Deer Park and Rookery are dealt with in the winter months by the garden staff.

The gardens areas now comprise:

Grass 2.0 ha (5 acres) of close-mown turf cut by gang and cylinder mowers, depending on the area. 1.3 ha (3 acres) of rough grass cut for hay or grazed.

Borders etc. 0.8 ha (2 acres) cultivated beds, mixed borders roses, etc.

hedges 8333 m² (90 000 sq. ft) hedges, mostly yew and some laurel and holly.

Paths/Drives 3.2 km (2 miles) averaging 2.5 m (8 ft) wide.

The remainder of the area, apart from the lake, is made up of light woodland, an arboretum and large banks of rhododendrons.

Management policy
The present head gardener, Peter Beagley, has been at Hall Place for eighteen years and during the period he had implemented the policy of a garden of 10.5 ha (26 acres) that can be managed by three full-time staff. Some of his techniques are described below.

Grass mowing systems. Long grass in the arboretum and among large specimen trees was, until 1981, offered to the tenant farmer for hay and he took up to 200 bales in a good season. The rate of cutting and removal with a forage harvester was equivalent to the speed of a gang mower. Surprisingly small areas were dealt with in this way, provided there were not too many obstacles (plate 8.9). Sheep are being tried as an alternative in 1981 restricted with simple posts and pig netting fencing.

The main lawns are cut with a three unit gang mower drawn behind a Fordson Dexter.

Plate 8.9 Hall Place. Long grass areas before cutting in July. Note the close-mown verge beside the drive. Sheep have been used to graze some of these areas.

Special lawns are cut with the cylinder mowers and all grass is boxed off. Ride-on mowers are not favoured and are not considered 'labour saving'.

Lake edges, banks and slopes are mostly cut with a hand-propelled Mountfield that is preferred to a Flymo, found at Hall Place to be lacking in 'guts' or staying power over long periods. A Kaaz Paice Setter (two-stroke) brush cutter was purchased in 1981 and is proving a very useful tool for banks and problem areas. Grass edges are still cut with long-handled shears. Mechanical edgers have been used, but are considered to be too much trouble.

Hedge cutting. This is done in late summer with two Tarpen hedge trimmers one 30 cm (12 in) blade and one 40 cm (16 in) blade, powered by a Jenny 110 V Generator.

Weed control methods. Herbicides are widely used, the main application being for the two miles of drives and paths. Here 'Casoron G' is applied as the granular material by hand, and approximately 75 kg (165 lb) are used per year. The use of this very effective granular herbicide has dramatically reduced labour costs. All the 'Casoron' is applied in one day as compared with four weeks for a simazine spray. The additional cost of the chemical is more than offset by the saving in time and manpower. For brushwood, brambles and problem areas, liquid applications of

S.B.K. 'Brushwood killer', 'Roundup' and 'Tumble weed' are applied by watering can which is considered safer than sprayer since there is little or no drift of the chemical.

Pest and disease control. Rabbits are a problem and some areas have to be fenced. Otherwise some spraying of the roses against mildew and aphids is done, using an 18 litre (4 gallons) Cooper Pegler knapsack sprayer.

Mulches. Heavy mulches of home-produced leaf litter are used throughout, especially on the rose and shrub beds where only hand hoeing is practised against weeds. The mulch creates a light easily worked surface and very shallow rooted weeds which can be dealt with quickly by the hoe. Leaf sweeping is still done by hand.

Lake area. The banks of the lake are planted with common alder (*Alnus glutinosa*), the roots of which support the banks greatly reducing or preventing erosion. In January these alders are pruned back hard to almost ground level, by hand.

The lake has three islands (man made) and these are cleared of undergrowth annually in February before the naturalised bulbs appear and birds start to nest. The only other operation is removing debris from the lake, and maintaining a correct water level. A recent interesting point affecting maintenance concerns the flock of about 150 Canada and Greylag geese in the lake area that are fed during the winter, but in the summer eat large quantities of short grass on the front lawns, reducing the amount of mowing. Apparently they seem to do little other damage and are not fenced or restricted. Feathers and droppings can look unsightly.

Staff management

All three staff including Peter Beagley are working gardeners. Each has a main area of responsibility to oversee in the gardens, but all three combine for main jobs like hedge cutting, weed control, etc. Each man has his own mower and own tools and meetings are held regularly to check progress. In the winter months, woodwork repairs and stonework are also handled by these men.

Visitors

About 5000-6000 people visit Hall Place each year mostly on the Charity Days or special groups by arrangement.

The High Beeches, Britain

Location: 1.61 km (1 mile) E. of Handcross, East Sussex. North off B2110 Handcross to Turners Hill

Owners: The Hon. H.E. and Mrs Boscawen

Opening: Groups by arrangement.

Background

A fine, mature woodland garden showing a continuity of rare and imaginative planting from the early twentieth century up to the present.

In 1849 Sir Robert Loder purchased the then extensive High Beeches estate and proceeded to enlarge the house and over a period of years laid out an extensive formal garden on level ground around the house. His grandson Colonel Giles Loder developed the existing woodland gardens from 1906 onwards.

The house was destroyed by fire in 1942 and after Colonel Loder's death in 1966, the garden and remains of the house and outbuildings were acquired by the present owners, who built a more contemporary and comfortable house on a new site overlooking the woodland garden. With very limited staff to help they have carried out a most effective and ambitious restoration programme concentrating on the woodland gardens.

The gardens and their management
Plate 8.10 shows the general character of the gardens comprising essentially Colonel Loder's original woodland garden with later developments and planting by the Boscawens.

Plate 8.10 Woodland and water habitats at The High Beeches

The framework or structure of the woodlands is composed of and characterised by the fine English oaks (*Quercus robur*), many well over 100 years of age and creating varying habitats of glade and shade, together with other native species such as ash and beech that also reach impressive sizes on these rich forest soils. The design is essentially informal, exploiting the natural contours and features of the site. There are some 10 ha (25 acres) of maintained areas, with further tracts of woodland and forest undeveloped as gardens.

The age structure of some of the canopy oaks and other trees and also of some of the original plantings does present problems. Some overmature or decaying specimens have to be felled and removed which is not easy in such a richly planted garden.

Staff. The 10 ha (25 acres) of woodland gardens and some additional gardens round the house are managed by one full-time gardener, and one part-time pensioner (who also works on the other woodlands) and the Hon. and Mrs Boscawen themselves, who are able to devote about 75% of their time to the gardens. In effect this means a total force of about two full-time people to manage the 10-12 ha (25-30 acres).

Management has to be in accord with the whole *character of the site* and the nature of the plant asssociations. This is an important point.

Some maintenance techniques

Grass areas. Three zones are maintained:

(a) Reasonbably close-mown turf cut to about 2.5 cm (1 in) for the lawns around the house and most access paths.
(b) The generally level grassy glade areas. A longer cut to about 5 cm (2 in) especially around shrubs and small trees.
(c) Meadow and natural areas. Here a long grass or hay meadow treatment is encouraged cut in late July with all mowings removed by hand.

Trees and shrubs. Apart from new planting the longer-term management decisions are about the treatment of overmature forest trees and some of the older rhododendrons and other more exotic species. Losses occur and the policy, especially with such a small labour force, is to remove casualties only when they occur or when they look imminent.

Weed control. Drives and paths are treated with the contact herbicide, paraquat at about monthly intervals or when weeds appear. Coarse grasses and vigorous weeds are 'restrained' with this herbicide especially in ditches and wet areas that tend to become overrun with weed growth. The use of paraquat is, however, discriminate depending on the herb layer. Brushwood and brambles are controlled when necessary with a June application of the translocated herbicide 2,4,5-T ('Brushwood killer') carefully applied. Shrub regeneration can be a problem especially of *Rhododendron ponticum* and even the common laurel (*Prunus laurocerasus*) and these are controlled by spraying in the growing season, every other year, with 'Amcide', a translocated and soil-acting herbicide for brushwood control. Bracken is a problem and has to be controlled by hand pulling and cutting. Bindweed (*Convolvulus arvensis*) can be effectively controlled by hand spraying the weed growth with a mixture of very dilute 2,4,5-T ('Brushwood killer') at two drops per ½ litre (1 pint) of water, applied when the flowers are just opening.

Wherever possible 'natural areas' of meadow and waterside flora are encouraged, where maintenance is reduced to the minimum and no chemicals are used. Regeneration or colonisation of desirable herb species, such as the blue willow gentian, cowslips, bluebells, wild orchids and a great variety of ferns and mosses, is also assisted.

Machinery and equipment
The policy is for a selected range of up to date mechanical aids without which the

Boscawens know they could not manage the gardens. These are the main items:

(a) A small tractor and trailer. Essential for haulage, and many other jobs. A middle- to long-term investment.
(b) A Springfield ZTR (Zero Turning Radius) 107 cm (42 in) rotary, 'sit on' mower. Very manoeuvrable and efficient for most of the grass areas in lawns around the house and level grass glades.
(c) A Flymo 75 professional model rotary hover mower with two rear wheels. Very useful for long grass and the steep banks and gradients.
(d) A Turner Flail hand-propelled mower. A heavy, robust machine used to a limited extent for brushwood and scrub and weed growth in the rough woodland areas. Useful for initial glade clearance.
(e) A Cooper Pegler knapsack sprayer for most of the herbicide work.
(f) A Mountfield Multitrim 37 for stream banks and long grass.

Plate 8.11 The High Beeches. A collection of most of the equipment used to maintain this large woodland garden. The wheeled 75 Flymo (2nd from left) and the Springfield ZTR rotary mowers are invaluable for the varied terrain. The Cooper Pegler knapsack in the centre does most of the spraying required

Visitors are welcomed by previous arrangement. There is an excellent guide book.

Great Comp, Kent, Britain

Location: Mid-Kent, 13 km (8 miles) W. of Maidstone, 3 km (two miles) E. of Borough Green off B2016 that leaves the A20 at Wrotham Heath.

Owners: Mr and Mrs R. Cameron

Opening: Regularly between April and October.

Background and development of the gardens

A good example of a comparatively large modern private garden created during the last twenty-five years and managed entirely by the owners, until quite recently.

Great Comp is an imposing seventeenth century house, of stone and brick but with no records of any large formal gardens of that period. When the Camerons purchased the property in 1957 some 1.8 ha (4½ acres) of gardens remained, with vestiges of an earlier more formal layout of the early twentieth century and a number of mature trees, especially limes (*Tilia*).

In 1962 an important extension to the garden was made by purchasing a 0.8 ha (2 acres) piece of market-garden land to the south east, and during the next ten years it was turned into an attractive, secluded sanctuary of woodland glades and cool shaded walks with under planting of many interesting and effective ground-cover associations. To achieve this transformation, the Camerons worked out a simple effective design on paper and then planted up most of the area quite closely with large numbers of fairly fast growing deciduous and evergreen trees such as silver birch, Scots pine, larch, spruce and various oaks and maples. The favourable soils and close planting caused the trees to grow rapidly and after five years or so there followed a thinning stage to implement the design by making the paths and the glades one sees today. This is a technique many more people should follow, not only to create shelter and enclosure, but to plant in advance of the ultimate design. (See also Chapter 3.)

Other features of the garden were gradually developed over the years, but particularly successful were the main vistas (plate 8.12) using flowing shapes in the

Plate 8.12 One of the main vistas at Great Comp

grass of massed heathers, conifers, and shrubs with carefully sited specimen trees or groups of trees. The present collection amounts to over 3000 different plants, many rare or unusual.

Low maintenance has not been the main objective, but in adopting the close boskage ideas of Michael Haworth Booth and using many original ground-cover associations, a style of garden has evolved which enables two people to maintain it very effectively. It is the close relationship between the character of the planting and the maintenance systems used that is a key to their achievement. Few hedges exist in the garden boundaries, division being created by screening associations of the rather taller trees and shrubs, carefully selected for contrast in colour and form and designed in such a way as to achieve most effective seclusion and shelter. Visual continuity is also achieved between these informal backgrounds and the more distant trees and woodlands beyond.

To encourage the undershrubs and ground flora, some thinning of the maturing tree cover is still being done.

Maintenance
Maintenance of the established planted areas has for many years now involved only a light clipping of the heathers and similar shrubs in April with hand shears, and occasional pruning of some shrubs and trees as they mature by removing overhanging branches and competing growth. One problem as a result of so much dense planting everywhere is that there is no safe site for localised bonfires to dispose of bulky prunings, and these do have to be carted some distance to the burning area! Some replacement of heathers is necessary from time to time, and also of the occasional shrub casualty.

The lawns for the most part are derived from the original meadow pasture, that has responded to good management over the years.

The close-mown areas are cut regularly with 60 cm (24 in) cylinder motor mower and a weekly cut is the norm throughout the growing season. The light soils encourage the grass growth, and so even the occasional cut (in good conditions) in the winter is done. The clippings are only boxed off during periods of rapid grass growth – usually May and June – and these are discreetly scattered among shrubs as a mulch. Turf weeds are controlled with an annual spring treatment of selective herbicide, using an 18 litre (4 gallons) knapsack sprayer. Clover is, however, accepted as inevitable on these light soils. The edges are cut with an Andrews Spin Trim battery-operated machine with great success. What would be a long and tedious business is done speedily and effectively with this machine. The soils are not stony, and the edges are kept in good condition too; important points to note for those considering using mechanical edge trimmers of this type.

Weed control. Simple and effective methods have been developed over the years at Great Comp to control weeds, helped by the well-drained soils. Bare soil areas in newly planted borders or on fallow ground neglected during the winter months usually become colonised with weeds. They are either buried by shallow digging with a spade, or more often a series of small pits are dug in the weeding areas and the weeds buried in these, having been skimmed off with a hoe, or spade or pulled by hand. This 'scoop and bury' method before the weeds have seeded works well in the light sandy soils at Comp. Another method is again by hand weeding, but this time the weeds are left in small unobtrusive heaps or 'lost' judiciously among the boskage and ground cover. When couch (*Agropyron*) is an occasional problem a larger heap is made behind the scenes, the couch incorporated in the middle of the heap and the whole given a strong dose of sulphate of ammonia. The couch apparently succumbs to this treatment! Weed control in established areas where little bare soil can be seen, is done by a combination of hand weeding and hoeing.

Chemical herbicides such as paraquat, are used on drives and paths, and for clearing areas of annual weeds, a selective weed killer such as 2,4-D is used as spot treatment against nettles, bindweed and the all too invasive buttercup.

Leaf sweeping is not considered a serious headache since there are not as yet too many large trees with heavy leaf drop, apart from the limes north of the house. The owners quite like to see the autumn leaves lying on the grass, at least for a time, and usually wait until the wind has blown the leaves into convenient corners before picking them up manually and dispersing them as a mulch in the planted areas. No special leaf sweeping gadgets are employed.

Herbaceous plants. The aim is for close-grouped planting of sturdy perennials and shrubs using robust self-supporting plants like *Euphorbias, Campanula lactiflora, Gillenia trifoliata* among bushy shrubs such as azaleas, viburnums and shrub roses. Even the trunks of small ornamental trees come in useful as natural support for shade-tolerant perennials.

Dead heading and cutting back of these perennials are usually not done until the spring. There are usually more important jobs to be done before this and in any case the winter effects of stems and seed heads of plants like achilleas, sedums and ornamental grasses are well worth having. They also offer a measure of protection.

Pest and diseases are seldom a real problem. Local greenfly attacks are usually dealt with by spot insecticide treatment. There is always some bird damage to buds of flowering trees and shrubs in the late winter or early spring, but it never seems to be on the same plants every year. Rabbits are becoming more of a nuisance despite the frequent sitings of foxes which seem to like close boskage borders as a habitat and hunting ground.

Cultural events
In addition to all these gardening activities, a barn and outbuildings have been cleverly converted into a small theatre and tea rooms, so that apart from serving delicious home-made teas to visitors, musical events and festivals are also held during the opening season. Visitor numbers are increasing.

Summary
The achievements at Comp are due both to the result of enthusiastic, and intelligent approaches to design and planting and to the organisation and the techniques of maintenance. The longer-term management aspects are not really a matter for immediate consideration, since the garden is comparatively new and still evolving. Another critical factor, which of course faces all gardens developed by individuals is their successive ownership and upkeep when the present regime ends.

Earlscliffe, Eire

Location: East, North East of Dublin City on North peninsula about 14 km (8.7 miles) from city centre.

Owner: Dr D. W. Robinson

Opening: By special arrangement with the owner.

Background and development of the garden
The only example in this group of case studies of a plantsman's garden of medium size maintained almost entirely by the extensive and successful use of chemical herbicides.

The house and original garden of about 1.2 ha (3 acres) date from 1870 and are sited on a coastal promontory some 60 m (66 yd) above sea level facing south across Dublin Bay and the Irish Sea. Despite the latitude of 53.4°N (equivalent to Liverpool and Lincoln in England) an exceptionally favourable microclimate enables the cultivation of a remarkable range of exotic, tender and half-hardy trees and shrubs and examples include *Eucalyptus, Acacias, Olearias, Leptospermums, Giant Echiums* and even bananas (no ripe fruit, however!). The soils are shallow, well-drained medium loams derived from shales and quartzite (about 25% clay and 4.5% organic matter in the top 8 cm (3 in). The rainfall is comparatively low at around 750 mm (30 in) per annum.

The garden until 1969 was a complex design of formal and informal areas based on Edwardian and later 1920s and 1930s intricacies with many small lawns, high hedges for enclosure and wind protection (the sea is less than 200 m (219 yd) away), herbaceous borders, rock gardens, rose beds, annual borders, bulbs, shrubs, and fruit and vegetable gardens. Three gardeners were originally employed to keep it all in shape.

Modification of the design
When the garden was taken over in 1969 by the present owner, a drastic revision of the design and maintenance methods was essential, to enable the whole area to be maintained by Dr Robinson with some part-time family help. He decided to introduce a herbicide regime as a major means of achieving this objective. The programme of conversion he adopted over the next five years or so was as follows:

(a) A number of lawns were eliminated by spraying the turf with paraquat and planting up with shrubs, trees and ground-cover plants directly into the killed sward (plate 8.13). Five of the eight small lawns were treated in this way.
(b) Internal hedges were gradually eliminated and replaced where shelter was required by informal plantings of trees and shrubs. *Pittosporums, Olearias, Grisellinias* and *Escallonias* were particularly effective for this purpose.
(c) Annuals and bedding plants were largely eliminated and their place taken by shrubs and some perennials known to be resistant to herbicides.
(d) A herbicide programme was imposed over the entire area and wherever possible the soil was left undisturbed after planting. The herbicide programme was not planned in detail in advance, but was modified as required to deal with the existing or anticipated weed problem.

Plate 8.13 Earlscliffe. A shrub area two years after planting into a former lawn. The turf was first killed with paraquat and the shrubs sprayed with simazine immediately after planting

Maintenance programme
Apart from the routine hand jobs of mowing the remaining lawns, clipping the few hedges and cutting back over-vigorous plants, the main operation is the application of suitable herbicides to existing and newly planted areas. The chief herbicide used in the first eight years was simazine, the soil-acting residual herbicide described in Chapter 2. This was applied to areas already cleared of perennial and actively growing weeds. In the early years the use of more powerful translocated herbicides as spot treatment was necessary to eradicate such persistent species as clovers (*Trifolium* sp.), bindweed (*Convolvulus* and *Calystegia*), ground elder (*Aegopodium*), and brambles (*Rubus* sp.), and also the regrowth of stumps of cut-down hedges. Newly emerged weeds were also controlled with contact herbicides like paraquat, and also by some hand hoeing. From 1970 onwards, the entire garden (except the lawns) was sprayed twice a year with simazine ('Weedex' or 'Gesatop') usually applied in March and July at 1.7 kg active ingredient/ha (1.5 1b/acre) including shrub borders, herbaceous borders and rock gardens. This is equivalent to 34 g of the 50% product per 100 m² (1 oz/100 sq. yd). A stronger rate of simazine at 11.2 kg active ingredient/ha (10 lb/acre) or 238 g of product/100 m² (7 oz/100 sq. yd) was used on paths and drives.

After seven years the simazine was replaced by another closely related residual, soil-acting herbicide atrazine ('Gesaprim'), which has greater contact effect on weed seedlings than simazine and is somewhat less dependent for activity on moist soil conditions.

The programme of residual herbicides used from 1969 to 1980 is shown in table 8.1.

Table 8.1 Residual herbicides used from 1969 to 1980

Year	Herbicide*	Number of applications per year
1969	Simazine	Two
1970	Simazine	Three
1971	Simazine	Two
1972	Simazine	Two
1973	Simazine	Two
1974	Simazine	Two
1975	Simazine	Two
1976	Simazine	Two
1977	Atrazine	Two
1978	Atrazine	Two
1979	Atrazine	One
1980	Atrazine	Two

*Applied at the rate of 1.7 kg/ha (1.5 lb/acre).

The method of application was by an 18 litre (4 gallon) Cooper Pegler knapsack sprayer spraying in straight lines marked by canes as a guide.

Both materials were applied as an overall spray, no attempt being made to avoid contacting the plant foliage with the spray.

Some results and observations. Dr Robinson is by profession a plant physiologist and horticultural scientist and he has used his garden and his maintenance systems with herbicides as something of an outdoor trials area, or laboratory, noting the effects of his regime over a period of twelve years since he took over the garden and testing the tolerance of specific ornamentals to new herbicides. Dr Robinson has made some most interesting observations for the particular soil and climatic characteristics of his locality. His methods have proved to be very successful. It was not found possible to control all weeds completely by chemicals, but generally few survived and these were easily removed by hand. After six years of simazine applications, resistant or tolerant weed species proved to be blackberry (*Rubus* sp.), *Oxalis*, and cleavers (*Galium*) and these were spot treated as far as possible with other herbicides.

Herbicide damage. Despite the large range of cultivated plants treated (over 200 genera of trees and shrubs are represented and many more species) very little herbicide damage has been recorded. The elimination of annuals and many susceptible herbaceous species has left those that seem to tolerate the residuals, such as *Montbretia, Helleborus, Hosta, Bergenia, Lamium, Sedum, Dianthus*, the hardy cyclamen and many hardy bulbs including narcissus, tulips, crocus and snowdrops, and some rock plants. Of the several hundred woody species treated surprisingly few showed signs of damage that could be attributed to simazine. Those species usually considered to be sensitive, such as *Syringa, Prunus, Senecio* and *Spiraea*, grew well with no signs of damage. Dr Robinson considers this is partly due to the soil type with its high clay and moderately high organic matter content.

Effects on soil. Although the soil surface becomes hard, cracked and crusted, the conditions did not have any harmful effects on the growth of plants. This is an important subject of especial interest to Dr Robinson whose research programme at the Kinsealy Research Institute, Dublin, (of which he is Director) has shown that even over long periods of herbicide management there are no apparent detrimental effects on soil condition fertility and structure. Rather the opposite, in that beneficial effects of no hoeing and no cultivation have been observed. There is less compaction, except for a thin layer at the surface, better drainage and also there is no mechanical damage to the upper root systems of woody plants, which frequently happens when hoeing or forking are the normal practice. A covering of species of moss that frequently develop is often welcome in gardens as it provides a pleasant surface to walk on and protects the soil surface from rain impact.

Seedling regeneration. Traditional regimes such as hoeing tend to destroy seedlings of exotic species as well as weeds, but some interesting regeneration has been taking place over the years in the herbicide-treated soil, of such woody species as *Cupressus, Myrtus, Berberis, Cotoneaster, Olearia, Escallonia* and *Erica*. It is possible that these seedlings may be of herbicide-tolerant strains that have developed over the years, and this might point to an interesting development of selected resistant strains for use in landscape work where maintenance by other methods is increasingly difficult.

Planting design and maintenance. Observations are continuously being made and fresh information gathered in the garden, and alterations and renewals of planting associations and specimens are continuously in progress.

The garden tends to be at its most colourful in the spring when the resistant bulb species are in leaf and flower and the many spring shrubs also, but with the enforced lack of many summer perennials, annuals and the softer plants, a more subdued summer effect may be the result, However, roses, fuchsias and hydrangeas are also tolerant of residuals so the scope is still considerable for trying out plant associations for summer and late-summer effects.

Longer term management. The original shelter plantings of *Cupressus macrocarpa* and pines and other species are getting past their prime and some trees have fallen or are gradually dying. However, new shelter plantings of *Eucalyptus, Olearias* and other species are being tried, and rates of growth are very impressive. Further simplification of the still quite intricate designs may follow with a reduction of the remaining lawn areas and hedges and the creation of larger banks of enclosing shrubs and ground cover.

Summary

This is the only example in these case studies of a garden maintained almost entirely by herbicides over a lengthy period of years. This regime suits the owner as a busy research scientist, with little spare time, but a great fascination for plants and their cultivation, but he does offer a most important word of warning 'success will only be achieved where the importance of good garden equipment and accurate application is recognised'. Also, the type of soil in a particular garden will affect the activity and the performance of the herbicides, and also the extent of the tolerance or susceptibility of the cultivated plants treated. The experience gained in this Dublin garden will undoubtedly be useful in many parts of Britain, and owners and gardeners should be prepared to try out these materials in view of the considerable savings in time, and labour they can achieve.

9
Prospective View

Throughout the long history of gardens the style and character of the gardens of each period have always been directly related to the economic and social life of that particular time. And that is the situation in the early 1980s as we move into an era of marked redistribution of wealth, of small gardens and of increasing burdens of economic pressure on those who own large gardens and estates. Those who regard large gardens as anachronistic and relics of the privileged classes from a fast vanishing era, may like to examine the important roles that large gardens and parks, are playing at present in Britain and also in some countries of Western Europe. Their historical and heritage importance is unquestionable. Lawrence Banks observes that:

gardens, parks, arboreta and designed landscapes are an integral part of our national heritage stretching back for more than four centuries. Together they form a unique British contribution to international civilisation.

Related to this historical role, is their educational potential that is enormous, though still not sufficiently exploited; particularly where gardens are part of the grounds of important historic houses.

They are also extemely important as 'Garden Plant Reserves' where many thousands of species and cultivars are cultivated. There are over 10 000 plant species in British gardens, from all over the temperate world, many of which are rare or facing extinction in their native habitat and to these must be added over 20 000 cultivars and Lawrence Banks quite rightly likens this 'heritage' of garden plants to our great national picture collections and museums, 'an educational resource of priceless value, and a genetic bank which could well be vital to mankind as a whole'. This highly important role has been recognised quite recently by the formation of The National Council for the Conservation of Plants and Gardens (N.C.C.P.G.) which aims to establish national collections of garden plants in conjunction with botanic gardens, universities, colleges and plant nurseries. The National Trust and private gardens and public parks. It is accepted that the nursery trade and botanic gardens will be unable in the future to hold all these unique collections, without the essential help of garden owners and their own private collections.

All gardens, and more especially those of larger size attached to houses of architectural importance have a design role, demonstrating historical and contemporary styles and trends and enabling garden designers and landscape architects to create original schemes or to incorporate 'new layers over the old'.

Gardens have an important commercial importance as tourist attractions and as unique places for passive recreation and leisure. About forty-nine million visitors were recorded in 1980 to historic properties, many of which include gardens.

Finally, for visitors and owners there is the important role of gardens as a refuge and place of escape, very necessary in the high-speed materialistic society that now characterises most of Western Europe. The refuge could also be for native wildlife since large 'natural' gardens perform an important role in this respect.

If these are some of the important present roles of gardens, what of their future prospects? The mounting costs of running gardens are becoming a very serious matter, when one considers that to employ only two gardeners at the time of writing costs about £10000 per annum in wages and overheads alone. The backlog of repairs to structures and the renewal of historic features, whether it be ancient trees or garden walls can amount to an enormous bill, usually beyond the resources of many owners today. Marcus Binney quotes dramatic figures in his publication *Elysian Gardens* to illustrate these problems with gardens in England. Visits to the great Renaissance gardens of Italy reveal a similar story.

Changes of ownership and the break up of family continuity often enforced by the pressures already described, have a disrupting effect on the maintenance staff and the long-term management of the gardens and parks.

The inevitable consequence is the acquisition of the property by an institution or commercial organisation, which may or may not see fit to maintain the gardens to the same standards. For some, drastic alterations reduce once fine gardens to mere institutional grounds.

However N.C.C.P.G. already referred to, is attracting an enthusiastic membership, and more important, the necessary funds from private sources, enabling it to begin its work. Membership of The National Trust, The Royal Horticultural Society, The Garden History Society and other garden-orientated bodies is increasing year by year, and the popularity of garden visiting has already been mentioned. Private individuals can do a great deal to launch a cause, and an excellent example is the work of Rosemary Nicholson and a few enthusiastic friends in funding the Tradescant Trust (1978) which has now a base at the restored redundant church of St Mary, Lambeth, London as a centre for a museum of garden history and a garden of the Tradescant period now being completed in the adjacent churchyard. Her group have stimulated great interest in the Tradescants and garden history. The concept of 'Friends' of a particular garden might be adopted more widely, as in the United States, to help with the running of a garden by providing labour and raising funds. Unemployed young people are being used under various government schemes for all kinds of work and more of these could well be used for some garden clearance and restoration work. There is still no national or regional basic training provision for gardeners, as opposed to commercial horticulturalists, and this is an urgent matter. Finally it must be said to quote Lawrence Banks that gardeners

'are by nature not normally assertive or politically active ... and so the threats of inflation and taxation still go largely unnoticed by the national press and the great mass of the British public.'

If all the energies and enthusiasms of the British gardening public:

can be harnessed and co-ordinated there is no reason why Britain's garden lovers should not achieve lasting successes comparable to those of naturalists in recent years in stemming the tide of erosion and decline.

References and Bibliography

Alpine Garden Society. The quarterly journal, Lye End Link, St Johns, Woking, Surrey.

Arboricultural Association Publication (1979). *Trees and the Law*, Leaflet No. 6.

Arboricultural Association. The Brokerswood House, Brokerswood, Nr Westbury, Wilts.

Bacon, L. (1980). '*Rock gardening—a dying art*', The Garden, Journal of the Royal Horticultural Society, **105**, Part 3.

Banks, L. (1977). 'Gardens under stress', in *The Garden, Journal of the Royal Horticultural Society*, **102**, Part 5.

Banks, L. (1980). 'Saving gardens and plants', in *The Garden, Journal of the Royal Horticultural Society*, **105**, Part 3.

Barry, R.G. and Chorley, R.T. (1976). *Atmosphere, Weather and Climate*, 3rd edn., London University Paperbacks, Methuen and Co. Ltd.

Bellchamber, P. (1979). *Scotland's Garden Survey Report*, published by Scotland's Garden Scheme, 26, Castle Terrace, Edinburgh.

Binney, M. and Hills, A. (1979). *Elysian Gardens*, published by Save Britain's Heritage, 3, Park Square West, London, N.W.1.

Bisgrove, R. (1980). 'Grasses and gardens', *The Garden. Journal of the Royal Horticultural Society* **105**, Part 4.

Blomfield, R. (1901). *The Formal Garden in England*. Macmillan, London and New York.

Bloom, A. (1960). *Perennials for Trouble Free Gardening*, Faber and Faber.

Bridgeman, P. H. (1976). *Tree Surgery*, David and Charles.

British Standards Institution, 101 Pentonville Road, London, N.1. Standards on Gardening, Horticulture and Landscape Work.

Brown, G.E. (1972). *The Pruning of Trees, Shrubs and Conifers*, Faber and Faber, London.

Burrage, S.W. (1976). 'The microclimate of the garden', in *The Garden, Journal of the Royal Horticultural Society, February 1976* **101**, Part 2, 91-5.

Cobbett, W. (1980 edition). *The English Gardener*, Oxford University Press.

Cook, R. (1981). 'Replant diseases', in *The Garden, Journal of the Royal Horticultural Society*, **106**, Part 6.

Cooper, J.I. (1979). *Virus Diseases of Trees and Shrubs* Institute of Terrestrial Ecology, Oxford.

Countryside Commission, The, John Dower House, Crescent Place, Cheltenham, Gloucestershire.

Crowe, S. (1959). *Garden Design*, Country Life, London. Second edition (1981) by Packard Publishing Ltd, 16, Lynch Down, Funtington, Chichester West Sussex PO 18 9LR in association with Thomas Gibson Publishing Ltd, 9A New Bond Street, London W1Y 9PE.

Dawson, R.B. (1959). *Practical Lawn Craft and Management of Sports Turf*, Crosby Lockwood.

Decker, P. (1974). *Pests of Ornamental Plants*, 3rd edn., Ministry of Agriculture, Fisheries and Food, H.M.S.O., Bulletin 97.

Dutton, R. (1937). *The English Garden*, Batsford, London.

Farley, N. (1980). *Handbook of Garden Machinery and Equipment*, Dent.

Farrer, R. *The English Rock Garden*, A classic work first published in 1918 and reprinted many times.

Fiennes, Celia. (1949). The Journeys of Celia Fiennes (Ed. C. Morris), Cresset Press, London.

Forestry and British Timber. Monthly publication, 25, New Street Square, London.

Forestry Commission, The, 231, Corstorphine Road, Edinburgh, EH2 7AT.

Garden History Society, The, The Secretary, 12 Charlbury Road, Oxford.

Greig, B.J.W. and Strouts, R.G. (1977). *Honey Fungus*, Forestry Commission, H.M.S.O., Arboricultural leaflet No. 2.

Grower Guide (1980), *New Cut Flower Crops*, No. 18, Grower Books, London.

Hadfield, M. (1960). *A History of British Gardening*, Spring Books, London, New York, Sydney, Toronto.

Harris, J. (1979). *The Garden*, Victoria and Albert Museum publication.

Harvey, J. (1979). *The Garden*, Victoria and Albert Museum publication.

Haworth Booth, M. (1961). *The Flowering Shrub Garden*, Farall Publications.

Health and Safety at Work Acts. See Bridgeman, P.H., *Tree Surgery*.

Hedging (1975). British Trust for Conservation Volunteers Ltd., Zoological Gardens, Regents Park, London.

Historic Buildings Council, Fortress House, 23, Savile Row, London.

Historic Houses Association, 38, Ebury Street, London, S.W.1. OLU.

Hudson, J.P. (1968). 'The plant and its environment', in *The Garden, Journal of the Royal Horticultural Society*, **XCIII**, Part 5; **XCIII**, Part 6.

Hussey, C. (1967). *English Gardens and Landscapes*, Country Life, London.

Jekyll, G. (1843-1932). Author of *Wood and Garden, Home and Garden* and other books that greatly influenced the use of more natural planting concepts and the use of foliage plants and colour schemes.

Jellicoe, G. (1980). 'Creative conservation', in *Journal of the Royal Society of Arts*, **CXXVIII** (5285).

Johnson, H. (1980). *Principles of Gardening*, Mitchell Beazley.

Lloyd, C. (1957). *The Mixed Border*, Collingridge, London.

Lloyd, C. (1970). *The Well-Tempered Garden*, Collins, London.

Lloyd, N. (1925). *Garden Craftsmanship in Yew and Box*. Ernest Benn Ltd, London.

Loudon, J.C. (1783-1843) and Loudon, J. (1807-58). Horticultural writers, journalists.

McClean, T. (1981). *Medieval English Gardens*, Collins, London.

Matthews, W.E. (1979). 'Removing tree roots', in *The Garden, Journal of the Royal Horticultural Society*, **104**, Part 2.

Men of the Trees, Crawley Down, Crawley, Sussex. Journal published in April and October of each year.

Ministry of Agriculture, Fisheries and Food (1976). *The Agricultural Climate of England and Wales*, Technical Bulletin 35, H.M.S.O., London.

Ministry of Agriculture. *Approved Products for Farmers and Growers* (annual publication), Agricultural Chemicals Approval Scheme, H.M.S.O.

Mitchell, A.F. (1972). *Conifers in The British Isles*, Forestry Commission Booklet 33, H.M.S.O.

National Council for the Conservation of Plants and Gardens, c/o The Director, Royal Horticultural Society Garden, Wisley, Ripley, Surrey.

National Trust, 42, Queen Anne's Gate, London SW1.

Natural Environment Research Council (N.E.R.C.) (December 1977). *Amenity Grasslands*, series 'C', No. 19.

Nursery Stock Manual. Grower Books, London.

Peace, T.R. (1962). *Pathology of Trees and Shrubs*, Clarendon Press, Oxford.

Perry, F. (1962). *Water Gardens*, Penguin/Royal Horticultural Society series.

Power Saw Association of Great Britain, 11, Park Mansions, Prince of Wales Drive, London, S.W.11.

Prockter, N.J. (1973). *Climbing and Screen Plants*, Faber, London.

Professional Gardeners Guild, The Gardens. Castle Howard, York, YO6 7BY.

Ramsbottom, J. (1953). 'Mycorrhiza and other fungal associations', in *Mushrooms and Toadstools*, New Naturalist series.

Roberts, E.H. (1980). 'Weeds from seeds', *Proceedings of Conference Weed Control in Amenity Plantings*, University of Bath.

Robinson, D.W. (1975, 1976). 'Herbicides in the landscape and garden' in *The Garden, Journal of the Royal Horticultural Society*, **100**, Parts 11 and 12; **101**, Part 1.

Robinson, W. (1870). *The Wild Garden.* The Scolar Press, London (Reprint of 1894 edn. in 1977.)

Royal National Rose Society, Bone Hill, Chiswell Green Lane, St. Albans, Hertfordshire. Its yearly publication *The Rose Annual* contains much useful information. See 'Resistance and susceptibility to black spot' in the 1979 editions.

Sales, J. (1978). 'The restoration and conservation of historic gardens', in *Conference Proceedings: The Management of Important Gardens and Parks*, Wye College, (London University), Wye, Ashford, Kent.

Sports Turf Research Institute, St. Ives, Bingley, Yorks. Many useful reports and publications on Turf grasses and management.

Stapeley Water Gardens, Nantwich, Cheshire. Comprehensive catalogue and advisory service.

Synge, P. (1976). *Collins Guide to Bulbs*, Collins.

Thacker, C. (1979). *The History of Gardens*, Croom Helm, London.

Thomas, G.S. (1976). *Perennial Garden Plants*, Dent and Sons Ltd, London.

Thomas, G.S. (1980). 'The influence of the rose on garden design', in *The Rose Annual*, Royal National Rose Society.

Thomas, G.S. (1980) 'The preservation of historic gardens' in *Journal of the Royal Society of Arts*, **CXXVIII** (5285).

Treasury, H.M. (December 1980). *Capital Taxation and The National Heritage*, H.M. Treasury, Parliament Street, London.

Tree Council, The. The National Tree Survey (1975). Tree Council, 35, Belgrave Square, London, SW1X 8DN.

Weed Research Organisation (W.R.O.). *Weed Control Handbooks*, Vols. I and II, Blackwell, London.

Wells, T., Bell, S. and Frost, A. (1981). *Creating Attractive Grasslands Using Native Plant Species*, Nature Conservancy Council, Attingham Park, Shrewsbury.

Williams, E.D. (1978). *Botanical Composition of the Park Grass Plots at Rothamsted 1856–1976*, Rothamsted Experimental Station, Harpenden, Herts.

Wright, T.W.J. (1976). 'Microclimate and plant selection', in *The Garden, Journal of the Royal Horticultural Society*, **101**, Part 5, 234-41.

Wright, T.W.J. (1978). 'Bedgebury Pinetum' in *Gardens of Kent, Sussex and Surrey*, No. 4, Gardens of Britain series, Batsford, London.

Wright, T.W.J. and Parker, J. (1979). 'Maintenance and conservation' in *Landscape Techniques* (Ed. A. E. Weddle), Heinemann.

Index